**This book is to be returned on or before
the last date stamped below.**

05. SEP 86   31. OCT 8   STORE

25. SEP 86

15. NOV 86   05. JAN 88

25. MAR 87

10. APR 8

JUL 87

35

WALLINGTON LIBRARY
Shotfield,
Wallington, SM6 OHY

081-770 4900

RENEWALS   *Please quote:* date of return, your ticket number
and computer label number for each item.

BOTH HANDS

BOTH HANDS

AN AUTOBIOGRAPHY

———∞∞∞◆∞∞∞———

GERVAS HUXLEY

C.M.G., M.C.

'I warm'd both hands before the fire of life.'
Walter Savage Landor

CHATTO & WINDUS
LONDON

Published by
Chatto & Windus Ltd.,
40–42 William IV Street,
London W.C.2.

*

Clarke, Irwin & Co. Ltd.
Toronto

SBN 7011 1651 X

Printed in Great Britain by
Ebenezer Baylis & Son, Limited,
The Trinity Press, Worcester, and London

CONTENTS

ILLUSTRATIONS

FOREWORD

Looking back on the memories of seventy years, I can only write with profound gratitude for the kindness that the Fates have shown me. Whatever my remaining years may bring, my life has been a singularly happy, full and lucky one. Born in 1894 into the small well-to-do intellectual upper middle-class in what was then the greatest and wealthiest country in the world, the first two decades of my life had as their background a home never disturbed by any shadow of domestic discord and an environment of privileged security that seemed so firmly based as to be impervious to any winds of change. Few, indeed, of the human race in any era can have been so fortunate in their youth as were I and my contemporaries of my nationality and class.

Since 1914 I have fought as a soldier throughout one world war, and, unlike so many of my age, emerged undamaged in mind and body; I have taken part, equally without hurt, in a second world conflict as a civilian. I have lived in an era of change unparalleled in human history, but though, in its course, I have seen the decline and fall of the greatest empire since that of the Romans, as well as a social and material revolution in Britain at its centre, my own little niche has remained virtually untouched by any but on balance beneficent developments, and I have wholly escaped the disasters and miseries that during these years have fallen upon so many of the earth's inhabitants. I have never known want, nor hunger, nor disgrace, nor the lack of well-paid and interesting work and satisfying leisure occupations, nor, except as a soldier the absence of any reasonable creature comforts. My health has been above the average and though, of course, there have been sorrows in the deaths of parents, near relations and friends, I have, for the last thirty-five years, been blessed with the love and companionship of a wife far more gifted than myself.

I am fully aware how little deserved my exceptional good fortune has been, and I can only hope that my son may be as fortunate, and that, fifty years hence, he may be able to record his own life in similar happy terms; but I fear that the hope is a slender one. To me it seems highly dubious that humanity will be capable of controlling the new immense powers that science is giving it. Even if human folly does not lead to complete self-destruction, my own little corner of the world cannot continue much longer to enjoy what remains of an already greatly eroded privilege. The challenge to my successors is the most formidable one that mankind has yet faced. No doubt it is an exciting one, but I am relieved to know that I shall not be called upon to take it up.

CHAPTER I

i

I WAS born on 6th April 1894 at 2 Queensborough Terrace, off the Bayswater Road where my parents had begun their married life; but when I was about three they moved to 39 Leinster Gardens, in the same neighbourhood but a larger and more convenient house and I have no remembrance of my birth-place.

My father, Doctor Henry Huxley, was the younger surviving son of the great Victorian scientist and humanist, Thomas Henry Huxley. He was just under six foot tall, slimly built, with a pleasant face rendered handsomely striking by a superb curling moustache. In no way academically brilliant, he brought to his profession a notable common-sense flair for diagnosis, supremely gentle and skilful hands and a deep understanding of and sympathy with the sufferings of his patients, to whom he was a loved and trusted friend as well as doctor. All children were his special devotees and his mere entry into the sick room would act as a tonic. Later in life I was to hear many testimonials to him from grateful patients. Here I would only quote, as an example of their devotion, one letter which I found among his papers after his death. It was written to him by Queen Victoria's daughter, Princess Louise, Duchess of Argyle, whom he attended for many years. She was the artistic member of the Royal Family and her letter accompanied a picture which she had painted. 'Could the picture speak,' she wrote, 'it would tell of thoughts and gratitude worked into it towards one who has helped me much (perhaps quite without knowing it) by his example of noble unselfishness and untiring devotion to his work. This I fear sounds arrogant but a little wee cat may look at a King, may she not?' When once asked what was the secret of being a good doctor, his reply was 'understanding people'.

Being without private means and wanting to marry, my father had entered general practice when he left St. Bartholomew's hospital, his father-in-law advancing him the money to buy a share in a Dr. Hames' West End practice. The partnership was, however, broken by my father after only a year or two when he discovered that Dr. Hames' fashionable treatments included abortions. But even in a very short space of time young Doctor Huxley's qualities, aided no doubt by his good looks and by his father's world renown, had so impressed patients that he had no difficulty in launching out on his own, and, until he finally retired more than fifty years later, he remained one of London's most sought-after general practitioners.

As a child I saw far too little of him owing to the pressure of his work. But if remote, he was to me a much loved and respected figure, blessed with a simple and pleasant sense of humour and, above all, utterly reliable. As a boy he had, I believe, been known for his quick temper, but this had been fully mastered, partly perhaps through having been brought up with five clever, teasing sisters, but more, I think, through his devotion to his father on whose high ethical principles and code of conduct he patterned his own life.

His working day started at eight-thirty when he went off in a hansom cab to make his first calls, but before leaving he always paid a quick visit to the nursery where my sister and I were having our breakfast. About ten his carriage and pair would pick him up at a pre-arranged rendezvous to carry him swiftly on his rounds till his return home to a hurried lunch about one-thirty. From two to four he was 'at home' to patients in his consulting room. A cup of tea on a tray and he was off again on his rounds, this time in a single-horsed brougham. He would get home about seven-fifteen, in time to dress for dinner at seven-forty-five. Changing into a stiff white shirt and dinner jacket was obligatory even at home when your wife was your only company. Immediately after dinner and a cigar he would get busy with his letters which would occupy him until bedtime, about ten-thirty. This was a hard enough day in all conscience, but frequently the night bell would ring and my father would be called out at one or two in the morning to a maternity case. Snug in bed, I would hear the bustle below as my father dressed and went out, to return white and tired for breakfast and for the start of another day's grind. Nor was Sunday a full day of rest, though the consulting room was shut on Sunday afternoons, and calls, after two, were only made for really urgent cases. What, I think, saved my father's health was his six to eight weeks' summer holiday.

My mother, born Sophy Wylde Stobart, was the pervading and dominating influence in our home. The Stobarts came originally from the Hexham area of Northumberland and had been hard-riding and hard-drinking small Northumbrian squires. Moving south to Durham, Mother's branch had prospered by adding coal to land-owning, and my grandfather Stobart, besides being chairman of Wearmouth and other collieries, had large interests in iron, steel, docks and shipping. He now lived in Pepper Arden, a large house near Richmond in north Yorkshire. All the Stobart men were tall and handsome with regular clear-cut features, and Mother inherited the Stobart good looks. Her mother had been the daughter of General Wylde. As a colonel in the British army he had taken a prominent part in the Carlist war in Spain on the side of the Queen and a special medal had been struck in his honour for raising the siege of Bilbao. He had also been at the British Court on the household staff of the Prince Consort. The Wyldes were originally Verderers of Sherwood Forest. One—Gervas Wylde from whom I acquired my christian name—had been an Andalusian merchant and a friend of Drake's. He had fitted out two of his ships to fight with Drake against the Armada and had invented a 'secret weapon', arrows fired out of muskets, for which he had received a personal letter of thanks from Queen Elizabeth.

From the Stobarts, besides her looks, my mother inherited her hard-headed business efficiency, but her Wylde ancestry brought her a vivacity and love of the arts which had no place in the Stobart make-up. She was possessed of great vitality and energy, and her strong character made her over-anxious to order the lives of her husband and children. This was, I think, welcome to my over-worked father but detrimental to us children in sapping our self-reliance.

My mother's and father's courtship had been a romantic affair. When she was twenty she determined to break away from the comfortable routine of her Yorkshire home where interests were confined to hunting and social life. Against her father's wishes she went to London to train as a hospital nurse at Saint Bartholomew's. It was a bold and unorthodox step in days when a nurse's training was definitely not considered a suitable one for young ladies from wealthy 'county' backgrounds and when a probationer's first year was mainly spent in scrubbing floors on hands and knees. At Barts she caught the eye of my father, a young house-surgeon, and they fell in love. My father had no idea of Nurse Stobart's family background other than that her father lived in Yorkshire, and he got a considerable shock when on going north to ask for her father's consent to the marriage, he was met at Northallerton station by a brougham with liveried coachman and footman and was ushered by the butler into his fiancée's imposing home.

Their first child—my sister Marjorie—was born in 1891. I followed nearly three years later. Then came a gap of five and a half years (broken, I believe, by miscarriages) before my brother Michael's birth, followed in eighteen months by that of my other brother Christopher (always known as Kit). Finally, after another five-year interval, came my younger sister, Anne. Because of the gap between us and the next child, Marjorie and I were inseparable companions, and she was the most even-tempered, kind and tolerant elder sister a boy could wish for. With straight dark brown hair and dark blue eyes, she was a Stobart in looks, but as my mother's Aunt Hamilton had remarked on first seeing her 'of the plainest type'. My own looks were definitely Huxley, though my most noticeable feature was a mop of curly red-gold hair. This was much admired by the ladies and a source of vanity to myself until I started going to school when I found that curls, and especially golden ones, were an object of scorn to other boys. I then insisted on my hair being so cropped that it soon lost most of its curl.

My father employed no secretarial help since Mother was determined to fulfil all such duties herself.

Besides her domestic, secretarial and social duties, she somehow found time to play an active part in the Invalid Children's Aid Association. She also kept up with new books and went to concerts and art exhibitions. The Mecca of art was the Private View day at the Royal Academy, and Alma-Tadema's Grecian marble ladies were the height of artistic fashion. 'Art' was close to us, in the person of our uncle, the Hon. John Collier, whose 'problem pictures' were the sensation of successive Royal Academies. These pictures, as large as life and twice as natural, each depicted with photographic fidelity some social topic. 'Repentance oft I swore', a woman clasping the knee of a man on a fire-lit sofa. The problem, what had she (or he) done? 'The Cheat', a card party of two men and two women in full evening dress. The problem, which of the two women had cheated and how? Each year the problem picture received columns in the Press and drew the biggest crowds at the Academy. I wonder where these huge canvases are now? But Uncle Jack was a very competent portrait painter, especially of men, and made a large income from his art. His first wife was my father's eldest sister, Maidie, a very promising artist in her own right, who died young, soon after the birth of her first child Joyce. Uncle Jack's best work was painted under her influence and some of his portraits of that time, notably that of my grandfather, were very fine indeed. Later, Uncle Jack married my father's youngest sister Ethel. At that date, a marriage to a deceased wife's sister was still not legal in England, so they were married in Norway whose laws were more enlightened. But their two children, Laurence and Joan, were bastards in English law until the passing of the Deceased Wife's Sister Act. Somehow, the illegitimacy of their birth got to my ears and greatly intrigued me.

We always spent Christmas afternoon at North House, Uncle Jack and Aunt Ethel's home near Swiss Cottage.

Uncle Jack's studio with its canvases and smell of oil paint was a fascinating place. Awe-inspiring, if not fascinating, were the life-size nudes, fleshy yet austerely proper, that hung on the walls of the dining-room.

North House was always fun. Both Uncle Jack and Aunt Ethel had bad stammers, but no stammer could check or blunt their flow of sharp but good-humoured talk. Memories of North House are compounded of laughter and the quick thrust and parry of personal remarks and repartee. In that cheerful, if slightly undergraduate atmosphere, even the dull and sober became witty and gay at least in my uncritical eyes.

North House grew most familiar to me when I was taken there to be painted by Uncle Jack. I can remember sitting, clad in a white suit with frilly collar, perched up at a wooden nursery table, supposedly playing with some large wooden soldiers (which I thought very inferior to my own lead ones) while Mother read aloud to me from *The Rambles of a Rat* and I sucked toffee.

One of my earliest recollections of our Leinster Gardens house and certainly the most vivid is that of a fire. I remember my father waking Marjorie and me in the night nursery and our being hurriedly taken down to the dining-room with an acrid smell of smoke filling the house. A bin of inflammable material had been left in the basement yard outside the kitchen. Somehow this had caught alight and the fire was merrily burning its way into the kitchen passage, when, after midnight, our next-door neighbour, providentially returning from some party, saw the flickering of the flames and roused our household. From the dining-room we watched a procession of firemen with hoses and buckets coming through the hall and descending the stairs to the basement. The fire was soon put out and little damage done, but I can remember with what self-importance I related every detail to my friends at the kindergarten next day. The incident left me for years with a dread of fire and many a time I woke up in the night and tiptoed to the door of my little bedroom to sniff the air for any sign of smoke. I also acquired an almost automatic habit, when sleeping in a new place, of examining and deciding on the best means of escape if cut off by fire.

The daily routine of children in our part of London included morning and afternoon walks in Kensington Gardens. Inside the Gardens, the Round Pond was easily our favourite. Here I sailed my toy boat and watched the other boats of all shapes and sizes. Other times we would trundle our hoops along the Broad Walk or round the shores of the Serpentine.

After nursery tea it was the invariable routine that we were changed into best clothes and escorted down to the drawing-room for an hour or so with Mother until bath- and bedtime. The hour was usually spent in being read aloud to by Mother, while I lay on the floor and scribbled drawings on half-sheets of note-paper. Mother had a great gift for reading aloud. Walter Scott's novels were our favourites. I suspect that Mother must skilfully have skipped dull passages, as we were never bored. Sometimes we had singing round the grand piano at the end of the drawing-room annexe. I can remember a book of children's songs with Kate Greenaway illustrations. There was also a book with one song in it about a dog, disguised as a doctor who came to visit his patient, an elderly cat. The words went 'Doctor Dog comes running, just to see her begs.' What precise portion of her anatomy constituted her 'begs' which the Doctor so badly wanted to see remained a perpetual source of secret wonder. I never ventured to ask what they were.

When we were bathed and in bed, Mother would come up to kiss us good night, while we tried to make her stay a little longer and tell us more stories of her childhood, which was always a subject of the most intense interest to us. Our great plea was for 'more about when you were naughty'. Crime and punishment indeed, always rated higher with us than virtue and rewards.

We fell asleep with the quiet sounds of Hannah in the day nursery reassuring us by her friendly presence and with her light shining through the just-open door. Often, from the street outside, would come the tinkling strains of a barrel organ or the louder music of a 'German band'. Barrel organs were, of course, London's main source of popular music, playing the latest tunes such as 'Daisy, Daisy' and her bicycle built for two ; or, at the beginning of the Boer War, that romantically sad ballad, 'Good-bye, Dolly Gray'. Most of the barrel organs were operated by swarthy Italians, and often had, as an accessory, a little monkey on a chain, dressed up in clothes and holding out in tiny paws a tin mug to collect the pennies of charitable music lovers.

Why the bands of itinerant musicians (usually three or four players) were all Germans, I don't know ; but they were. Both barrel organ grinders and the German bands lived on the pennies (and I suppose an occasional 3d. or 6d.) given to them—sometimes, no doubt, by non-lovers of this type of music to make them go away ; and I can only suppose, from their numbers, that it must have been a paying profession.

Treats varied our routine. Some Sunday afternoons we were taken to the Zoo, on others we visited one or other of the South Kensington museums. In the entrance of the National History Museum is a statue to my grandfather, Thomas Henry Huxley. I can just remember its unveiling ceremony by the Prince of Wales (afterwards King Edward VII), when I watched my father and his elder brother, Uncle Leonard, in frock coats, shaking hands with Royalty. My principal recollection of the event, however, is of my cousin Aldous, overcome by excitement, being sick into the only available receptacle—his father's top-hat. How sad it is that one's memories of great events are so often confined to the most trivial incidents. I can, for instance, remember being taken to the Reginald Smiths' house at the top of Park Lane to watch Queen Victoria's funeral procession, but my only distinct recollection of the occasion is of finding a green caterpillar in my salad and of being rebuked for drawing loud attention to it.

The greatest treat of the whole year was the Drury Lane Pantomime. A large crowd of Huxley relations always made up a party for it, including the Colliers and Julian, Trev and Aldous, Uncle Leonard's three boys, and other cousins. We went, of course, to the matinée and sat in the Dress Circle.

The Drury Lane Panto was then in the heyday of its glory, with Dan Leno and Herbert Campbell as its star comedians. The show lasted a good four hours, so we got full measure. I was most impressed, I think, by the unimaginable splendours of the 'transformation scenes' when serried rows of gorgeously attired supers marched and countermarched and made patterns of colour up and down the huge stage.

Shopping with mother was one of our more common treats. The usual route was down Leinster Gardens and along Westbourne Grove to the Bank where Mother would pay in the cheques from patients. Thence we usually went to Whiteley's, the first of London's great department stores. The biggest thrill that Whiteley's ever provided was the murder of Mr. Whiteley himself in his own store by a young man who claimed to be his illegitimate son. We had been in Whiteley's that morning and I can remember seeing, from our nursery window, Whiteley's house flag, with its globe, at half mast in mourning for the dead proprietor.

Marjorie's and my first school was a kindergarten run by a Miss Moore. I greatly enjoyed going there and the pleasures of learning to count with beads strung on wires and of clay modelling. When I was six I went to Norland Place, a large day school for boys and girls off the Bayswater Road towards the Shepherd's Bush end. Marjorie had already preceded me there. The headmistress was Miss Langhorne, an imposing white-haired lady, but I remember best my form mistress, Miss Winter, of whom I was very fond. Again, I greatly enjoyed school as represented by Norland Place—a 'real school' this time and therefore the source of much pride. We had prayers every morning and exercise books stamped with the school crest and motto.

After two years at Norland Place I went for a year to Wilkinson's, a well-known boys' day school in Orme Square, Bayswater. Wilkinson's was the school referred to in Barrie's *Peter Pan*, and his adopted boys George and Jack Llewellyn Davies were contemporaries of mine there. I used to sit next to Jack in form and cordially disliked him. Mr. Wilkinson, the headmaster, was a ferocious figure with sweeping moustaches, and I can remember his scorn when, at Mother's request, I asked him if we had a Whitsun holiday, but I much liked my friendly form master Mr. Toller, and got on well in his class We had organized games at some suburban playing fields, reached by bus and I was introduced to soccer and cricket without much success. But Wilkinson's also had—daily I think—a game of its own played in Kensington Gardens. This was a kind of Prisoners' Base and I loved and excelled at it, being, for my age, a very swift runner.

My chief recollections of my Wilkinson year are out of school ones. My great friends were Nick Wadham and two Nott Bower boys, sons of the Chief Constable of the City of London. All our homes were close to each other. The four of us formed a 'gang', partly for mutual support in school, but more for offensive operations outside. We always went to and from school together and our return home was a very lengthy progress, full of alarms and excursions, since we chose the most circuitous route possible by ways that led us through slum districts in order that we might wage war against 'cads', in which term we included all boys of inferior social status. We used to flaunt ourselves in the cads' haunts in order to pick fights with them and to this end always carried sticks or umbrellas.

So far as I remember, the contests were more in the nature of running fights than pitched battles. Ringing door bells and then scooting off was another way of enlivening our slow progress home. In the winter we bought 'whizz-bangs' —little explosive paper bags which went off with a loud bang when thrown hard on to the pavement. Armed with these weapons, we had endless fun in startling old ladies, dogs and other prey. It was in company with the gang that I first smoked. Nick Wadham purloined two of his father's cigars, each of which we cut in half and puffed with—astonishingly—no ill results.

Looking back, I am not surprised that, after a year at Wilkinson's, Mother decided that I must be sent to a boarding school in the country.

For dancing and deportment, Marjorie and I went to Miss Wordsworth's famous dancing classes. Dressed in my best I reluctantly and clumsily learned the polka, the Highland Schottische, the Barn Dance, the Gallop and the Valse (in those days 'reversing' was unknown or definitely bad form and one just went round and round), and the 'Lancers'. Miss Wordsworth, who was reputed to have one glass eye, was a tartar for discipline and her pupils never strayed from the path of exemplary behaviour.

Marjorie learned the piano, but my musical education was limited to going to a Miss Mills' solfa classes. Regular riding lessons were also part of our curriculum. We started in an indoor riding school and later used to join a party, led by a riding master, that walked, trotted and cantered in Rotten Row.

I had little illness as a child, apart from ordinary childish ailments, such as tummy upsets to be treated with cod liver oil and Dinneford's Milk of Magnesia, and coughs and colds for which the remedy was ammoniated tincture of quinine with its hateful bitter taste, or, in the case of chest colds, a loathsome linseed poultice tied round one's neck in a muslin bag as hot as could be borne and almost choking one with its smell. An attack of ringworm on my head was enjoyable rather than otherwise since it involved a daily bus journey to the City for treatment at St. Bartholomew's hospital. I can remember minor operations for tonsils and adenoids, but principally because the anaesthetist, Dr. Macdonald, had no roof to his mouth. His intriguing method of speech (which I tried to imitate) provided some compensation for the ordeal of chloroform and ether with its long-lingering sickly-sweet smell and its aftermath of violent vomiting.

Spurred, I suppose, by seeing an elder sister read, I was eager for books and their magic, and reading was one of my childhood stand-byes. The Tenniel-illustrated *Alice*, *Robinson Crusoe*, *The Swiss Family Robinson*, *Black Beauty*, the George Macdonald books—*At the Back of the North Wind*, *The Princess and the Goblins* and *The Princess and Curdie*— were all very early favourites, as were Hans Andersen's and

Grimm's fairy stories and Miss Molesworth's and Charlotte M. Yonge's books. A little later came Henty's historical novels and Fitchett's *Deeds that Won the Empire* and his *Indian Mutiny*. Marjorie was a subscriber to *St. Nicholas*—an American children's magazine of outstanding quality—and I became an equal *St. Nicholas* addict and was thus familiar at a very early age with the American scene. On railway journeys we were sometimes given the *Strand Magazine* to look at, which, at that time, usually contained a brand-new Sherlock Holmes story. Our own travel-taste, however, ran more to highly coloured 'comics'—*Ally Sloper's Half Holiday*, the *Rainbow*, etc. *Punch* was, of course, an institution in our home and we had the complete bound volumes from its start. These provided a really valuable background, even for my childish mind, to the whole social and political history of the Victorian age.

In my own childhood, the outstanding public event was the Boer War. I remember a map of South Africa pinned up in my father's consulting room, with little flags stuck in to mark the position of our armies. I remember, too, helping to hang flags out from our balcony for victories, and seeing the City Imperial Volunteers marching off in khaki with their Australian-type slouch hats. But my chief memory of the war is of the little lapel buttons that all right-minded children wore. The buttons had on them a picture of one or other of the British Generals—Lord Roberts, Kitchener, Buller, White (Ladysmith's defender), Baden-Powell, etc. The wearer of a particular general had of course to stand up for his favourite against the supporters of rival commanders. It was unfortunate that Sir Redvers Buller was my choice. The legendary aura of Queen Victoria brooded over all Britons, even children. I saw her driving once or twice, and well remember my parents' hushed tones when they told us of her death. As I have told, we watched her funeral procession and were to have seen King Edward's coronation, but this was postponed, and we were away on our summer holidays when the event took place and had to be content with a village sports meeting and the present of a coronation mug.

Each year, soon after Christmas, Marjorie and I were packed off to Eastbourne in the charge of our nurse in order to benefit from the sea air. We were well wrapped up for the train journey from Victoria Station since, on the Eastbourne line, the non-corridor compartments had no form of heating other than iron footwarmers filled with hot water which, on request, a porter would place in the carriage.

Eastbourne's bracing air was not the sole reason for our parents' choice of a seaside resort for us. It was to Eastbourne that Grandpater had retired for the last years of his life, building a house there, Hodeslea in Staveley Road, Meads. He had died in 1895 but his widow, our beloved 'granmoo' as all the family called her, still lived there, and, while Marjorie and I and Hannah stayed in lodgings, our day's routine invariably included a visit to 'granmoo'. Since I was only a year old when my grandfather died, I had no first-hand memories of him, but he was always a very vivid figure in my childhood from my parents' talk of him. My father lived all his life under Thomas Henry's influence and, on her marriage, my mother had at once fallen under his spell. From my earliest days it was his example that I was taught to try to follow. At Hodeslea his study was kept undisturbed as he had used it.

I think that my father was 'granmoo's' favourite child and he and my mother were devoted to her. We children dearly loved her kindly wrinkled face with her thin grey hair covered by a white lace cap, and her eyes twinkling behind steel spectacles. Our daily visit to her was indeed always 'fun'. She would play lively tunes on the piano for us and there was at Hodeslea a grand game of which we never tired consisting of fishing with little rods and lines for cardboard fish on a board. I well remember, too, a delightful illustrated children's book whose rhymes we got to know by heart.

Eastbourne in the nineties, in my childhood recollection, was composed of kindly landladies who gossiped with our nurse, of clean red-brick sidewalks, of gravel paths with low evergreen hedges, and the red-brick dullness of The Parade, crowded with invalids in bath chairs pushed by old men. The Parade must have been the scene of the story my father used to tell of 'granmoo' following a brood of her grandchildren and exclaiming, 'How nice it is to see one's posterior walking in front of one.'

At Easter and for August and September, Marjorie and I were sent north to 'Pepper'—Pepper Arden—where our Grandfather Stobart lived with his unmarried daughter, our Aunt Amy, as hostess. My first really clear memory of Pepper dates from August 1899 when I was five and a half years old. Our nurse had taken Majorie and me there to be out of the way while Mother was giving birth to Michael in London, an event of which we were left in such complete ignorance that even the alteration in the shape of Mother's figure as her pregnancy advanced escaped our notice or was otherwise explained away. What, at Pepper, I vividly remember is being summoned to the drawing-room as Aunt Amy had something very exciting to tell us. Speculating on what this could be, we ran downstairs to be informed that we had a little baby brother, a piece of news which we thought a sad let-down as we were perfectly content with our family as it was and did not much like the thought of the changes that this unexpected addition would be bound to bring about. How and why the baby had joined our family was, of course, completely veiled in mystery.

Pepper Arden was a great ugly barrack of a Victorian house, bought, I believe, by my grandfather mainly because he got it cheap, after he had relinquished the lease of the lovely Elizabethan Norton Conyers, the ancestral house of the Grahams where my mother had spent her childhood. But to us children Pepper was paradisical. I suppose its most welcome attribute was that it was so large that we were able to lead there lives largely severed from those of our parents or grown-up relations.

Our world was the nursery and servants' wing. All the first-floor rooms in this wing opened out of a long corridor, glorious for races and games. At one end was the day nursery, with barred windows looking out on to part of the gardens. My chief memory of the nursery's contents is of an oleographic picture of a dove holding a branch in its mouth. The wording below the picture said, 'The voice of the turtle is heard in the land.' Why the turtle and what its voice was like were a constant puzzle to me. Next door, along the passage, was a big night nursery and then a series of maids' bedrooms. At the side of the far end of the passage a locked door led to the menservants' wing. At the nursery end, a door opened into the main part of the house. The windows of the corridor looked out on to a cobbled square courtyard.

Most of the inhabitants of the maids' rooms were our close friends and allies. The head cook was, however, an exception, dignified by the honorary title of 'Mrs'. We were forbidden to invade her demesne with the threat that we should swiftly emerge 'with a dishcloth tied to our tails'.

Certain figures stand out in the hierarchy of the Pepper servants. First was 'Bestie'. Her real name was Swainson. She had been my mother's nurse and was now housekeeper. She had, of course, her own sitting-room where her meals were brought to her in solitary grandeur. Clothed in rustling black silk, she was a formidable woman with a more than formidable tongue but also with a remarkably soft heart which I knew well how to exploit. From Bestie's waist there dangled a load of keys, some of which opened the various store cupboards of which she was mistress. Many a fig, raisin, or sweet biscuit did I cajole out of her. She was addicted to saws and sayings. Fruit, for instance, was 'gold in the morning, silver at noon and lead at night'. When put out, she would declare that she'd been thrown 'into a canary fit'.

Then there was Parkin, the butler, a man of amazing talent in my admiring eyes. Apart from butlering, he was an expert portrait photographer. He could also cut hair, and, in his range of rooms where silver was endlessly polished and where one footman was employed solely for cleaning and trimming the paraffin lamps, Parkin had a stringed musical instrument, something like a zither on which he was an expert performer.

There were also various nieces of Bestie's, the female element in a large family of house painters who lived in Richmond. One of them was Maggie, who became our undernurse when Michael arrived and subsequently Michael and Kit's nurse. Annie and Florrie were two of Maggie's sisters. They were my earliest loves, especially Florrie. Annie was one of Pepper's numerous housemaids and I used to creep into her warm bed on many an early morning.

I could not now say whether the gardens were beautiful or not, but they were a source of endless pleasure to us children. One of the lawns was, of course, devoted to croquet, but we did not share in this 'grown-up' game. Our chief recreation was a swing in a piece of wild garden where blue convolvulus rioted up a bank. We also had a lair in a thick patch of shrubbery where there was a tangle of hops which we used to use as food in our games of keeping house. There were tall brick walls covered with fruit trees, yielding unripe apples and pears to our greedy hands. A favoured play-place was a large conservatory, opening out of the billiard room. Here we used to sail little homemade boats of walnut-shells on the water tanks.

The chief feature of Pepper Arden was a very large hall, two storeys high; and the chief feature of the hall was a stuffed tiger in one corner on which we proudly rode. Near the tiger was the gong. It was our ambition to make it reverberate with the skill of Parkin, but all attempts to do so were promptly squashed. The gong received its first beating of the day in the summons to family prayers before breakfast. My grandfather promptly appeared, prayer book in hand and proceeded to the dining-room where prayers were held. Guests and family would hurry downstairs. Then, headed by the junior under-house or kitchenmaid and with the rear brought up by Parkin and Bestie, a procession of the domestic staff would file into the hall from the servants' quarters and on into the dining-room. Family and guests sat or kneeled at chairs, the servants at benches brought in by the footmen. The prayers were always read by Grandfather. Back to the nursery we children then went for breakfast, while the grown-ups got down to an enormous meal laid out in plated dishes on the sideboard.

The gong was sounded again for lunch, then for 'dressing'—three-quarters of an hour before dinner—and finally for dinner itself.

I don't know how many rooms Pepper contained, but it must have been a very large number. There was, of course, no central heating nor electricity. The living-rooms were lit by paraffin lamps and the bedrooms with candles. In the evening rows of little silver candlesticks were put out in the hall. With these the grown-ups lighted their way to their bedrooms. In the night nursery the candle cast long wavering shadows and when it was blown out the smell of hot wax lingered on.

Pepper contained only one bathroom—my grandfather's —a huge room with a sunk bath, and we in the nurseries, equally with the guests in the best bedrooms, had our baths in large enamelled tin tubs in front of the bedroom fire.

Galsworthy's *Forsyte Saga* gives one a good idea of the Stobarts—solidly rich and hard men of property—with my grandfather as the principal figure. Grannie had been dead for some years before I first visited Pepper, but her features were familiar to me from her portrait by Herkomer which hung in the dining-room. She was, I believe, a woman of great vivacity and unconventional spirit. When she was over seventy, she committed suicide. Her reason was apparently her utter boredom with Pepper and with the business and sporting atmosphere in which she was compelled to live in company with Stobarts having no intellectual interests. She found an old pistol and got the gamekeeper to show her how to fire it. Then she shot herself.

Grandfather Stobart was well over seventy in the days I remember him. But he was still a fine figure of a man, tall, broad and heavy with strong regular features and a wonderfully clear pink complexion. He always looked as if he had just come out of a cold bath. I think we were rather frightened of him, but he had an endearing custom of hiding grapes which the grandchildren had then to find. Black grapes were usually hidden in corners of some groups of black statuary which adorned the dining-room.

I can remember him best sitting upright with all his eighteen stone on the back of a big weight-carrying horse or driving in the dogcart and teaching me the names of trees.

Next in importance to Grandfather came Aunt Amy, Mother's elder and unmarried sister. Like my mother, she must have inherited her spirit from the Wyldes for she, too, was a rebel against the conventions of the day. In her case, Art had been the channel. She had left home to study painting under Herkomer at Bushey and had led what was then probably referred to as the life of a 'bachelor girl'. In the eyes of county Yorkshire, she was unusual and definitely 'advanced'.

Aunt Amy had a well-deserved reputation for unfortunate remarks. At dinner one night, when the ladies were leaving the table, she called out to my cousin Hugh, just seventeen— 'Well, Hugh, are you staying with the men or coming to bed with the ladies !' On another occasion, visiting Pepper between a round of country house visits, she proclaimed herself 'Just a bird of paradise'. She was a keen and good amateur actress, but once gravely offended a very stuffy old dowager staying at Pepper by disguising herself as a young Frenchman and making open and violent love to the dowager until the latter fled to her bedroom and locked herself in. Altogether Aunt Amy was great fun and we children were very fond of her.

There were five Stobart uncles (Mother's brothers) all married and all, except Uncle Will, with children, so that Pepper usually housed a number of our cousins. The most familiar to us were Winifred and Dorothy, the youngest daughters of Uncle Douglas, Mother's eldest brother. They were a great deal at Pepper, because of the unsatisfactory nature of their mother, Aunt Isabel, a blowsy dark-eyed Irishwoman whom Uncle Douglas had married in Winnipeg and who was definitely 'not quite a lady'. Winifred and Dorothy were jolly, hearty girls, much given to teasing a small boy. I can remember well being questioned by them as to what I supposed happened to my dinner after I had eaten it. I replied with appropriate gestures that it started down my throat and came eventually out at my toes. I can see them now, doubled up with laughter and making me repeat my theory to the grown-ups.

The biggest tease was Uncle Harry, Mother's youngest brother. But he was also great fun and we were very fond of him and of Aunt Bessie, his wife, a Canadian by birth, as was Aunt Margaret, Uncle Fred's wife. Grandfather had profitably invested money in a business in Winnipeg and three of his sons had worked in it and married Canadian wives. Uncle Fred—a rare visitor in those days as he still lived in Winnipeg—was enjoyable because of his Canadian accent. Uncle Frank was, however, the most successful and richest of the Stobart brothers with his Durham colliery and railway interests. He and Aunt Mittie's two older children Hugh and Kate were our seniors in age. Kate we greatly disliked because of her stuck-up ways, but we were fond of Ralph, the youngest child and our contemporary.

Finally there were Uncle Will and Aunt Frances. Uncle Will—Major Stobart—had been a heavy dragoon until forced to retire through illness. He still preserved a heavy-dragoonish air but was especially kind to us as he was very devoted to Mother. Typical of the cavalry mind of those days was his letter to Mother when she got engaged to my father. Professor Huxley was at the height of his international renown, but Uncle Will's sole comment on his son was, 'Are you sure that he's a gentleman?'

Aunt Frances was a brusque figure who hid her kindness beneath a rather sharp exterior. I remember complaining that I couldn't drink my milk because of the skin on top and that I should be sick if I tried. 'Very well,' said Aunt Frances, '*be* sick, but out of the window!'

It was at Pepper that religion first loomed large in my life. My father, as one would expect from his upbringing, was an agnostic. Like Grandpater his code of ethics was a very strict one, but he had no use for organized religion. The Stobarts were however strong and conventional Anglicans of the low

Church persuasion, in which tradition Mother had been brought up and confirmed. But after her marriage she gradually adopted my father's agnosticism. All her children were however baptized, and though in London we never went to church, Mother used to read Bible stories to us on Sundays. At Pepper, however, religion was taken very seriously. Prayers every week-day morning, while on Sundays secular books and games were barred and only 'improving' books allowed, mawkish tales of good little children being taken early to Heaven. I am afraid that I wallowed in this sort of sentiment. There was usually some sort of a 'companion' living at Pepper—an elderly indigent spinster or 'decayed gentlewoman'. I do not know what her precise function was but she inevitably became a butt for Grandfather's common-sense arrows. These ladies were zealous in imparting religion to children and we had many quasi-religious stories read to us on Sunday evenings in the morning-room.

Church on Sunday morning at Cowton was, of course, a compulsory affair to which the whole household walked across the Park. For a long time I cherished a vague idea that Mr. Parker, the clergyman, and Jesus Christ were akin, since Mr. Parker wore a reddish beard of precisely the form in the picture of Christ in my prayer book. Later I learned that there was a strong feud between my grandfather and Mr. Parker. Grandfather was low Church, Mr. Parker, high. On one occasion, observing lighted candles on the altar at Matins, Grandfather marched up the aisle and blew them out, remarking audibly that he wasn't going to have candles wasted in daylight.

Altogether, life at Pepper was a very pleasant and comfortable business, wrapped in a complete economic and social security that seemed to be so grounded that nothing could ever shake it.

CHAPTER II

i

O NE autumn evening in 1944, I travelled down by rail from London to see my father in his new house at Shackleford. After leaving Guildford, the train stopped at a dark little station and I heard a porter's voice calling out 'Farncombe, Farncombe'. For a moment I was back forty years, with that empty feeling in the pit of my stomach, hearing the same cry that marked the end of happy holidays and the return to Hillside, my preparatory school, to the certain and uncertain miseries of a new term.

'Miseries' is an exaggerated word to use, except as a contrast to the holidays, since I was very far from miserable all my days at my preparatory school. The sharpness of the transition from home comfort, privacy and freedom to the prison atmosphere of school would wear off after a short time. What I could not escape, I would accept and endure, passively without rebellion or regret. School life had undoubtedly its pleasures as well as its pains, but it was a life lived at a different level from home, where happiness was keyed so much higher and where unhappiness was so rare and minor a thing.

I suppose that those thrice-yearly transitions were good for me. At least they enured me early to making the best of the inevitable and forced to stand on his own feet a small boy of very unadventurous character who would never have taken any plunge by himself. All the later dives into the unknown that I have had to undertake were, I believe, made far easier by such early initiation into acceptance of the lesson that, in the ultimate, a human being must rely on himself alone.

Anyway, my initiation began in the autumn of 1903 when I was nine years old. In spite of a toughening year at

Wilkinson's in London, boarding school was very much of an unknown—and hence alarming—country. But there were compensations to offset apprehension. Boarding school marked a definite stage in the exciting career of growing up. there were new and more grown-up clothes ; a wooden play-box with one's name on it in black letters ; a silver pencil from Marjorie ; tips from Grandfather and various aunts— more money than I had ever had in my pocket before ; above all a pleasant sense of being important and of filling the centre of the home stage.

My departure for Hillside took place from Pepper Arden. Mother came south with me and also escorted my cousin Ralph Stobart who, like me, was going to his preparatory school. I was given *The Three Musketeers* to read in the train, but the distraction of thinking of what lay ahead was too much for the book, and I have never succeeded in reading it since.

All I can remember of my arrival at Hillside is entering a large classroom full of boys and sitting on a wooden bench beside my cousin Aldous—also a new boy—who was weeping copiously at leaving home. I myself was much too excited and over-awed by the novel surroundings to indulge in tears. Besides Aldous, there were two other new boys whom I knew ; Lewis Gielgud whom I had often met at children's parties and whose parents were very old family friends ; and Nick Wadham, who had been a fellow-member of our Wilkinson's gang.

Hillside had about fifty boys from eight to fourteen years old. The headmaster was Mr. Gidley Robinson—commonly known as 'Gude'. He may once have been a good headmaster. In 1903 he was old and definitely past his best. He had a silver-haired wife, an amateur artist of some merit, who radiated a forlorn sweetness, much despised by the boys. Mr. Taylor was the senior member of the resident staff. While other masters came and went, he was a permanent fixture. I think he was a thoroughly frustrated and embittered man, conscious of having got into a blind alley unworthy of his gifts, but unable to escape from it. Nevertheless he was a

good teacher, genuinely fond of boys and we liked and respected him. The other permanent member of the staff was
Mr. Jacques—or 'Jacko' as he was nicknamed. This kindly
soul was the science master and lived in Godalming. 'Jacko'
was born to be the butt of small boys who ragged him un-
mercifully. Another non-resident master was Mr. Macintosh
who taught music—a bespectacled old buffoon ; while the
two Miss Noons from Godalming supposedly taught drawing—lines and circles with chalk on blackboards—to bored
classes. The remainder of the staff were transients who only
came to Hillside in the hope of getting a better job elsewhere
as soon as possible. Finally there was 'Ma' James, the matron,
an irascible ill-educated old woman, whose favourite phrase
was 'stop your imperence [sic] or I'll report you'. I admit that
she must have been sorely tried.

'Gude' being old and tired, supervision was lax, with the
result that the older boys were free to indulge their unpleasant habits at the expense of the smaller fry. One custom
was to range the small boys at one end of the large classroom (the only sitting-room for the school) as target while
the elder boys fired at them with catapults, using hard little
paper pellets as missiles.

Fighting was a frequent pastime promoted among the
juniors by the elder boys, either as individual fights or as
team contests. One favourite form of the latter was for a
couple of older boys to go round asking the juniors whether
they were 'mushrooms' or 'pears', that is circumcized or un-
circumcized. The two sides would then be ranged against
each other and made to fight for the amusement of the
seniors. New boys were, of course, mere dirt. Anything they
did or said was apt to be labelled 'cheek', to be punished by
arm-twisting, buffets or kicks. At night, the dormitories
provided good fun for the seniors. Running the gauntlet
with wet towels flicked at the victim's bare back, beatings
with slipper or hair-brush-back for imagined offences, cold
water poured into beds, such were samples of these diversions.

There was of course absolutely no privacy nor any chance
of reading a book or any other quiet pursuit. I can remember

my dismay on one of my first days at being chased out of a civilized lavatory on the dormitory floor—where I had gone in order to read in private Mother's first letter to me—and being driven to the communal earth-closets on what was known as 'the Hill'.

Life at Hillside proved too much altogether for some little boys. I recall two who came the same term as I did and were removed by their parents after passing one or two terms almost permanently in tears. Weeping was, of course, no defence against the general bullying, but only increased the zest and zeal of the tormentors. The best protection was an assumed indifference to torment coupled with sycophantic approbation of the bullies when their efforts were directed against some other wretched infant. One had to practise the arts of lying and insincerity and to abandon any moral bravery in the effort to survive in comparative peace.

I was very lucky in having the staunchest of friends in my cousin Aldous, and an ally—albeit one of no power—in Lewis Gielgud. Together, Aldous and I were a less vulnerable target than we would have been singly. We were also both big for our age.

By virtue of being three months older than Aldous, I was Huxley Major and he Huxley Minor. Strange to say, I retained my seniority in the classroom and was always a place or two higher than Aldous in form, but this, I think, must have been due to his rather frequent absences through illness.

In the memorial volume that Julian edited after Aldous' death I wrote a piece in the course of which I tried to describe Aldous in our Hillside days. 'Aldous,' I wrote, 'possessed the key to an inviolable inner fortress of his own, into which he could and did withdraw from the trials and miseries of school existence. Fleeting though these were, they seemed to most of us to darken not just the moment but the whole of life. Aldous was able to put them into perspective. Never can I remember him losing his self-control or giving way to violent emotion as most of us did. It was impossible to quarrel with him. Any waves of ill-natured spite or temper broke up at once when they met the shore of his integrity and complete unselfishness. Another factor which helped him to preserve his remarkable sense of proportion was the deeply interested curiosity with which, even at that age, he regarded the behaviour of the world and his fellows. If we somehow felt that Aldous moved on a different plane from the rest of us, it was not that he held aloof from his fellows. On the contrary, he was the most companionable of companions, and a full sharer in all our schoolboy nonsense, only with nonsense more imaginatively nonsensical than anyone else's.'

It is with Aldous that all my memories of Hillside are inseparably connected, and in those years a bond was forged between us that lasted throughout his life and that no length of absence ever weakened.

The food at Hillside was thoroughly bad. My stomach still turns at the thought of the breakfast porridge full of greenish, sour-tasting lumps. The meat at lunch was generally considered to be horse. Between lunch and breakfast next morning, all we had was thick chunks of bread at tea, thinly buttered and with a scrape of jam.

Games took place on the playing field on the crest of the hill and in a separate field just beyond. We played soccer in winter and cricket in summer. I liked soccer, but cricket, for the small fry, was turned into an occasion for further torments. A missed catch or failure to field a ball was the invariable excuse for the use of the stumps on the hinder portion of the offender. Most of us, I fancy, heartily loathed the game. Nevertheless we all kept little scoring books in which we played endless games of 'paper cricket' between our favourite county sides or teams representing the Universe versus the Rest. What I enjoyed most was the Athletic Sports, held each summer term. Being very tall and slim built I was by far the fastest runner of my age and won, each year, a collection of silver gilt trophies.

There was a corrugated iron gymnasium on the playing fields and a carpenters' shop. Gymnasium classes were dull and unimaginative, but the carpenters' shop was fun even for boys like myself who were unhandy with their fingers. The shop was in charge of a dear old carpenter and I turned out book ends and pipe racks to be given as Christmas presents to parents. Once a week, in summer, we used to go to the Charterhouse swimming bath and, in spite of the lack of any proper instruction, I gradually learned to swim after a fashion.

On Sunday mornings, arrayed in large stiff 'eton' collars and little black 'eton' jackets, and grey striped trousers, the whole school marched down the hill to Farncombe Church. We were given 3d. a week pocket money on Saturdays, but one penny had to be reserved for the Church collection. Unfortunately, though I suspect designedly, the collection was made on a plate by one of the masters, thus preventing offerings of buttons. With the remaining twopence we were allowed to buy sweets from the matron. Prudent boys kept back a caramel or two for sucking in church during the sermon. Shortly after I had left Hillside, Mother handed on one of my 'eton' suits to my brother Michael for use at his prep school. Michael was rather fussy over his clothes and I can remember his fury of indignation at finding the remains of a half-sucked caramel sticking in the lining of one of the waistcoat pockets.

After lunch on Sundays, Aldous and I were allowed to walk over to Priors Field, the girls' school which had been started by Aldous' mother, my Aunt Judy. At that time it was only a few years old and was a modest affair, though rapidly expanding into the large and very successful school which it soon became. My cousin Joan Collier was there (Marjorie went there later) and Aldous and I were friends with many of the girls as well as with the mistresses. Aunt Judy herself was a gracious if slightly alarming person wearing pince-nez. Uncle Leonard was also always there on Sundays. During the week he went up to London every day, where he worked in the publishing office of Smith Elder's. Then there was Aldous' old nurse, a German from East Prussia, who was in charge of Aldous' young sister Margaret. Julian and Trev—Aldous' elder brothers—had already left Hillside and, in term time, were away at Eton. The home-like atmosphere of Priors Field was a glorious change from Hillside, as was the excellent tea we enjoyed. The rest of Hillside went on a country walk, accompanied by one of the masters. Aldous and I had to partake in this, when, as happened quite frequently, some infectious disease at either school kept us from going to Priors Field. In summer such country walks were made enjoyable by Mr. Taylor who was an expert butterfly and moth hunter and who encouraged a like enthusiasm amongst the boys. So most of us went armed with butterfly nets and killing bottles and Mr. Taylor gave a prize for the first specimen of any species captured.

At Hillside there were three or four dormitories, each with ten or twelve beds and a large room divided into cubicles for the oldest boys. Kneeling down by the side of the bed to say prayers was compulsory night and morning. At night small boys used to make their prayers as lengthy as possible, since only when kneeling at prayers was there sanctuary for them. Every morning, winter and summer, we had to have three quick dips in a cold bath and once a week each boy had a hot bath at night.

The teaching at Hillside in my first years there was uninspired. It certainly failed to evoke any enthusiasm in me and I only worked at my lessons for fear of the punishments that were freely dealt out to delinquents. Punishments were, in order of leniency, keeping in, writing lines and canings. These latter were always inflicted on the hand—a particularly painful proceeding on a cold day. Latin was taught to the youngest ; Greek a little later. History teaching followed the dreary practice of concentrating on pre-Tudor times, with endless names of Saxon Kings and dates to be learned parrot-wise, together with the reading of a few irrelevant anecdotes, the parts failing to fit into any pattern or to make any long-term meaning at all. 'English' consisted of learning by heart and reciting third-rate poems such as the 'Wreck of the Schooner *Hesperus*', Southey's 'Battle of Blenheim' or Campbell's 'Mariners of England', together with dull grammar and parsing. Geography was reduced to learning lists of rivers and capitals. Nor was there any encouragement to boys to read or learn for themselves. There was no library ; no place or time for reading. Out of school and organized games hours, the boys filled in their time by ragging or playing such traditional games as 'cheesers' with horse-chestnuts in autumn, whipping tops in winter, and stump and paper cricket in summer. Another winter game was played with pen nibs, the opponents pushing their rival nibs along a desk or the floor with the object of inserting the point of the nib under the tail of the opponent's nib and then flicking the opposing nib into the air. If it fell upside down it became the property of the other side. If not, the game went on. So the vogue was for very sharp-pointed nibs, low on the ground, impossible to write with, but very effective as fighters.

End of term was celebrated by 'the Last Supper', of which the mainstay was large bowls of trifle, followed by a 'Penny Reading', in which the staff, with very varied degrees of competence, entertained the boys with songs, recitations and sketches. The audience, on the last night of term, was very far from critical.

> 'One more day and where shall I be ?
> Not in *this* Academy
> No more lessons, nor more sums
> No more'—etc., etc., *ad lib*.

sang each joyous boy at the thought of respite from Hillside for the holidays.

This then was the background of my first two years at Hillside. During World War II, I was travelling down to Kemble and found that Michael Sadleir, who was sharing the carriage with me, had been at Hillside just before my time. He confessed that he still looked back with loathing at his schooldays there and I found that his recollections were much the same as mine. 'Bulstrode' in Aldous' *Eyeless in Gaza* is a thinly-disguised Hillside and the schoolboy characters are an amalgam of some of our school fellows.

The autumn term of 1905 marked a great change at Hillside. When the school reassembled, it was under a new headmaster. 'Gude' had at last retired and his place was taken by Jimmy Douglas, aided by his brother Sholto and by his sister. The change was wholly to the good. Jimmy Douglas was a comparatively young man; a first-class cricketer—in the holidays he went in first for Middlesex and made many runs; keen, energetic and good with boys.

Sholto I always disliked, despite a certain glamour that he possessed from having served in the Yeomanry in the Boer War. He was stupid and narrow-minded and obsessed with the worship of games.

With the new régime, there also came to Hillside a young master, Hugh Parr, who made a vast difference to my life. He afterwards went back to Clifton, his old school, and was killed in the 1914–18 war, as was Sholto. Hugh Parr was a very good teacher, who really enjoyed encouraging the adolescent mind, particularly in anything relating to literature and art. He was always ready to discuss any subject with us and never laughed at us or treated us as children. He must have also had a very lovable personality to have inspired such real warmth of affection among so many of us.

The whole atmosphere of the school quickly altered. Certainly as I grew to be an older boy, we seniors never practised any of the bullying so lavishly dealt out to us as juniors. That sort of thing was no longer done. New boys no longer spent their time snivelling in corners. Lessons became much more interesting. The school had concerts and acted Shakespeare plays. No longer did we troop down to dreary Farncombe Church on Sundays, but had our own service in the Dining Hall. Our food improved, too, and we were encouraged to buy extra fruit with our pocket money. Certainly my last three years at Hillside were very much happier than my first two.

As I have said, acting was one of the new ventures of Jimmy Douglas' régime. Each Easter term we performed parts of a Shakespeare play before an audience of parents and friends, the principal role being given to Lewis Gielgud, as befitted a great nephew of Ellen Terry. Our first essay was from *Julius Ceasar*, with Lewis as Mark Antony. I acted the part of First Citizen and Aldous that of a messenger. The next year's play was from *The Merchant of Venice*. Lewis was Portia and Shylock was acted by P. L. Vian (Admiral Sir Philip Vian of the late war). My part was Gratiano, while Aldous' pathetic rendering of Antonio moved the old ladies in the audience to tears. My last year, scenes from *Richard II* were chosen, with Aldous as King Richard and myself as John of Gaunt. Aldous' performance would undoubtedly have made the most stony-hearted weep. Unfortunately an epidemic of mumps intervened and no play could be performed.

There were also great improvements in the teaching of English. Instead of parsing, we read Shakespeare plays aloud, taking the parts in turn. Under Hugh Parr's guidance essays were also set and written, while the reading of books and of poetry was encouraged. Even history was allowed to advance beyond the Tudors.

In the winter of 1906–7, the seed that Hugh Parr had been sowing blossomed forth in the form of a literary magazine, with Lewis, Aldous and myself as joint-editors. I wrote the magazine out in longhand on a jellograph machine, and some fifty copies of each issue (there were three I think) were rolled off. The contents were short stories, essays and verse. Aldous' contributions to each issue were a poem and a short story with illustrations by himself. Even then, his verse had maturity. I remember a poem called 'Sea Horses' that began :

> 'At a canter we dash at the shingle,
> At a gallop we charge the sea-wall,
> With mad exultation we tingle
> For we, we can overcome all.'

Lewis' verse was of a decidedly lush character. One of his poems began :

> 'Let us away to the East
> On the breast of some Orient Beauty'

—certainly a novel form of transport. I have quite forgotten what my own contributions were, except for one poem about a seagull which, floating on the waves, watched a liner passing, whose passengers (possibly anticipating an egg shortage) 'nightly on their beds do lay'.

Aldous and I now shared a double cubicle. Being 'in cubicles' was a great improvement on the ordinary dormitories. Besides providing an element of privacy, they afforded scope for acrobatics, the top of the partitions furnishing a sort of tightrope on which one could walk with the palms of one's hands pressed against the ceiling. Another 'cubicles' pastime was the sailing of little boats with matchstick masts and paper sails along a convenient gutter running outside the top of the windows. Aldous describes this in *Eyeless in Gaza*. Every evening Jimmy Douglas used to come round to put the lights out and before doing so used to ask us a couple of general knowledge questions—a most admirable practice.

With so expert a coach as our new headmaster, enthusiasm for cricket naturally increased and I became a member of the eleven. Rugger was also started in the Easter term and here my fast running gave me a great pull. I also played outside right in the soccer eleven.

In class, Aldous and I passed rapidly into the top form. Lewis Gielgud was the head of the school in the year ending with the summer term of 1907, when he left with an Eton scholarship. Next term I went to Rugby to try for a scholarship, but my attempt was unsuccessful. At Easter, however, when I sat for the common entrance examination, I had the satisfaction of passing top into Rugby.

In September 1907, I succeeded Lewis Gielgud as head of the school. Aldous was second. Lewis had been a weak and ineffective head and I returned to Hillside after the summer holidays full of the most splendid and autocratic resolutions, which I at once proceeded to put into effect. This time the school was certainly going to know who was its head boy and such a model of a head boy would never have been seen before. In fact, the masters wouldn't have anything to do except just teach in class. I can well imagine how quite intolerable this priggishness must have been to my unfortunate contemporaries. At any rate, it roused them before long into a full-scale rebellion. The storm burst one Saturday evening just before 'prep' when all the school was assembled in the big classroom. Without warning a volley of books was hurled at me from all corners of the room, accompanied by boos, hisses and insults. During 'prep', a junior and weak master barely kept the storm down and, on his departure, it burst forth anew. No one would speak to me, but the moment my back was turned, a concerted chorus of taunts would be shouted. I had had no idea of the unpopularity which my well-meant efforts had engendered and the shock to my vanity was considerable. But Aldous' loyalty to his unpopular cousin remained unshaken and I can remember how that night, after lights-out in cubicles, he momentarily silenced the pack with a shout of 'You dirty skunks and cowards'.

The next day, Sunday, I was ostentatiously shunned. The masters knew, of course, what was happening and went out of their way to be friendly but they realized that they would only make matters worse by open interference. Hugh Parr was really understanding and, in a long talk, showed me the mistake of abusing power and how 'hubris' brought its own downfall. The storm gradually blew over, but I had learned a lesson and walked much more warily. Nor have I ever since been tempted to become a dictator.

At the end of the Easter term of 1908, I left Hillside to enter Rugby.

ii

I do not really know why Mother had chosen Rugby for my public school, since we had no family connection with it other than that my Aunt Judy (Aldous' mother) was Dr. Arnold's granddaughter and that my least successful Stobart uncle—Douglas, the eldest—had gone there. Anyway she had rejected the choice of Eton, on the one hand, and of Bedales co-educational school on the other, at both of which I had cousins. She considered Eton too much of a playground for the rich and Bedales too 'advanced' for a normal boy, though my father's sisters, Aunt Rachel and Aunt Ethel, were loud in their praise of what Bedales had done for their sons. Mother's final choice had lain between Rugby and Marlborough, but on a visit to the latter in winter she had been put off by the cold and comfortless conditions. Rugby had therefore been chosen and I never regretted her choice.

Founded in 1567 as a grammar school to serve local needs, Dr. Thomas Arnold, appointed headmaster in 1828, had created the tradition that made Rugby world famous and that had set the pattern for the nineteenth-century English public school system. Its aim was to foster religious and moral principles and gentlemanly conduct as well as scholastic ability. The Arnold tradition was still very much alive at Rugby in my day.

Dr. James, the headmaster when I entered the school, was known as 'the Bodger', a nickname which became the generic term for all future headmasters. A stout, squat bachelor with a vast grey beard, he was a remote and alarming figure to whom I never even spoke. It seemed to me, and I think was largely true, that it was the house-masters, exercising an 'imperium in imperio', who were the real rulers of the school. They still owned their boarding-houses, of some fifty boys each, as their private property. They were mostly outstanding men, since Dr. James, as one of them later told me, would not consider an application for an assistant mastership unless the applicant held a first-class honours degree from Oxford or Cambridge. Under James, Rugby enjoyed perhaps the highest reputation of any public school and there was never any difficulty in filling its full complement of some 600 boys, although higher entrance standards were required than in any other school except Winchester, while superannuation was rigorously employed to weed out boys who subsequently failed scholastically.

The school's site on the high ground on the southern fringe of the town was by no means a bad one, with the Close and its fine elm trees forming the core round which lay the school buildings and the boarding-houses. Unfortunately the school buildings were unworthy of Rugby's high standing. The Headmaster's House and Old Big school at the town end of the close were pleasantly undistinguished old stone buildings, but in the late 'sixties a new Chapel and schoolrooms, library, etc., had been built to accommodate the school's ever-growing numbers. Butterfield had been the architect and his creations, based, I believe, on his admiration for Sienna Cathedral, were in fussy multi-coloured brick, and quite hideous. The further large school buildings, put up in my day, followed Butterfield's pattern. The boarding-houses scattered round outside the close had been built as cheaply as possible as private speculations by their original owners and had no architectural pattern or merit. In consequence, Rugbeians could derive no aesthetic pleasure or benefit from their surroundings.

I had heard that Rugby was supposed to be a 'tough' school. I did not find it so. My house, Steel's, may have been exceptionally civilized, but I do not think that conditions were substantially different in other houses. After Hillside, Rugby seemed to me to be a most pleasantly adult place, where one's fellows—always spoken of as 'men'—behaved with good sense and where one had far greater freedom than one had ever previously enjoyed. Every boy had a 'study', a double one shared with another boy for the first two years, but subsequently a single one to himself. At night all boys slept in dormitories, each holding some fifteen boys and each presided over by a member of the VIth form. Entry into the VIth conferred the prefects' powers though which, since Arnold's day, the school had been ruled under the masters.

Bullying or anything but the mildest form of ragging was completely unknown, at least in Steel's House. Any manifestation would have been firmly and promptly put down by our House VIth who closely supervised everything that went on and were imbued with an almost priggish sense of responsibility. They had the power of beating, but in my day it was very rarely used. In my own two years in the VIth I think I had only once to use it. Such was our tradition of orderly conduct that during my years there was never a case of a caning of any boy by the assembled House VIth in their sitting-room which was the final punishment allowed before recourse to our housemaster. Smoking, card-playing or drinking were wholly 'taboo', not for fear of punishment but just because such things were not 'done'.

High-minded endeavour in work and in games set the general Rugby tone. One result of this code was the suppression, at least in any overt form, of the homosexuality which, as I was subsequently to learn, flourished in many other public schools of the day. I can remember my surprise at hearing my Etonian cousin, Hugh Stobart, declare how thankful he was that his plain looks had debarred any senior boy from conceiving a romantic affection for him; and I found it difficult to believe, when I read the book just after the war, that Alec Waugh's *Loom of Youth* could have given a true picture of Sherborne. At Rugby, in my time at least, if any older boys cast sheep's eyes on attractive-looking juniors, they kept their feelings hidden; and scope for such attachments outside one's own House was denied because of the strictly-enforced convention that, except in the classroom or in school games, one mixed only with members of one's own House.

Heterosexual experiments were never even talked about, far less practised, while 'dirty' jokes were simply considered bad form. Indeed, from the veiled references to 'impurity' which fell from preachers' lips in sermons in Chapel, we were given to understand that sex in any form was to be shunned as a shameful corruption of the good Christian life of hard work and play which Rugbeians should lead both at school and when they went out into the world. Whether such an embargo on any frankness about sex and the natural impulses of boys attaining and passing puberty was really healthy or desirable is another matter. In me it developed an attitude to sex that I found hard fully to banish in later years, and that was to affect my future relationships with women. At the time it created for me a private and disturbing world of sexual fantasy whose only outlet lay in occasional secret and shame-ridden masturbation.

It is true that in my time at Rugby there was one homosexual scandal that resulted in the expulsion of one older and one younger boy. The whole episode was, of course, shrouded in mystery by the authorities. I can only remember the strained atmosphere that prevailed and my Housemaster darkly referring at House evening prayers to Bunyan's words—'there but for the grace of God goes John Bunyan'.

The two other school scandals in my time had no connection with sex and were, therefore, the subject of open though generally disapproving discussion. Personally I viewed both with an amusement wholly foreign to the view taken by the authorities. The one concerned a member of the VIth form who, when it came to his turn to read one of the lessons in Chapel, undertook for a bet to perform the task wearing batting gloves. This unusual habiliment was spotted and reported by a master. Dr. David, the then Headmaster, took so serious a view of what he felt to be sacrilege that the boy was threatened with expulsion, but finally the punishment was reduced to loss of all VIth form powers and privileges.

The other scandal was occasioned by two senior Vth form boys. Reacting against what they considered excessive zeal of the master commanding the school Officers' Training Corps in ordering some extra parades, the two boys removed the buttons from their uniforms and gave the lack of these essentials as their excuse for not turning out. When it was discovered that the loss had been self-inflicted the whole Corps was paraded and, in a scene reminiscent of Dreyfus's epaulettes of rank being publicly removed, the culprits were made to stand forward and commanded to leave the Corps which they had disgraced.

Having passed top in the school entrance examination I was placed on arrival in upper middle I, the top form of the middle school. I found the work easy except for having to master the new pronunciation of Latin which had just been introduced, and at the end of the term was given a remove into the upper school's lower Vth on the classical side (the upper school being divided into 'classical' and 'modern'). Altogether my first term was a very enjoyable one, and I spent many happy half-holidays tasting to the full the liberty given to us by being allowed the use of bicycles on which to explore the Warwickshire countryside when not booked for a compulsory game. The sole bar to my enjoyment was the one that was always to make the month of June something of a misery to me. The curse of hay fever from which I had suffered since childhood was far worse in Rugby's midland country air than it had been at Hillside, and my perpetual sneezing was now accompanied by such bad asthma at nights that every June I had to be removed to the sanatorium for a short spell.

C. G. Steel, my housemaster (known as 'Pussy' or 'the cat' from a supposed, but I think, fictitious, habit of creeping round the house in carpet slippers in order to trap malefactors) was a strong personality, a man of wide culture with a lively and very well-informed mind, who felt that in taking up teaching for financial reasons in order to marry young, he had frustrated his ambitions. His wife was equally, cultured. She came of a well-known Oxford family—the Prices—and one of her sisters was supposed to have been the original of the red-haired girl in Kipling's *Light that Failed*.

In those days an ample domestic staff removed most of the burden of running a boarding establishment from the back of the housemaster and his wife. At Steel's we had a butler with two junior assistants, known as, 'Bens'—a matron and under-matron, a supply of housemaids and a fully-staffed kitchen department. It was always supposed that the profits accruing to a housemaster from the fees paid by the boys he boarded allowed him a comfortable retirement after some fifteen years, and that the more indigent housemasters, especially those with large families, unwarrantably increased their profits by starving the boys. At

Steel's the food supplied was of good quality, well cooked and served, but as was the custom, after supplying breakfast and lunch (at which free beer was provided), bread, butter and tea were the only rations for the rest of the day, the boys being supposed to furnish any further eatables that they wanted such as potted meats, sardines and jam out of their own pockets. Moreover for a fag, breakfast and tea were usually very hurried meals, since it was one of his duties to make toast for his VIth form master at the big roaring fire in the Hall. While the fag was thus able to make a piece of toast for himself, the prior duty of supplying the needs of his master left him late and in a weak position to take advantage of the food supplied by the House. A fag's other special duty was to keep his master's study dusted and tidy, while he was also at the command of any member of the VIth who shouted 'Fag'. At this call all the fags rushed to the caller and the last comer had to perform whatever errand was required. Being in the upper school I was only a fag for my first year. When I entered the House, Steel had been its housemaster for seventeen years and had long made it one of the best Houses in the school.

Before acquiring my own study I shared one with a classical scholar with whom I had nothing in common in either tastes or background, though we got along amicably enough. In fact I made no attempt to establish any intimate friendships at Rugby. Equally, however, I made no enemies, but maintained a pleasantly companionable relationship with my fellows in and outside my House. In any case few Rugby friendships would have survived the 1914–18 war in which over 700 Rugbeians lost their lives, the mortality being greatest among my own contemporaries who provided the army with its expendable junior officers.

In work, the end of my second term brought a change that I think was all to the good. My one term essaying the foothills of the upper reaches of the classics convinced me that such interests and abilities as I possessed would be better catered for on the modern side. With Steel's and my mother's agreement the transfer was arranged, and in the

Grandfather Stobart

'Grannie' Stobart

My mother and father (circa 1905)

"Granmoo"
(T. H. Huxley's widow)
in her eighties with my
brother Christopher and
sister Anne

My father in his late
seventies

Easter term of 1909 I found myself in the modern Vth form presided over by G. F. Bradby. There I spent a most happy year. 'G.F.', large, stout and walrus-moustached, was a delightfully friendly and intelligent teacher. A novelist and poet, his *Dick* was already a minor classic among books about boys and his later *Lanchester Tradition* was, I think, equally good. In my day there was no science side, but chemistry and physics formed part of the modern side's curriculum. Since science was despised as a subject, the science masters, even at Rugby, were of very poor calibre, headed by the absurd old bearded 'Puff' Cumming who taught chemistry. The mere sight of 'Puff' provoked any right-minded boy to rag him, nor were opportunities lacking among the welter of benches and elementary chemical apparatus. I certainly learned little chemistry and penetrated even less into the mysteries of physics taught by a thoroughly third-rate and unpleasant master whose sole response to my genuinely puzzled questions was to tell me not to be impertinent.

At the beginning of 1910 I moved up into the top form of the modern side. Steel now also became my form master since he presided over the modern XX, lower XIth and upper Bench. He was an excellent and always inspiring teacher. Amongst other things, unusual for those days, he set a general knowledge paper every Monday morning. Having realized that his questions were mainly derived from the previous week's *Spectator*, a careful study of that periodical in the school library over the week-end enabled me to perform very creditably on Monday mornings.

During my last two terms I became a History specialist, forsaking for this purpose the barren fields of chemistry and physics. There were, I think, only three History specialists and we had the good fortune to be taught by 'Tiger' Hastings in the study of his little house in Horton Crescent, where we read our essays and enjoyed enlivening discussions led by 'Tiger', whose great gift, I think, was his ability to sift the grain from the chaff and to help us grasp the fundamental causes of historical developments.

From my earliest boyhood reading about real people and real events had always made more appeal to me than any works of imagination. History, dealing with such realities, had always been my best subject, however badly and uninspiringly it had been taught. Now I even welcomed memorizing in my spare time comparative tables of dates of European history as the necessary framework for mastering the wider issues which were the subject of our sessions with 'Tiger'; and I was convinced that if I had any academic qualifications it was in the field of History that they must be pursued. Next to History, I always most enjoyed English literature, especially poetry and drama. Here too, I was lucky at Rugby both in the time devoted to the subject on the modern side and to the quality of Steel's teaching. The set books, such as a Shakespeare play, Tennyson's *In Memoriam*, or Milton's *Samson Agonistes* were not just conveniences for making us learn long passages by heart. Steel gave them depth and meaning and imbued us with a real feeling for words and thoughts. *The Oxford Book of English Verse*—my copy was given me by Mother in 1906—had always been my favourite bedside book, and I knew much of it by heart. Thanks to Mother and my home surroundings, I was much more widely read all round than most boys of my age, and at Rugby, Steel had the admirable good sense to forbid all magazines in his House, so that we had to concentrate our spare-time reading on books in the very well-stocked House library.

At the end of 1910 Dr. James was succeeded by A. A. David, Headmaster of Clifton. David, also a cleric but married, was a much younger man and, I have been told, instituted a number of reforms. But he must have proceeded cautiously in his first two years since I was unconscious of any changes, and David remained almost as personally remote to me as James had been, even though by now I was a senior. What was important to me was becoming a member of the VIth when I was only sixteen and enjoying two years of the powers and privileges that membership of VI bestowed—wearing a white straw hat, owning fags to clean my study, make my toast and run errands for me, being in charge of a dormitory and having the use of the House VIth room with its newspapers and periodicals. So far as I was concerned it was still my combined house and- form-master, Steel, who represented Rugby's magisterial authority, and the much closer contacts that I enjoyed with him in my last two years as one of his senior boys only steadily increased my admiration and affection for him.

Another very pleasant memory of those last years is of the House plays that Mrs. Steel sponsored in the Easter terms and that, at the time, were a novelty at Rugby. With members of the House VIth as the actors she produced scenes from Sheridan's *Critics* and, the next year, from *Twelfth Night*. My roles were the crazy heroine 'Tilburina' in the *Critics* and Sir Andrew Aguecheek in *Twelfth Night*. Mrs. Steel was also musical and trained our successful entry in the newly established inter-House singing competitions.

In games, my overgrown height—I was 6 feet 4 inches tall before I left—was a handicap and my only distinction was in running. Here I won medals for the sprints in the under 15's, under 16½'s and finally in the open events, carrying off in my last Easter term the school quarter-mile cup. That term I was also a member of the school long-distance Running VIII, journeying to Uppingham and to Shrewsbury to take part in inter-school matches.

One activity that was taken very seriously was the Officers' Training Corps to which all able-bodied boys belonged and in which I eventually rose to the rank of sergeant. There were many drills in the Close and a yearly inter-house drill competition. There were also field days for which we entrained to take part in combined mock-battles with other school Corps. These were enjoyable occasions and were made the more so by the discovery, which Archie Lutyens and I made, of the devastating shrapnel effect of firing a round of blank ammunition into a large cowpat. The Corps had, too, its royal occasions. I well remember the parade and inspection by King Edward VII when he visited the school shortly before his death and my shock at hearing the

very guttural Germanic voice in which he asked the Headmaster to grant us an extra week's holiday in honour of the
event.

One other Rugby memory perhaps deserves chronicling.
It concerns Rupert Brooke, whose father was a Housemaster. I was never in the school with him, as he left Rugby
for King's, Cambridge, in 1906. But he had returned to
Rugby for a short spell early in 1910 in order to act as temporary Housemaster of School Field on the sudden death
of his father. At the end of 1911 his first book—*Poems 1911*
—was published. The volume was to sell nearly 100,000
copies in the next twenty years, but it was received with
shocked horror by the Rugby authorities. I well remember
even the liberal-minded Mrs. Steel expressing at lunch at
our House VIth table her sympathy with poor Mrs. Brooke
for the shame that Rupert had brought on her and the
school.

The uproar was, of course, due to the inclusion of several
'unpleasant' poems in the volume, such as 'Libido', with its
line, 'and your remembered smell most agony'; 'Jealousy'
with 'its lips that can't hold slobber'; and 'A Channel
Passage', which describes only too vividly a sea-sick lover
vomiting 'old meat, good meals and brown gobbets'.
Naturally I surreptitiously bought the book which also contained such fine poems as 'Dining Room Tea', and being at
that time enthusiastic about Masefield's *Everlasting Mercy*
and *Widow in the Bye Street* was not unduly shocked by
any of Rupert's verses. What was surprising to me was that
so dull a man as his father and so spinsterish a woman as his
mother should have begotten Rupert, and that Rugby
should have produced an aesthete and a socialist, especially
in the case of one who had been such a good athlete and a
member of the XV and XI.

It was only in 1912 during my last two terms that I met
Rupert. Steel's had acquired a young and attractive house-
tutor named H. S. Wilson who had been at Cambridge with
Rupert and like him was to die in World War I. On two
occasions, I think, I had lunch on a Sunday with Wilson in

his 'digs' when Rupert was a fellow guest and I can well remember the beauty of his features and the fascination of his talk. Needless to say I did not inform my housemaster of those meetings.

I left Rugby at the end of the summer term of 1912 when I was eighteen and a quarter. Mother had decided that my destined career was to be the Foreign Office and, having no contrary ambitions, I was content to accept her judgment. First, however, must come Oxford and during my last term at Rugby I had gone there and successfully passed the general matriculation examination for entrance into the University, though this had included a Greek paper for which I had to refurbish my Greek abandoned four years earlier. But Oxford for me meant Balliol where both Uncle Leonard and my cousins Julian, Trev and Laurence had been and where Aldous would also be going in the autumn of 1913, and Balliol's standards were so high that, alone among Oxford colleges, it had its own reputedly stiff entrance examination. Steel wanted me to stay on at Rugby for another year as head of the House, but Mother had another plan with which I readily agreed. This was to get special tuition in History after the summer holidays and so sit for a Balliol scholarship in December, with the object of doing well enough to be excused taking the Balliol entrance examination. Then, I would go to Germany for the first seven months of 1913 to live with a German family so as to attain a real proficiency in the language against my subsequent Foreign Office entry.

Looking back from the distance of fifty-five years I think that Rugby left me two principal legacies, one good and one bad. The latter was to encourage my natural tendency to conformity to the accepted conventions of my time and class. I have never been a rebel and have always found it easier to say yes than no, and in my formative years at Rugby I was only too happy to gain the approval of masters and fellow Rugbeians by being the complete conformist. Only in one particular did I stray from the norm. Alone among my contemporaries in my House, I refused to be confirmed in the Church of England and accept articles of faith which my reason rejected. But my rebellion in this respect was, in reality, no more than conformity to my strong family tradition of religious nonconformity which I had imbibed from my grandfather's writings and example and from my father's own attitude. It is only fair to say that my housemaster brought no pressure on me, though I can remember being reported to him by a bigoted classical master with whom I ventured to argue in his scripture class about his insistence on a literal interpretation of some Old Testament story.

Rugby's good legacy, for which I have ever since been grateful, was the inculcation of the habit of work for work's sake, and the realization that, however seemingly dull or trivial the task, its honest fulfilment brought its own enjoyment and reward, while idleness only created boredom and unhappiness.

iii

Throughout my school years my life was divided into two wholly separate worlds. Six times a year I crossed the dividing line between them. Back at home I sought at once to bury school associations under the pleasure and comforts of my family life. Back at school I plunged into the routine of work and games so as to leave no time for vain home regrets. Such a deliberate apartheid also involved friendships. It is true that in holidays from Hillside, my apartheid rule was broken in favour of Aldous, Lewis Gielgud and Nick Wadham, but they had been pre-school friends. No Rugby friendships were, however, allowed to invade my home privacy. Nor at home was I ever forthcoming about my school life. Questions received short and evasive answers even in my early unhappy Hillside years. I imagine that my father and mother never closely questioned me since, in company with most other parents of the day, they shared the comfortable belief that their son was 'very happy at school'.

Christmas holidays were normally spent in London, first

at 39 Leinster Gardens and then, from 1908 onwards, at nearby 51 Porchester Terrace, a much larger and more attractive house, standing on its own with a garden, mainly at the back, which was large enough to hold a full-size tennis court and which led to our own mews where a motor-car had replaced my father's horses, though my mother still kept her horse and carriage.

While Aldous was still living at Priors Field, my companion in the Christmas holidays was Lewis Gielgud, whose family lived in Kensington. His mother—an old flame of my father's—had been Katie Lewis, the daughter of a once wealthy draper (Lewis and Allenby). Her mother, Kate, was Ellen Terry's sister and might have been an even greater actress than Ellen but for her retirement from the stage on her marriage. Lewis' father, of Lithuanian refugee descent, worked on the Stock Exchange and had a gift for impro-visation at the piano. Lewis was the eldest of the family. Next came Val, then John and finally a girl, Eleanor. Lewis in the holidays was always a nattily dressed man about Town. One of his great assets as a companion was his ability to extract free matinée seats from his theatrical relations. Thus it was that he and I saw his great uncle Fred Terry and Fred's wife Julia Nielson in the immortal *Scarlet Pimpernel*, and yet another early theatrical memory is going with a large party to the dress rehearsal of Barrie's *Peter Pan*.

Mother looked on the theatre as education rather than entertainment for her children. Thus I was regularly taken to Tree's Shakespearian productions, in which the staging and costumes were more memorable than the play and its words. But the highlight of the Christmas holidays was the evening when my Godfather Dighton Pollock took me out to see the latest musical comedy at Daly's. Dighton, a bar-rister member of the famous legal family, had been best man at my father's wedding and was one of the handsomest men I have ever seen. He was then still unmarried and, before the theatre, he and I would dine in full evening dress (in my case my 'Eton' suit) at Kettners restaurant before proceeding to see the latest musical comedy.

Christmas holidays took on a new turn in January 1911, when, immediately after Christmas, Marjorie and I joined the Colliers' Swiss party at Montana. Winter sports had only recently begun to be popular, largely, I believe, through the efforts of Sir William Lunn whose travel agency booked whole Swiss hotels for his so-called Public Schools winter sports club. Lunn had a strong publicity sense and offered special concessions to well-known figures whose presence at his hotels could be publicized. One such was Uncle John Collier, and he and Aunt Ethel headed a large party of friends and relations. The Swiss fortnight made a glorious ending to the Christmas holidays. At Montana the winter sunshine, hot at midday, seemed perpetual except for the occasional and welcome snow-storm which laid a fresh and deeper surface of pure white over everything. All day long the expert skaters cut their elaborate figures on the skating rink at the side of the hotel, while elderly gentlemen, the devotees of 'curling', called 'soop it oop' in phoney Scottish accents as they swept the ice with their brooms in the path of the stones. But it was for the new sport of skiing (then pronounced 'sheeing') that most people, including all of us younger ones, came to Montana. Ski-instructors were then unknown and we learned to ski the hard way on the nursery slopes through many a tumble and by watching the methods of more practised performers. Eventually came the glorious moment when one seemed to be flying effortlessly through the air at immense speed.

Uncle Jack's party reproduced in Switzerland the gay 'North House' atmosphere of chaff and repartee, enlivened at dinner by bottles of 'asti spumanti' which then seemed to me the choicest of wines. After dinner there would be dancing and, on one evening, a grand fancy dress ball. There were nights, too, when we dragged our toboggans up a mountain road to the hotel at Vermala, there to drink mulled claret, and thus fortified to hurtle down the road to Montana in the keen frosty air with the bright stars lighting our way.

For at least a fortnight of every Easter holiday Mother would take the family away from London, usually to Devon or Cornwall. We always took our bicycles with us. The combination of train and bicycle constituted, I always think, the perfect way of exploring a countryside.

Four outstanding Easter holidays were partly spent abroad. The first and most unforgettable, if only because it was the first time I had ever been abroad, was in 1906, when Mother and Father, Marjorie and I went to Grasse in the hills inland from Cannes. Our visit had very nearly to be cancelled as Mother caught influenza, but with her usual courage she insisted on travelling even though she had a high temperature. It was, of course, a tremendous excitement to cross the Channel, to see French gendarmes at Calais Pier and to hear a foreign language spoken. We spent the afternoon in Paris at the Hotel St. James and Albany, a highly respectable resort of the English, where Mother was put to bed before we travelled on that night from the Gare de Lyons. Marjorie and I shared a *wagon-lit*, another great excitement as I had never slept in a train before. I fell asleep to the long melancholy hoot of the French engines, and woke in the night to hear 'Dijonville, Dijonville', being called as the train stopped. Next morning there was break-fast of croissants, rolls and coffee in the *wagon-restaurant*, and the blue Mediterranean sparkling in the sunshine as the train ran along the coast to Cannes where we left it to drive up to Grasse in a hired car.

We had brought our bicycles with us and, with Mother soon recovered, we explored the foothills of the Alps, their slopes covered with wild flowers and the air aromatic with sharp scents, visiting such spots as the Gorge de Loup and lunching at restaurants in little walled hill towns like St. Paul. In Grasse itself there were the hotel gardens to walk and sit in, full of lovely flowers and palms and other exotic trees, and visits to the scent manufacturers and a wonderful preserved fruit factory. In the evenings, being still in my Dickens phase, I read the *Tale of Two Cities* and *Dombey & Son*. It was, I think, the best of all my Easter holidays.

My other Easter-time journeys abroad took place while I was at Rugby. On the first, Mother took Marjorie and me to Italy. Two nights in the train brought us to Naples. Someone had once told me that to avoid infection from bad drains it was advisable to spit when one encountered an unpleasant smell. Trying to follow this advice in Naples very soon left my mouth too dry to make continued expectoration feasible. Like all English tourists of the time we were armed with the red volume of Baedeker's guide with its comprehensive lists of all the sights worth seeing, starred in order of merit, with Pompeii first. Mother, an indefatigable sightseer, was also the delight of the guides showing parties round each spot. She was the visitor who placed herself next to the guide, asked all the appropriate questions and listened with rapt attention to his stories. I regret to say that Marjorie and I, ungrateful and self-conscious little snobs, used to trail at the back of the party to try to avoid being connected with Mother in front.

Leaving Naples we stayed for a few days at Sorrento, and went by steamer to Capri. From Sorrento a two-horse hired carriage drove us to Amalfi, whence we had an unforgettable visit to Paestum with its temples lying deserted in the desolate marshes.

On the way home we stayed for a few days in Florence where the pictures in the galleries and churches made a lasting impression on my hitherto unformed tastes. We visited, too, Perngia and Assisi, and in the latter, quite unspoiled on its hill, the spirit of St. Francis still seemed to linger.

Next Easter Mother took us to Fontainbleau. We again took our bicycles with us and explored the huge and lovely forest, on one occasion following a Boar Hunt, the hunt servants splendidly attired in green and carrying great round horns on their shoulders. Before coming home we gaped at the vast wonders of Versailles and had a few days sightseeing in Paris.

Finally, in 1912, my cousin Laurence Collier and I formed a history reading party, staying at the Villa Serbelloni, the Bellagio hotel on a bluff overlooking Lake Como, and combining our reading with rowing and steamer trips on the deep blue lake and with long walks over the hills starred with spring flowers. I remember seeing with incredulity the headlines in the Italian newspapers announcing the sinking of the *Titanic*. I remember, too, an encounter with a charming elderly American lady, a fellow guest in the hotel. Thinking to please her I spoke of my great admiration for Abraham Lincoln. 'Young man,' was her reply in the soft slow accent of the deep South, 'say no more. That man was the fiend incarnate.'

The long summer holidays were the high spot of these school years. At their start, their eight weeks seemed to stretch so far ahead as to put out of mind the inevitable return to school at their end.

In 1905 and 1906 we went to the Lake District, my parents taking a six weeks' lease each year of Mirehouse, a square substantial Victorian mansion belonging to the Spedding family and standing a little way back from the shore of Lake Bassenthwaite. In 1905 we shared the lease with Uncle Leonard, Aunt Judy and their family, and, at the end of the summer term, I travelled by train to Keswick with Uncle Leonard, Trev and Aldous, taking our bicycles with us in the van. From Keswick on Lake Derwentwater we rode our bicycles to Mirehouse. It was Aldous' and my first view of mountain scenery and I remember the enthralled excitement with which we gazed at the lovely shapes of the Lakes' mountains boldly outlined against the evening sky. At Mirehouse Aldous and I shared a bedroom. Far from our close school companionship leading to boredom with each other's holiday company, my memories of this first Mirehouse summer are all of the fun and interests we shared—hunting for moths with a light after darkness fell in the garden ; damming with boulders a mountain beck above the lake and making pools and waterfalls with Julian and Trev as architects ; icy cold swims in the lake ; a triumphant whole day's expedition on foot when, under Uncle Leonard's leadership, we climbed Saddleback ; gay evenings when we took part in 'Nebuchadnezzars', a form of charades, produced and directed by Julian, who must just have been leaving Eton, and a very grand Etonian friend, Neville Bland.

By the summer of 1907, my father had bought a Renault of the famous early model which was one of the first really reliable cars. That year we rented a house in Kinross with fishing on Loch Leven and rough shooting, including some grouse, on the hills. The rest of the family travelled north by train, but I had the great thrill of driving up from London with my father. We left at 6 a.m., and after a second breakfast at Stamford and a sandwich lunch, got to York in time for an early tea. In spite of its over-heavy and over-high landaulette body and its small engine, the Renault never faltered over the 200 miles, achieving a speed of thirty miles an hour on the flat. The speed limit on all roads was still twenty miles an hour, but we avoided the police speed traps at several well-known points. My father sat in front with his chauffeur, while I reclined on the comfortable back seat with the half-hood open, reading the *Story of Scotland* and watching hens scattering, dogs barking and horses shying as we rolled on leaving a cloud of white dust behind us. After a night in the Station Hotel at York we reached Kinross comfortably by tea, crossing the Firth of Forth by the Burntisland ferry.

I had been given a lovely little double-barrelled 20-bore gun for my thirteenth birthday and in the Easter holidays had had practice lessons with clay pigeons as the target at the gun-maker's shooting school. Having a good eye I had very soon attained a respectable proficiency, and this summer holiday I started my shooting career, which was to bring me much enjoyment with never a thought or regret for the victims. Indeed it was not for very many years, after two World Wars, that the, I suppose, atavistic pleasure in the chase and the kill ceased to please, and killing game in any shape or form became completely distasteful to me. On Loch Leven I was also introduced to fly-fishing. Both my father and mother were keen and good anglers but though I enjoyed paddling the boat for them, I had not the patience for the sport and found fishing terribly slow and boring as compared to shooting. The first live victim of my gun was, I think, a rabbit, bowled clean over as it ran, but I well remember the thrill of watching my first grouse tower and fall dead as my father, Dighton Pollock and I walked over the rough Kinross moor.

For the summer holidays of 1908 and for the next five Augusts and Septembers we leased Balder Grange, a pleasant grey stone gabled house, standing on a bluff overlooking a stream which joined the Tees some five miles up the river from Barnard Castle. We rented Cotherstone grouse moor, which, though small, was very well-stocked, and our opening day's bag would be as many as forty brace, driven over butts under the firm direction of Foster, the keeper, a bluff, outspoken character who had been a Durham miner.

At this distance I can no longer disentangle the six very happy summer holidays I spent at Balder. My memories are of hot August days on the moor with the grouse calling in the heather, the thrill of watching the birds flying swiftly towards my butt and the satisfaction of seeing my chosen targets tumble dead to my shots. At lunch time the ladies joined the party for a splendid picnic meal in the lee of a stone wall with the morning's bag laid out on the ground watched by the dogs. For the last two or three Balder years I had my own retriever, Ben. He and I were inseparable companions all through the holidays and he never disgraced me by running in when in September we walked up partridges and hares in the grass fields and roots. Apart from the shooting, Balder memories are compounded of bathing in the ice-cold pools of the stream, of long-drawn-out doubles at tennis, of the laughter and shouting and running at 'I spy' among the yew hedges in the garden, and of long lamp- and fire-lit evenings in the tapestry-hung sitting-room playing rhyming and other games with pencil and paper. There were expeditions, too. A favourite one was by car through Middleton-in-Teesdale to the great High Force waterfall. Once each holiday at least, the more ambitious of our party tackled the long and rough walk on by Calder

Snout and over the desolate moorland to High Cup Nick where the ravens circled croaking above the rocks and where we suddenly came on the panorama of the Lake mountains raising their lovely outlines beyond the broad green valley at our feet. In the valley Appleby was our goal for tea and the train back to Barnard Castle.

My godfather, Dighton Pollock, was a regular guest for the 12th of August, when the other guns for the opening three days' shooting, besides my father and myself, would be General Sir John Steevens, a very old friend of Aunt Amy's, and Uncle Harry Stobart who motored over from Witton-le-Wear. A regular visitor for later shoots was Mother's cousin, Sir John Ross, Chief Justice of Ireland, who told delightful Irish stories in a broad brogue but who was a poor shot and, as such, somewhat despised by Foster the keeper, no respecter of persons however eminent. There were other shooting visitors, but Dighton Pollock and Sir John Ross were my favourites and not solely because they never failed to tip me a golden sovereign when they left.

CHAPTER III

i

I N mid-September of 1912 I started my coaching for the
Balliol scholarship examination. Mother had found my
coach, an ex-Oxford History graduate (Third Class Honours)
in his late twenties. He was an amiable character but so dim
and lacking in personality that I cannot now even recall his
looks or name. It had been arranged that he and I should
initially lodge at the Mill House at Cutmill near Godalming,
a pleasant old farmhouse with a water-wheel on a small lake
noisy with duck of many kinds, where we were the only
lodgers. I read assiduously, though my coach's uninspiring
mind and conventional knowledge contributed little to my
history studies. Indeed I found his chief use was as my partner at Puttenham Golf Course where we played every afternoon. I was, however, a complete novice and his almost
equal lack of proficiency was no aid to improving my game.

After a month or so at Cutmill we moved to lodgings at
West Runton on the Norfolk coast where we followed the
same routine of reading and golf. In December I went to
Oxford for the examination in which, though just failing
to win a Balliol scholarship or Exhibition, I did well enough to
have been given a scholarship at one of the other colleges in
the Group examination had Balliol not been my sole choice.
Anyway my papers were good enough to achieve my aim in
gaining me exemption from the Balliol entrance examination. This hurdle cleared I left England to start my seven-
months' sojourn in Germany.

Through the good offices of Fräulein Richard, Mrs. Steel's
companion at Rugby, I went as a paying guest to the Wendtland family in Leipzig. Herr Wendtland, a blond down-to-
earth East Prussian from Königsberg with no back to his head,
was the Secretary of the Leipzig Chamber of Commerce

and had recently moved into a commodious official flat on the top floor of the Chamber's new building in Leipzig's big central square. Frau Wendtland, a shapeless mountain of a woman with short grey hair, took refuge from household duties by insisting on the delicacy of her health and on her artistic temperament, inherited she claimed, from her father who had been the Director of the Weimar State Opera. The management of the household was therefore left in the very capable hands of Herr Wendtland's spinster sister. The Wendtlands had one child, Mäusi, an exceedingly spoilt fat little eight-year-old girl.

From my arrival I was overwhelmed (almost literally in the case of Frau Wendtland) by kindness and was treated as one of the family. The Wendtland's table groaned with rich food and I early learned to take only a small first helping of any dish, since when it went round again a refusal of a second helping led to anxious and prolonged inquiries as to the state of my stomach. Particularly cloying were the cream-filled cakes and pastry that constituted the last course. No one in the household bothered about taking exercise and I contented myself with a daily walk in a large and pleasant park. As none of the Wendtlands spoke any English, my German perforce soon became conversationally fluent, and for written lessons in the language I went, on Frau Wendtland's recommendation, to an elderly Fräulein Luxemburg in her little flat.

Frau Wendtland had, she told me, hesitated to suggest Fräulein Luxemburg for fear that I might object on the grounds that she was a Jewess. I remember my complete surprise at thus being confronted with the anti-semitic prejudice that was so absent in England but that was already so strong in Germany. I also improved my German by buying and wading through the German librettos of some of the repertory of operas which were performed by the Leipzig city-subsidized Opera Company.

I had bought a season ticket at an absurdly cheap rate for a twice-weekly stall at the Opera and this provided my chief evening recreation, in the course of which I must have

Portrait of G.H. by John Collier, 1899
G.H. winning the Open Quarter Mile at Rugby, 1912

G.H., 1917

Shooting in Scotland, 1907,
my father, G.H., my
godfather, Dighton Pollock,
my sister Anne and Aunt
Netty (father's sister)

seen thirty or more different operas. Apart from the occasional star guest-singer, the standard of the Leipzig company
was not notably high and the singers made rather heavy
weather of French and Italian operas, being at their best in
Wagner. From this perhaps over-intensive course in Opera I
came to the personal conclusion that Grand Opera in trying
to combine, as in Wagner's *Ring*, great music, great drama
and realistic spectacle all in one, was apt to be often boring
and occasionally ridiculous, and that I enjoyed Wagner's
music much more when orchestrally performed and removed
from the artificial distractions of the stage. Where I was
really musically fortunate in Leipzig was in being able to
attend the famous Gewandhaus concerts when Nikisch conducted in succession all the Beethoven symphonies.

The weeks passed pleasantly enough. I met with nothing
but apparent goodwill towards a young Englishman and his
country from the Wendtlands' friends and from some very
hospitable students at the University who entertained me at
a number of beer-drinking parties. Many of my hosts
proudly displayed strips of white sticking plaster on their
cheeks covering cuts acquired in the fashionable student
duels. These were fought with razor-sharp sabres and their
main object seemed to be to mark the duellists for life with
ugly scars on their cheeks, since this part of the face was
alone left unprotected.

I found much to admire in this pre-war Germany, the
tradition of honesty and hard work that prevailed in all
classes, the respect for law and social order and the sense of
security which this gave, though the proliferation of titles
among the professional classes, so that everyone and his wife
seemed to be Herr Geheimrat this or Frau Professor that,
did strike me as somewhat absurd. I admired, too, the Germans' pride in their country and its achievements and was
spared that unpleasant manifestation of German patriotism,
the adulation of the Army Officer class, since the Wendtlands'
circle did not include any representatives of these self-
consciously superior beings. Only once was I made aware of
an undercurrent of ill-feeling against England, an ill-feeling

that I think arose mainly from jealousy, and this was when, to my anger and disgust, the newspapers, reporting the death of Captain Scott on his return from the South Pole, ascribed the disaster to his having stocked his expedition with champagne and whisky at the expense of food and fuel, and sneered at the British for making him a hero.

The hot summer came and, accompanying it, my hay-fever and asthma returned in force, though an expedition with Fräulein Wendtland to Eisenach and the pollen-free air of its pine forests provided some relief. Then suddenly one night at the end of June I suffered what I and the hastily summoned Wendtland's elderly doctor thought to be a heart attack. After I had been made to lie flat in bed for a week the doctor decided that I was well enough to risk travelling back to England, and I was duly put on the train for the Hook of Holland with a label attached to a button of my waistcoat reading 'wenn etwas passiert, bitte telegrafieren sofort an Herr Doktor Wendtland, Handelskammer, Leipzig' (if anything happens please telegraph at once to Doctor Wendt-land, Chamber of Commerce, Leipzig). In this role of an interesting young invalid who was putting on a brave face despite the warning of sudden death attached to his waist-coat, I reached home to be promptly given a thorough exami-nation by my father. It was a somewhat humiliating relief when he laughingly told me that there was nothing what-ever wrong with my heart and that indigestion from too much heavy food and light beer, coupled with too little exercise, had been the cause of my 'heart attack'.

At the end of July the whole family went north to Balder. Lewis Gielgud came to stay in September and I took him to Uncle Frank's at Marske Hall, near Richmond, for a couple of days' partridge shooting. Lewis, who had been at Magdalen for a year, much appreciated Uncle Frank's grand style of living and was, I remember, particularly impressed when Uncle Frank, looking at the tea tables laden with scones and cakes, rang the bell and demanded of the answering footman why, in addition to honey, only one kind of jam had been pro-vided. Lewis and I then travelled south together to join

Aldous for a fortnight's reading party at Cutmill before the Oxford term started.

Aldous' and my ways had parted in 1908 when I went to Rugby and he to College at Eton, but we had kept up a lively correspondence about our respective schools and holidays. Aldous had then suffered two shattering blows. First the death from cancer of his mother, my Aunt Judy, to whom he was the more devoted since Uncle Leonard, his father, had never been of much help to him. Shortly afterwards, when run-down after influenza and out on a field day with the Eton O.T.C., a streptococcus infection from dust attacked his eyes. Had penicillin been discovered, it would, no doubt, have cleared the whole thing up in a very short time, but as it was, the Eton authorities neglected his condition and he had almost completely lost the sight of both eyes before my father was informed and brought him to London to see specialists. He had, of course, to leave Eton and I had seen much more of him as he often stayed with us in the Christmas and Easter holidays. His courage and complete absence of self-pity in facing the disruption of his life and, for a time, almost total blindness won my intense admiration, and despite his handicap he continued to be the most delightful and fascinating of companions. By 1913 the sight of one eye had so much improved that, with the aid of a magnifying glass, he was no longer dependent on Braille for reading, and a typewriter helped him to write. He had succeeded in passing the Balliol entrance examination and, to my great joy, he and I were going up together as fellow-commoners.

Our Cutmill reading party was a very happy prelude to Oxford ; and one Saturday evening we bicycled over to Hillside to entertain the boys of our former school with a short play whose plot we concocted beforehand, but whose words we left to the inspiration of the moment. Our somewhat feeble jokes provoked a volume of laughter and applause that was only explained when Jimmy Douglas, still Hillside's headmaster, told us that the boys thought that Lewis had been deliberately giving an impersonation of one of the less popular masters.

Oxford and Balliol proved to be every bit as agreeable as my imagination had depicted. Oxford itself was still the old University City, little changed over the centuries and untouched by the industrial growth with which Morris and his motor-cars were soon to begin to swamp it. Horse-drawn trams trundled up the High, otherwise almost empty of traffic except for bicycles which formed the main means of locomotion. Balliol, though its undergraduates numbered well under two hundred, was one of the largest Colleges and was at the peak of its fame, giving its members a conviction of their intellectual and general superiority over the rest of Oxford, while Oxford, we felt, was much superior to Cambridge, its only possible rival, since 'red-brick' Universities were wholly outside our ken.

Balliol's master was Strachan-Davidson, a bearded and somewhat remote old-world figure of great dignity and courtesy. He presided over an exceptionally gifted and remarkable collection of Fellows such as A. L. Smith (his successor as Master), 'Sligger' Urquhart, Cyril Bailey, Pickard-Cambridge and Harold Hartley, together with the gigantic Neville Talbot, Balliol's Dean. Our relations with these Dons were of the closest. Their rooms and homes were always open to us and they were our friends and confidants as well as our tutors.

A few years earlier, drunkenness and rowdyism had been fashionable among the Balliol 'bloods'. Under the influence of Neville Talbot and such scholar athletes as Ronnie Poulton from Rugby the tone had completely changed and the example of our second and third-year betters such as Harold Macmillan, Victor Mallet, 'God' Wedderburn, Godfrey Elton and Gerry Hopkins now discouraged any manifestation of noisy insobriety.

Together Aldous and I excitedly explored our brave new sophisticated Balliol world. All freshmen had rooms in College and Aldous' 'sitter' soon became the rendezvous of the first-year contemporaries who formed our set. They included Philip Nichols and Rob Cross from Winchester, Bernard James from Rugby and Robin Holway and Geoffrey Madan from Eton. Lewis Gielgud from Magdalen and Jack Haldane from New College were also often to be found there, Jack looking like a great shaggy bear and matching his wit with the bawdiness of his repertory of songs. Instinctively Aldous' contemporaries must have recognized the originality and distinction of his mind with its catholic tastes and its curiosity about all things and all men. They were drawn to him, too, by his unassuming friendliness, his complete lack of any pretensions and the gaiety that his company always engendered. What did we talk about? University and College gossip was, of course, the main subject, followed by books, art and music. No one confined their purchases at Blackwell's to text-books, and 'musts' for Balliol bookshelves included the plays of Shaw, Synge and Galsworthy, Masefield's narrative poems and works by Chesterton, Belloc and Wells. Collected editions of Stevenson were very much in favour and, to a lesser degree, sets of Kipling, while hardly a bookcase failed to hold a copy of the first volume of Compton Mackenzie's *Sinister Street* and we eagerly awaited the publication of the second volume dealing with Michael Fane at Oxford. My own special pride was a very handsomely bound *Pepys' Diary* in eight volumes. So far as art was concerned, most of us had decorated our rooms with Medici prints of classical pictures, but Aldous had pinned over his mantelpiece a large French poster depicting a group of nubile nude girls by a seashore.

For music we always went to the Balliol Sunday evening concerts in Hall which were then an Oxford feature, and all queued up to get seats in the theatre for the annual visit to Oxford of the D'Oyly Carte Gilbert and Sullivan Company. I also found one or two friends such as Willy King, already an aesthete, who shared the interest in Opera which I had formed in Leipzig. But what intrigued Aldous most was the novelty of the tempo of the syncopated music that had recently arrived from America. He had an old upright piano in his 'sitter' and on it he entertained us by strumming the accompaniments to our singing of such popular numbers as 'The Wedding Glide', and 'He'd have to get under, get out and get under his little machine'.

What now surprises me is that I have no recollection of our ever discussing political topics, whether national or international. Most of us embraced a mild and indifferent Toryism and joined the Union, though I only remember Aldous and I attending one debate. This was out of curiosity to see what went on there, and was the limit of our interest and that of our friends in proceedings in which a small minority of undergraduates passionately sought advancement for political ambitions of which we were wholly free. Looking back it seems extraordinary that we should have shown such a complete lack of concern with the current issues that were so deeply affecting our country and the world, issues such as Irish Home Rule and the Ulster rebellion and constitutional crisis, women's suffrage, the Balkan Wars and their threat to the peace of Europe or Anglo-German Colonial and Naval rivalry.

> 'Alas, regardless of their doom
> The little victims play.
> No sense have they of ills to come
> Nor care beyond the day.'

Gray's lines well describe our attitude, and the possibility never entered our minds that the days of our self-centred, carefree and secure way of life were already numbered.

On arrival, all freshmen had been canvassed by the Captains of the various College athletic clubs anxious to win recruits for their particular sport. Persuaded by the magnificent Wedderburn, Captain of the Oxford eight, I opted for rowing, though totally unacquainted with its skills. So I spent most afternoons on the river, being coached first in pairs, then in fours and finally as a member of the Balliol second Torpid and Eights boats. Of all forms of 'shop' I think rowing must be the dullest, but it was healthy as well as brain-relaxing to share with my fellow oarsmen the training table in Hall with its special diet and to have to refrain during training from tobacco and alcohol except for a glass of beer. In the Summer term tennis furnished additional exercise and I found a very pleasant and well-matched singles opponent in Humphrey Parsons, a Balliol first-year Rhodes Scholar from Tasmania.

My work, with A. L. Smith as my tutor, proved as agreeable as my leisure. A.L. was a splendid history teacher and his critical discussions of the papers I wrote for him never failed to be stimulating. Moreover he held the just belief that his pupils would gain more from sessions with him than from taking notes at lectures given by other University professors, so that I was gratefully spared the chore of attending in cap and gown at these functions. It was, too, encouraging to gather from him that he had every hope of my attaining a First Class Honours degree. Carrying a load of recommended vacational reading I set off before Christmas to spend the four weeks vac in a pension at Munich where I could combine my reading with improving my command of the German language. Munich was a lovely city, with its fine baroque buildings, its splendid art-galleries and its wide snow-covered streets lined with little dark-leaved Christmas trees. A special pleasure were the Mozart Operas superbly staged and performed in the intimate little Prinz Regenten theatre. It was there that I first heard Mozart's light-hearted *Il Seraglio* which has ever since remained my favourite opera.

At Oxford my allowance of £250 a year was amply sufficient to meet any reasonable needs with enough to spare to buy clothes at Adamson's and books at Blackwells, and I had no occasion to take advantage of the almost unlimited credit that Oxford shops were happy to extend to undergraduates.

At an early date Aldous and I had become frequent visitors to Cherwell, Professor and Mrs. Haldane's home off the Banbury Road, where Mrs. Haldane kept open house for all friends of her son Jack and his sister Naomi. Short, square, energetic and vital, Mrs. Haldane had a great love and understanding of young men and women. The 'Prof.', Mrs. Haldane's husband, a brother of the Minister for War in the Liberal Government, was a tall, stooping scientist of great distinction. He seemed to live in a remote academic world and it was only at meals that we encountered his usually silent presence. Mrs. Haldane's hospitable roof gave us our only contact with young women. There were, of course, women's colleges at Oxford but they belonged to a different world from the strictly monastic society of the men's colleges, and the only time we even cast eyes on their inhabitants was when they came on their bicycles to University lectures. But at Mrs. Haldane's we had the enjoyable company of Naomi and her friends.

My memories of the summer term of 1914 will always be linked with Mrs. Haldane's garden running down to the River Cher. There a group of Naomi's friends, including her future husband Dick Mitchison from New College, rehearsed and performed to an invited audience a short play written by Naomi, followed by excerpts from the *Frogs* of Aristophanes, in, I think, Gilbert Murray's translation. Aldous and I had parts in both. In the latter he was Charon, with me as his slave and Lewis Gielgud as Dionysus. Lewis was also our producer and stage manager. In retrospect it seems as if the sun must always have been shining that summer so that our rehearsals were followed by gay picnics in punts on the river. To add a spice to my own happiness, I fancied myself in love with Naomi; it was a pleasantly mild and un-demanding form of love that was free from any pangs of jealousy or passionate desire and was satisfied by enjoying the presence of its object. An especially happy and hilarious farewell evening river picnic followed the plays' final per-formance. It was the end of term, and poling our punts back in the warm moonlight we planned further play acting for next summer and bade each other good-bye until we should all meet again in October. Little did I think that it would be five long years before I again set eyes on the few survivors of that happy company.

During June the one fly in my ointment had been, as in other Junes, the curse of hay fever. As soon, therefore, as term ended, I made for the pollen-free seashore. With her usual efficiency Mother had arranged for me to go to a pension in Dieppe where I would be able to improve my French while reading my history. I passed my days very pleasantly, bathing, walking on the cliffs, reading Anatole France and Pierre Loti and translating Sherlock Holmes stories into French for exercises with Madame. I remember how much I enjoyed Anatole France's *Isle des Penguins*, and the short stories in his *Étui de Nacre*, especially 'le Procurateur de Judée', the irony of whose last line made a special appeal to me. Most evenings I went to the Casino where I gambled innocuously at *boule* with five-franc pieces, never winning nor losing more than a few francs an evening. There were concerts, too, at the Casino, and I remember the audiences' enjoyment of the refrain of a low comedian's song :

> 'Ma femme est blonde
> Pour tout le monde
> Excepté moi.'

A few other English guests at the pension came and went but I avoided them and chose the company of the family who spoke no English to the advantage of my fluency in French. Nor did I find it unhelpful in this respect that Yvonne, the younger daughter, seemed to be nourishing a growing affection for me, obviously encouraged by her mother.

The news I read in the French papers about the murder of an Austrian duke and his wife at Serajevo appeared to offer no significance for me personally. There had been Balkan troubles for a number of years without more than local repercussions. I was beginning to look forward to joining the family early in August at Northfield, a house on St. Abb's Head on the Berwickshire coast which Mother had rented for July and August together with loch fishing and rough shooting, when, without warning as it seemed to me, the sky grew black with war clouds. Mobilization orders were posted up in Dieppe, and soon Yvonne and I were handing chocolates and cigarettes to the reservists in their blue and red uniforms as they entrained at the station.

It was all exciting, but this was conscript France, not England, preparing for a European war, and I still had no sense of personal involvement. England's wars were fought by her professional soldiers and sailors and even if she became a combatant a twenty-year-old second-year undergraduate would be back at Oxford continuing his studies. But I was keen to see what things looked like in Paris. A young married German-Swiss lady had left her nine-year-old son Willi at the pension while she visited Switzerland. Urgent and agonized telegrams came from her imploring Madame to send Willi home before it was too late. Inquiries at the station revealed that owing to mobilization all normal train services were suspended and the boy could clearly not risk travelling alone. So I volunteered to escort him to Paris and see him on to a train for Switzerland at the Gare de Lyons. I also had conceived the idiotic idea that from Paris I might travel to the Eastern frontier and spend the next part of the vac seeing real war at first hand as a free-lance unofficial war correspondent.

Willi and I succeeded in reaching Paris after a very slow journey in a crowded unscheduled train. The city was in a turmoil and I had the greatest difficulty in getting Willi from the Gare de Nord to the Gare de Lyons and even more in fighting my way through the frenzied mobs that were besieging any train for Switzerland. Late that evening, however, I succeeded in hoisting Willi into a train in charge of a friendly and motherly Swiss lady and her daughter.

Next morning I went early to the Gare de l'Est in pursuit of my own ends. I found that the military had taken complete charge of the station. No civilian trains were running and my efforts to travel by train towards the frontier were rudely rebuffed. Short of proceeding on foot there was nothing I could do to further my absurd plans. Sadly abandoning them, I was lucky to be able to find standing room in the corridor of a train back to Dieppe. The atmosphere there had changed in the three days I had been away. The French were now doubting whether England was going to join them in the war and Englishmen were greeted with hostile looks. It was time, I felt, for me to get back home. Next morning, amid tears from Yvonne, I embarked on the Newhaven boat and arrived in London in time to leave my luggage at Porchester Terrace, empty but for a housemaid, and join the vast crowd outside Buckingham Palace celebrating England's declaration of war that day and cheering King George and Queen Mary when they appeared on the balcony.

CHAPTER IV

i

AFTER a night at Porchester Terrace I travelled north to join the family in Berwickshire. There I found the same general excitement about the war and the same lack of any feeling of direct personal involvement that matched my own mood. 'Business as usual' was the nation's slogan of the moment, and in that spirit I went on with my history reading in preparation for my return to Balliol in October. The garden of our rented house ran to the edge of the steep cliffs of St. Abb's Head and a winding path led down to a row-boat alongside a little stone jetty. The North Sea was icy cold and full of floating jelly-fish, but we all bathed heroic-ally. Much more enjoyable was rock-pigeon shooting from the boat. The birds, disturbed by our shouts, seemed to dis-appear into the folds of the cliffs in their swift and almost vertical upward flight, so that to hit them while standing in the swaying boat was no mean feat. It was fun, too, to go out in the early morning with local fishermen and to bring back cod to be cooked for breakfast straight from the sea. Bernard James, my Rugby and Balliol contemporary, soon joined us. The Jameses were old family friends and though, being in different houses, we had not seen much of each other at Rugby, Bernard and I had always got on agreeably and shared many tastes.

It can only have been a short time before our pleasantly detached view of the war was shattered by Kitchener's call for all fit young men to volunteer for service. In spite of my father's insistence that we were much too young, Bernard and I at once felt that we must answer the appeal. Hearing that a public schools camp was being organized at Tidworth on Salisbury Plain as a refresher course for ex-O.T.C. cadets, we hastened there and found many old friends in the Rugby tents.

The camp was commanded by Colonel Frank Buzzard, an artillery and staff officer who had recently married my cousin Joan Collier. We all implicitly believed his pronouncement that the retreat from Mons, tidings of which were now arriving, was a deliberately planned and skilful withdrawal so as to trap the Germans and defeat them in one great decisive battle. The news of the Marne seemed at the moment to confirm such optimism. Convinced as we were by Norman Angell's confident predictions in his *Great Illusion* that a modern European war, for economic reasons, could only be of short duration, our main fear was that the fighting would be over before we had a chance of joining in, even though Kitchener had spoken of volunteering for three years' service.

After ten days in the camp, drilling, and, in turn, commanding platoons, we were invited to fill in a form applying for a commission as second lieutenants, stating the branch of the service of our choice. Bernard and I opted for the infantry as most likely to get us to France soonest, his preference being for a London regiment, while I, thinking of my half-Yorkshire descent, entered any Yorkshire regiment as my choice. (Bernard was given a commission in a newly forming battalion of the Middlesex Regiment in Kitchener's army. With the battalion he went out to France early in 1916 and was killed in July of that year on the Somme.) Then we were medically inspected. To my shocked surprise the doctor said that he would only pass me fit on condition that I underwent an operation for varicocele.

I had never heard of the complaint which, I learned, was a condition of the testicles that would cause trouble if the sufferer stood too long on his feet; nor had I ever experienced any discomfort. I at once agreed, however, to have the operation. The camp broke up that day and I telegraphed my father to ask his advice. His answering telegram told me to see Sir Victor Horsley in Cavendish Square. Sir Victor, the famous brain surgeon, and his family were old friends of ours and he had operated on me at home for a hammer toe a year or two earlier. I found him most reassuring, saying that he would at once get me a bed in a nursing home and would perform the minor operation himself. In a week, the operation over, I was recuperating at Aunt Amy's house at Greystoke near Penrith when my orders arrived. Dating from the 15th August 1914 I was commissioned as a second lieutenant in the Special Reserve of Officers and was to report to the 3rd (Special Reserve) Battalion of the East Yorkshire Regiment at Hedon near Hull. Hastening back to London I bought my uniform at Thresher and Glenny's, had my photograph taken in uniform and travelled north again to start my army career.

The battalion to which I reported had formerly been the militia battalion of the East Yorkshires. In pre-war days its men had enlisted for a short annual period of training, usually because they were out of work and wanted the money. With its headquarters at Hedon, a small town a few miles east of Hull, the battalion was combining its role of supplying reinforcements to the two regular East Yorkshire battalions, both in France, with the duty of guarding a stretch of the coast from Spurn Head to Bridlington.

At Hedon, I was joined by a number of newly-commissioned Special Reserve officers and we were placed under the aegis of Major Kino, an officer from the 1st Battalion, a cheerful little man of obviously semitic origin. Only two or three of us came from major public schools and I was the only one from Oxford or Cambridge, which may well have accounted for my very cordial reception at the hands of the Colonel and the adjutant. I soon made a particular friend of Peter Reynard, a Harrovian. He was the younger son of a well-known local fox-hunting squire but had inherited none of his father's tastes. His own were preciously aesthetic and he had drifted on to the stage where the summit of his achievement had been the chorus in musical comedy. He was very amusing company and he and I enjoyed hilarious evenings in Hull at the Alexandra Theatre where repertory companies regularly performed melodramas, with the audience hissing the villain and cheering the hero and heroine. 'Won't you marry me, Clifford?' begged the heroine in one such drama. Sir Clifford, the villain, replying amid boos from the audience, 'What a silly little puss it is !' It must have been also at the Alexandra Theatre that Peter and I watched with fascination a fat elderly lady garbed in a Union Jack sing a patriotic song with appropriate gestures. 'My boy's not tall, my boy's not small, he's just the boy for me. He's not in the Army (military salute). He's not in the Navy (naval salute and hornpipe). He's in the Royal Artillery' (bow and arrow gesture).

Week after week drafts of officers and men were being sent to France. My turn came a week before Christmas. I was given a very unpleasant typhoid injection, which created a high though short-lived fever and a very swollen and sore arm, and granted four days' leave before reporting at Grimsby to take a draft of the Manchester Regiment out to France. The family had gone to Somerset to spend Christmas with Uncle Will and Aunt Frances at Nynehead Court where they had lately moved from Yorkshire. I joined them there to say my farewells, and on 22nd December caught an early train to London. Aldous had learned of my movements and to my joyful surprise I saw his tall stooping figure on the arrival platform at Paddington. His eyesight had, of course, debarred him from any kind of military service and in October he had gone back to a Balliol deserted by all his friends. I could have wished for no better companion for my last hours in London. A good deal of the gilt had now worn off the gingerbread of the war which seemed to have got permanently bogged down in the mud of a trench line stretching from the Channel to the Swiss frontier. No end to the conflict seemed in sight, however distant, and the two or three East Yorkshire officers I met at Hedon who were back sick or wounded from Flanders told of wet and cold and boredom interrupted by the unpleasantness of shelling and sniping.

Aldous' comforting detachment from the war and the assurance that his familiar presence gave me of a friendship so enduring that it made our differing circumstances seem ephemeral, matched my mood of resignation to whatever the Fates might have in store for me. Together we did some last-minute shopping and, after a good lunch, he saw me off from King's Cross in the Grimsby train.

Reporting in the evening to the orderly room of the 3rd Manchesters in Grimsby, I learned that Lieutenant Moore of the Manchesters and I were to take charge of a draft of some 200 men leaving at 1 a.m. from the station. Meantime, I was given some food and a shakedown on a camp bed. We paraded at midnight and had some difficulty in entraining our charges, many of whom were drunk and some violent, our short march to the station being impeded by a number of their shrieking female friends, armed with hatpins, who tried to break the ranks. Nor was Moore a cheerful companion. A regular officer, he had been slightly wounded in France and his experiences at the Front had, he said, cured him of any desire to return there.

No one knew the destination of our unheated train with its locked carriage doors, but I remember it stopping at Basingstoke some time next morning, where tea and sandwiches were provided, and realizing that we must be on the way to Southampton. Moore and I mustered a very cold and miserable rabble of a draft on the quay there and embarked them on a small steamer with the red hand of Ulster on its funnel. Early next morning—Christmas Eve—found us steaming slowly up the Seine to Rouen where we marched our men up to the vast tented encampment on a hill above the town where reinforcements of officers and men were assembled to wait for a few days before being sent up to the front line formations. Infantry subalterns were in short supply and were being posted to any regiment whose need was greatest, so that I had no assurance of joining the East Yorkshires and finding some friendly faces from Hedon. Moore left for the Front next day, and I shared a tent with three strangers and messed with a motley collection from many regiments.

It was a miserable Christmas in a cold, wet and depressing place, though on Christmas night, a concert party brought some relief by performing in a vast marquee and singing,

'Sister Susie's sewing shirts for soldiers' and other topical numbers. The next evening thinking that it would be foolish to be killed with my virginity intact, I walked down the hill into the town and, over a drink in a hotel, picked up (or was picked up by) a good-looking black-haired woman. But when we got to the door of her apartment I found I had lost all desire for any closer relationship with my companion who now seemed hard and avaricious. Pressing some money into her hand I left her abruptly and walked slowly and sadly up the hill to the camp—still a virgin.

Next day my orders came. To my joy I was to join my own 1st Battalion at Houplines, a village just north-east of Armentières and I would be met at a railhead, west of Armentières, by the battalion transport taking up the rations. Eventually I found battalion headquarters in a more or less undamaged cottage on the outskirts of Houplines and reported to Colonel Clarke and Captain Anderson, the adjutant (in the last war he was to command a corps in North Africa). They were warmly welcoming, and gave me supper and a mattress on which to sleep in my 'flea-bag'. Only an occasional rifle shot or a burst of machine-gun fire or the crump of a stray shell disturbed my sleep, and before dawn I was walking over the open with the adjutant to join 'D' Company in the front-line trench. Major Kino, my old friend from Hedon, was commanding the Company. With him were two subalterns, Hawkesworth and Willis. The former had joined the Regiment straight from Sandhurst at the outbreak of war; the latter had been a sergeant in the Grenadier Guards and had recently been given a commission. Both were first-class officers and, in their respective ways, very agreeable companions, though I naturally had more in common with Hawkesworth with his public-school background.

'D' Company was also lucky in its sergeant-major, McKenna, a pre-war N.C.O. of the best and most reliable type. There were one or two other good pre-war sergeants but the men were a very scratch lot, mostly either little-trained and ill-disciplined militiamen or aged reservists. I remember one toothless and wheezingly asthmatic veteran, wearing a pre-South African War medal, who could only eat the hard ration biscuit by dissolving it into a mush in his mug of tea. I envied the officers of the territorial Queen's Westminster battalion in our Brigade, whose rank and file— all keen pre-war territorial volunteers and nearly all potential officer material—were models of soldierly behaviour in or out of the line. However, Sergeant-Major McKenna found me a very pleasant and willing batman in Private Prest whose faithful companionship and willing service added greatly to my well-being. One of our jobs as subalterns was to censor all the men's letters home, and it was interesting to me to learn from comments in them that the men preferred to be led by officers like Hawkesworth and myself, who came from a different social class, than by much more experienced promoted rankers, no doubt largely because the latter were too familiar with the men's thoughts and ways.

Besides the 1st East Yorkshires and the Queen's Westminsters, the 18th Brigade of the VIth Division comprised the 1st West Yorkshires and the 2nd Sherwood Foresters. The Divisional Commander, his headquarters far back in some comfortable château, was such a remote figure that I have no recollection of his name. Nor did he or any of his staff ever visit us in our trenches. But I had hardly been in the line a night before I came across our Brigadier and his Brigade Major making their muddy way along my platoon's sector. I recognized them at once as being Brigadier-General Stephens and Major Alan Paley, both of the Rifle Brigade, whom I had last seen when I entertained them to tea in 1912 in my Rugby tent at our O.T.C. camp at Tidworth where they were in charge of our cadet contingent. To my great pleasure the recognition was mutual and they gave me a very friendly welcome to their Brigade.

The Armentières sector of the front held by the three Brigades of the VIth Division was at that time a quiet one, largely owing to the low-lying swampy nature of the ground in which both our and the German trenches were sited. They were divided by a no-man's-land generally varying in width from 200 to 500 yards, though in a few places much closer. The land was too wet for any deep trenches to be dug and even our shallow ones needed continual baling out. Our protection against bullets and 'whizz-bangs', as the German high velocity shells were called, was a sandbag and earth parapet built well above ground level and requiring constant repair. Very tall people like myself had to develop a permanent stoop to keep their heads under cover and if I inadvertently stood momentarily upright the hiss of a sniper's bullet passing my head would, as often or not, provide a sharp reminder of the folly of my forgetfulness.

Our 'dugouts', for officers and men alike, were merely shallow dens scooped out just below the parados and roofed with sandbags on top of corrugated iron. The latrines were slits of muddy trench leading back from the parados. They must have been highly insanitary and gave so little cover that no one lingered over performing his natural functions.

From what we could see through our periscopes of the German trenches being baled out and repaired, the enemy's front line was in much the same condition as ours. In no-man's-land, immediately in front of the opposing trenches, a tangled mass of barbed wire, some in rolls, some attached to stakes formed the protection against raids or heavier infantry attack. From our front line one or two shallow communication trenches led back across the fields to the nearest houses in Houplines but they gave so little cover that in practice the only safe movement to and from the rear was above ground in the hours of darkness.

Each battalion in the Brigade usually had a spell of four days in the line followed by four days in reserve in the remains of houses in Houplines. Though the village had been evacuated by its former inhabitants, some of the houses were more or less intact so that, in reserve, we were at least dry even if we had little protection from the German 5·9 heavy howitzer shells with which the back areas were bombarded at intervals. When in reserve we could visit Armentières which was still largely undamaged and still inhabited by those of its civilian population who braved the risk of shelling

in order to make money out of the troops by keeping open
their shops and estaminets which did a thriving business
with omelettes and alcohol, mostly thin acid beer. It was
remarkable, too, how close to the front line the peasant
farmers still persisted in cultivating their fields even though
these became increasingly pitted with shell-holes. In
Armentières a disused laundry housed the Divisional baths
to which we marched in order to soak ourselves in vats of
soapy water and thus rid our bodies of lice while our clothes
were being steamed for the same purpose. Early on, while I
was marching to the baths at the head of 'D' Company, I was
suddenly almost felled by a blow between my shoulders.
Turning, I found the blow's deliverer to be gigantic Neville
Talbot, our Balliol Dean and now an Army Chaplain, whose
long strides had caught us up and who, recognizing me, had
thus typically accompanied his loudly bellowed greetings. It
was heart-warming to see him and, marching with him to
Armentières, to get news of Balliol and Balliol friends, a few
alas already killed.

The novelty, interest and adventure of being in the front
line and the glamour I attached to my having attained this
honourable position well in advance of most of my civilian
contemporaries, at once lifted the mood of depression that
had accompanied my last days in England and my journey
to Rouen. I found exhilaration in the carefree good companionship of my fellow soldiers. All of us, officers, N.C.O.s
and men, were 'in it' together, dependent on each other, and
sharing the same good or bad experiences. Even the rations
seemed to me at first to be excellent fare—the bully beef, the
Maconochie meat and vegetable tinned stew, and the bacon,
the scent of whose frying over charcoal fires in buckets so
deliciously sharpened my early-morning appetite. True the
square ration biscuits were iron-hard, but they were made
palatable by the plum and apple jam plentifully spread over
them; true also that all our water had to be so heavily
chlorinated that its sickly taste could not be disguised even
in the very strong brew of tea that accompanied our meals,
but when laced with the precious rum that came up with the

rations after dark and that was so carefully shared out, our supper tea made a most heartening and agreeable drink. I felt indeed extremely fit, my young body being at first unaffected by the conditions of wet, cold and mud that took their toll of older men.

In the past, I had often felt a keen sense of pleasure in being alive, induced by such commonplace experiences as waking up to a fine summer morning or walking out in the sharp frosty sunshine of a windless winter's day or being greeted by the flames of a log fire chasing the shadows as I entered a warm room on a cold night or, at any time, just by an upsurge of vitality from my youthful health. But the future and all the promise it held out for the repetition of such pleasures had always been an important element in such current happiness. Now, for the first time, I forced myself to live wholly in the present, and the refusal to allow any thought of the morrow to enter my mind made far more intense the feeling that it was good just to be alive at all and gave an extra zest to the moment and an extra perceptiveness to my senses. That what I now write is not just old age throwing a rosy glow over the distant past is proved by a letter that I wrote to Mother at the time. We were writing to each other almost every day, but of all my letters only this one has survived. It is dated 24th January 1915 and reads :

'We came back last night into the same section of trench as the time before—this was quite pleasant as it made the task of relieving the West Yorkshires a comparatively easy one. It is extremely difficult when the bit of trench is unknown to one—and as we always relieve in the dark an untidy muddle is often the result. Last night, when we relieved about 6 there was a bit of a moon and the place was further lit up by the glare of a hayrick on fire in the German lines about 500 yards away. One could see black figures trying to put the fire out, and our men kept up a continuous rifle fire at them but without much result, I think, as it is impossible to sight the rifle in the dark. My platoon got settled in very quickly and well and I found myself in the same nice little dug-out as before, where I can be warm and comfortable at night with the aid of my flea-bag and blanket. The 4 officers divide up the night from 6 to 6 into watches. Last night I was on from 12–3 a.m. and during one's watch one has to be outside and walking up and down the whole time. Tonight I shall be on from 9–12. At 6 a.m. everyone stands to till 7.15 when day sentries are posted and we go off to breakfast. The trenches are still very wet, in spite of 3 bitterly cold days without any rain. Most of the water springs up from the ground I fancy, or trickles through broken drains of the field, which is very low lying and flooded. Constant baling has to be resorted to, and during the night the floods gain on one horribly. We get very wet walking up and down the trench in our watches, as, in the dark, it is impossible to see where you are going. Before coming in last night we were all issued these wonderful little furry coats of goat skin. You have probably seen pictures of them in the papers. I have a dark brown one, and look like a cross between Robinson Crusoe and the Pantomime Cat. The men are too funny with theirs, crawling about on the parapets, and pretending to be monkeys, and thrusting up hairy arms for the Germans to see! The coats smell some, but are certainly warm. My tunic is extremely uncomfortable when I have 3 waistcoats on, as it is far too tight across the chest, so I have taken it off and am wearing the furry thing instead. We were working at draining from 9–12 and this afternoon the men have been having a sleep before setting to work on repairing the parapet as soon as it is dark. I have been lying in my dug-out writing this and tootling on a mouth organ, a supply of which some kind and unknown benefactor has sent out. I tootle hymn tunes with much success. We are given the usual corned beef to eat, but as a matter of fact we are living on our potted meat and cake, with a bottle of Benedictine which we got in the town. There is no fresh water to be got, and we are reduced to trench water—1 part water to 2 parts mud. It is always boiled and taken in tea or cocoa, so I suppose it's all right, thought it has a distinct 'tang' and leaves a muddy sediment all round the top of the cup. Sausages, and again sausages, would be very welcome. We are all very inane and very cheery. Trench life reduces one's brain to nothing and one can do nothing but laugh and be fatuous. It's very cold and feels like snow. My hands are frozen writing this and I must get out and see that my sentries are all right and awake. Very best thanks for the gloves, they are rippers.'

Unquestionably I was actively enjoying my first experience of war.

It was not very long, however, before the glamour began to be eroded by the monotony of trench life in the cold and wet of a Flanders February. The conditions in which we lived led to a steady loss of officers and men from sickness, apart from the odd casualties caused by shells and snipers' bullets.

In 'D' Company Major Kino was the first officer to be sent back sick. His successor in command of the company was Captain Inglefield, a very pleasant regular from our 2nd Battalion. Unfortunately, he did not last long, being succeeded by Major Slater, an elderly 'dug out' from some reserve pool of officers. His only previous experience of warfare had been in the Boxer Rebellion in China, which he had taken part in suppressing as an officer of the Hong Kong garrison artillery. His formation's possession of ammunition wagons had given its officers a great advantage in the loot of the summer palace in Pekin, enabling them to carry off booty too bulky for removal by less fortunately placed competitors. Major Slater had thus, as he told us, got away with enough bar silver to enable him to retire from the army in comfort. Moaning incessantly at the hardships which he was now compelled to endure, he spent most of his days scratching for lice in the mat of greying hair that covered his chest. Mercifully it was only a week or two before he persuaded our battalion medical officer that he was too ill to carry on. He departed unmourned by anyone. Hawkes-worth now took command of the company but it was not long before sickness also removed him. Meantime 'D' company had acquired another subaltern, Muhlig, commis-sioned like Willis from the ranks, from some Lancashire line regiment. Although Willis and Muhlig were both much older than I and, of course, experienced soldiers, my commission antedated theirs, so I took on 'D' Company's command. No one could have wished for more efficient and loyal supporters. The three of us got on very happily and 'D' Company's reputation stood high with the Colonel and Adjutant.

In the meantime I had acquired a new qualification as the battalion's bomb expert. The authorities had rightly come to the conclusion that, in the context of hand-to-hand fighting up and down a trench, the rifle was of little use as a weapon. The infantry were therefore to be also armed with hand grenades which could be thrown over the traverse from one bay to the next thereby killing any enemy advancing up or retiring down the line of trenches. I imagine that the Ger-mans must have first thought of this new type of warfare, as they already had an efficient form of stick bomb which they were beginning to use. In reply our sappers were manufacturing bombs from old jam tins filled with high explosive. A detonator with a length of black time-fuse attached had to be inserted into a hole in the top of the tin by the would-be user of the bomb, who then had to light the fuse with a match and wait till the fuse had begun to emit its sputter of sparks before throwing it at the enemy. Until our factories in England were able to supply proper bombs we had to make do with these home-made contraptions, which, through accidents, caused many more casualties to our own troops than they inflicted on the enemy. In the just belief that it would be safer to be in charge of these bombs in action than to be an onlooker, I had volunteered for in-struction by the divisional sappers in their use. I was given a wide berth by my friends when I subsequently proceeded to demonstrate the bombs to an officer from each company, but I was lucky in avoiding the accidents that were so easily caused by careless handling of the highly sensitive detonators or by faulty fuses.

The Germans had also begun to use trench mortars, most unpleasant weapons which lobbed large high explosive shells into our trenches. Being able to see these objects coming over, though uncertain where they would land, only seemed to add to their viciousness. In reply our Division formed a trench mortar company equipped with sapper-made mortars. Visits from members of this Company earned no popularity when they chose to fire their weapons at the Germans from one's own sector. As soon as they had loosed off their weapon they moved off elsewhere leaving us to await the inevitable retaliation by the German mortars directed against the area whence our mortar's fire had come.

It was while I was in command of 'D' Company and I think some time in March that I wrote for Mother a description of a typical day in the trenches. She had some copies typed for circulation round the family and one copy turned up a few years ago. Here it is :

A DAY IN THE TRENCHES

'Pass it along, Sentry: "D" Company, stand to, Mr. Huxley.' This is the formula which begins the day. I have been on duty since 2.30 a.m. and it was with a sense of relief that I sent the message along the line, for the long night is almost past and there is a freshness and thrill in the air which proclaims the coming dawn. The sentries stoop down and lift up the blanket flaps which cover the entrances to the dug-outs. 'Stand to. Come on, up yer get !' Unkempt and dirty and with many a yawn the men crawl out. Some are slower in getting up than others, but round come the non-commissioned officers, peering into every hutch to see that no slacker is hiding inside, hidden beneath a pile of blankets. In a short time the whole length of the trench is thickly lined with men, each at his own station.

In front the line of the enemy's trench begins to show up black against the sky. Paler and paler grows the night, and soon the eastern clouds are fired by the rose of the dawn. The enemy must be standing to as well, for with the dawn their shots come over thick and fast, singing and whirring overhead, hitting the ground with a bang, or striking the parapet with a loud plonk.

As soon as it is really light I send the order down. ' "D" Company day sentries.' At once the whole line springs into bustle and activity. Fires are made up in the braziers, dixies are put on to boil the tea, the welcome and warming tot of rum is issued and the scent of frizzling bacon begins to pervade the air. Only the day sentries, one for each section, still stand fully equipped at the parapet to continue the unceasing vigil. I stroll back to the headquarters dug-out in the centre of the line, and find the servants up and busy making the fire to cook breakfast. Inside, the little stove needs replenishing. My feet are cold as ice, and although I try and get a doze it proves an impossibility. Along comes the Company Sergeant-Major. 'Here is the indent to be signed, sir.' A list of what we require in the way of material has to be sent in to battalion headquarters by 8 a.m. Today we are requisitioning for 300 sand bags, 2 huts, 5 hurdles, 10 planks, and a roll of barbed wire. These materials will be brought up by the engineers or our pioneers to Pontbaillot farm just behind our lines, as soon as it is dark, and we shall use them to improve the trench.

The telephone operator blocks the entrance to the dug-out. 'Message, sir.' It is from battalion headquarters. 'Please report any fresh digging by the enemy during the night.' Out I go with my field glasses and gaze earnestly at the enemy's line from different parts of my trench. Yes—on the right there—they have dug what looks like a listening post in front of their trench, and there on the left is some fresh wire. Breakfast is ready by the time the report has been sent in and Willis and Muhlig arrive. They were on duty earlier in the night and have been sleeping the sleep of the just. The inevitable fried egg and bacon is brought in, and tea, the wonderful army tea, with iridescent colours floating on top and a thick scum round the edge. Then there is ration bread, sometimes toasted if the fire permits, and marmalade from home. Breakfast over, there is time for a quiet pipe before the business of the day begins. The morning is grey and cloudy and inclined to be cold, but breakfast has warmed us up and we can once more feel our feet. Life has begun to be worth living again. I look at my watch ; it is 9 o'clock and time for rifle inspection. Muhlig and Willis take 15 and 13 platoons on the right, I take 14 and 16 on the left. The rifles are surprisingly clean. They have been out all night, they have lain in muddy places and have been handled with muddy fingers, but the men have spent an hour on them and they come up for inspection as if for a peace parade. With the rifles, the ammunition and bayonets are inspected, as dirty ammunition would mean a jammed rifle in an attack. That was how the Durhams lost their trenches in October.

The inspection over, I set the men on to work that can be done inside the trench. There is always water to be baled or pumped out, for although there was no rain last night there are springs and old drains which soon fill the trench. Then we can make places for the two huts that are coming up tonight in sections, and there is a traverse or two to repair. Other work, such as filling sand bags or mending the parapet, has to be left till dark when the workers can leave the trench without being shot.

A buzzing in the air makes us look up ; one of our aeroplanes is flying over to have a look at the enemy. The big biplane is well known to both sides. The pilot is supposed to be a French officer, familiarly called 'the mad major'. He begins to hover high up over the German lines. A rattle of musketry and machine-gun fire is opened at him, of which he seems not to take the slightest notice. Now he swings round and flies along the enemy trenches. He must have come within the province of one of their anti-aircraft guns, for a ball of white smoke suddenly appears in the sky some way from him, and 'wumph' comes the report of bursting shrapnel. On he sails majestically, with the fluffy white balls all around him. Some are just below him, some just above, but none ever find their mark. Presently he disappears, a black speck merging into the grey of the sky.

Every man is now at his job—baling or digging or building—and the sentries at their posts, firing an occasional shot at anything moving in the German lines. I take up my glasses and peer cautiously over the parapet. Immediately in front, the ground is bright with a litter of tin cans of every description thrown from the trench. Then comes our high barbed wire and then the low trip wire. Beyond there is some 300 yards of muddy field with a ditch and some wire in the middle, and then the thick German wire with the brown line of their trench a little way behind it. Just opposite us the German lines run in front of what was a big white farm. Our guns are always blazing at it, and now little more than the white walls remain standing. The 'Quatre Hallots' is its name on the map, but throughout the Brigade it is known as the 'Four Harlots'. To the left of the farm are two haystacks and then the German lines curl right back in front of a row of poplars to the ruined village of Frelinghien. To the right there are a couple of red farms, also in ruins and more poplars. The whole country is perfectly flat, except behind our left beyond Ploegsteert wood where rise the hills crowned by Messines. Behind our trench there runs a track across a big field to a road where stand the ruins of Pontbaillot farm. Beyond there are a couple more fields and then the houses and factories of Houplines and the shell-pierced chimney which marks our billets.

Through my glasses the loopholes in the German trenches are clearly visible. Their trenches must be as wet as ours, as a bucket keeps on appearing above the trench, from which an invisible man pours water. Borrowing a rifle I have a shot or two at the bucket, and the baling stops. I have only fired two or three shots, but the German snipers have spotted where they have come from and their shots come pinging over the place where I have been standing. There is a lot of banging going on a little to our left and I can see our heavy shells dropping into Frelinghien in clouds of orange smoke. 'Brrrrr'—a German aeroplane is hastening over to try to spot our guns or to drop a bomb or two on Armentières.

Shortly before twelve the Sergeant-Major comes round again. 'The casualty return to be signed, sir,' and the welcome return, 'Casualties nil', goes in to headquarters. At 12 o'clock I pass the word down to knock off work. Fires are made up in the braziers and the Maconochies or tinned stews cooked for dinner. The sky has been growing more and more lowering and a few drops of rain have begun to fall. Soon the only too well-known downpour begins and I retire to the company headquarters dug-out to join Willis and Muhlig and wait for lunch. Harder and harder comes down the rain. Drops collect on the planks of the roof and begin to drip down, first in one place and then in another, till there is hardly a dry spot left, and the dug-out echoes to the melancholy drip-drip. Lunch comes in, but it is an unappetizing mess of tinned stew, and water drips down into the plate and into the tea. The little stove has been put out by the rain and our feet grow colder and colder. Nothing however seems to daunt the German snipers and one, doubtless well sheltered and dry, perversely selects the roof of our dug-out as his target. We three sit and shiver and wonder what on earth made us join the army. Protected by macintoshes our bodies are fairly dry, but nothing can mitigate the torture of frozen feet. 'Bang-whizz-bang.' Our guns have opened fire. Anywhere is better than the dripping dug-out, and we hasten out to see what they are firing at. 'Right on their trenches, sir,' says the sentry. 'Bang-whizz-bang,' and a cloud of black smoke and brown earth springs up on the enemy's trench, just in front of the 'Four Harlots'. 'Poor devils,' is our comment, as the guns work along the trench opposite. After firing about ten rounds they stop and things quieten down again. I walk along the trench to see that everything is all right. Most of the inhabitants are in the shelter of their dug-outs, but the sentries, clad in macintosh capes still keep an unending look-out. We return to the dug-out to try to doze, but our feet are far too cold. A faint bang—peu eu eueu eu—crescendo and diminuendo. Another bang! 'That the enemy! Where are they shelling?'

'Just to the right of our billets, sir.' Again the shell comes whistling overhead. This time we see smoke and dust coming from the roof of a house before we hear the bang. Unfortunate Houplines is getting it again. For some little time the shelling goes on. Up in the air appears one of our aeroplanes and the Germans guns cease firing. Ours soon take up the tale, shelling somewhere behind the enemy's trenches, presumably after the guns. Over on the left the enemy create a diversion by dropping some 'Black Marias', a large percentage of which fail to go off, and so the game continues all the afternoon. The rain begins to slacken and then stops. The stove is relighted and with the advent of tea our drooping spirits revive. Suddenly up comes a Sergeant. 'There's a man been hit, sir. Private Smith got it in the head. I am afraid he's done for.' I walk along the trench to where the man has been shot. There is quite a little crowd, which I disperse. Private Smith is lying in the bottom of the trench supported by a Corporal who has roughly bandaged him with a first field dressing. A bullet has apparently come through the sand bags and hit him in the side of the head. His face is a greenish white save where the blood is oozing through the bandage in red patches and his breath comes in great stertorous gasps which shake his whole frame. Mercifully he is unconscious. There is nothing to be done but to telephone for the stretcher bearers to come down as soon as it is dark, and when they arrive they have only a lifeless corpse to carry away.

The dusk begins to set in and with it the enemy's snipers increase in number and vigour. The line of the enemy's trench begins to grow misty. ' "D" Company, night sentries.' I pass the order down, and the night watches begin, every third man being on sentry relief throughout the night. The darkness comes quickly and with its advent the shots from the enemy grow fewer and fewer. A telephone message from battalion headquarters is brought in stating what we are to expect in the way of material. This I hand on to the Sergeant-Major who collects a party and goes off to bring the material up. Word is passed down for the platoon

Sergeants to send their parties for the rations. Presently the Quartermaster arrives, bringing the mail and the rum. Letters and parcels are eagerly opened and the next half-hour is spent in reading letters and any papers that have also come. As soon as rations have been drawn and issued by the platoon Sergeants and the material brought down, the night's work is begun. Sand bags are filled from behind the trench and dark figures can be seen on the parapet putting on sand bags and shovelling earth. The hurdles are used for riveting the sides of the trench, the planks are laid down as footboards and the huts are put together in the places already dug for them. It is supper time by now and we return to the dug-out to find an angry message from 'C' Company complaining that we have taken 200 of their sand bags. This we at once deny. There is great competition for material, and the first to get to the farm generally takes all he finds.

There is the inevitable tinned stew for supper, but cocoa sent from home forms a welcome change from tea. After supper the work has to be continued, and the men need constant supervision. I send out a patrol to see what the enemy are doing, as they are rather quiet. In half an hour the patrol is back again, reporting that the Germans are hard at work on their barbed wire. As we ourselves are busy we do not fire on them ; it would only make them retaliate in kind. At 9 o'clock the orderly Corporal comes along with a list of the sick whom he is going to take with him to see the doctor in the billet. A roll of barbed wire has come up with the stores. Taking out a Lance Corporal and a Private I go out to put it up in front, first being careful to pass down the message, 'Mr. Huxley and two men are going out to the front.' If this precaution is not taken one is liable to be shot at by one's own sentries. The Lance Corporal has brought some stakes with him and the Private carries a mallet. The stakes are driven in and the wire wound round and joined up. It is a dark moonless night, but the starlights go shooting up incessantly in front—to the left, to the right and even more or less to the rear—so oddly does our line curve round Armentières. Occasionally one comes shooting up from the trenches in front, for all the world like a rising cock pheasant, and we fling ourselves flat in the mud, as it lights up the whole ground with a bright white light. Away beyond Messines, at St. Eloi perhaps, can be heard the thunder of big guns and the faint rattle of rifle fire. An occasional bullet from in front strikes the ground with a smack. Across the strip of neutral ground is wafted the sound of hammering as the enemy's barbed wire is driven in, the Germans being engaged in the same pursuit as ourselves. Only 300 yds of open field divide us, and yet we are further apart than the two poles, for between us lies the valley of death. It is 10 o'clock by the time we have finished, and most of the work in the trench has now been done. I am on duty first tonight, till midnight that is to say, so I return to Company head-quarters dug-out, and making up the fire, sit down to read a newspaper and start censoring the men's letters. 'No. 15 and 16 sections, 16 platoon, all correct, sir.' It is eleven o'clock already, for every hour during the night the N.C.O.s on duty, two for each platoon, have to come and report to the officer on duty. I go out again and after sending out another patrol, go the round of the sentries. Every few yards stands a dark silent figure peering out towards the front and firing an occasional shot if he hears or sees anything suspicious. Some are shaken by incessant coughs, some are stamping their feet in a vain attempt to keep them warm ; but all are mute and uncomplaining, and now that the men have grasped their duties things run smoothly enough. Presently the patrol comes in to report that the enemy have stopped work-ing on their wire and that all is quiet save for the occasional sniper. Midnight, and the voice of the N.C.O. comes down, 'Next relief.' The sentries stoop to the dug-outs and wake up the next man, and not till he is up with equipment on and bayonet fixed can the old sentry leave his post. I go along to Willis' dug-out and tug at his leg till he gives a grunt. 'Quarter past twelve, Willis.' At last I make for my own dug-out where Prest has got my blankets ready and in I crawl to sleep for five hours the sleep that only those who have been up and busy for twenty-two hours can appreciate.

April came bringing increased activity all along our front as the land began to dry out. My battalion was in reserve in Houplines on my twenty-first birthday. I celebrated it by taking Willis and Muhlig to lunch in Armentières in one of the restaurants that was still open, though the town was rapidly becoming deserted by its civilian inhabitants as more and more houses were wrecked by shell-fire. After lunch we went to a horse-show organized by Division. It was a very different coming-of-age from anything that I had imagined on my twentieth anniversary, a coming-of-age lived wholly in the present and deliberately excluding any thought for a future which I believed I should be very unlikely to experience. I remember marking the occasion of my birthday by writing a letter to Mother and Dad to be delivered to them only after my death. It expressed no regrets but only my great gratitude for their having given me such a wonderfully happy childhood and youth.

Shortly afterwards I handed over command of 'D' Company to Captain Gervas Markham, one of our regular officers who had been wounded in the early days of the war and who had now returned to the front. He proved to be a particularly agreeable red-haired man in his late twenties, as well as an extremely smart and efficient officer. He and I at once became very good friends. Censoring the men's letters home, I was interested to find how pleased the remaining old regular soldiers were to have one of their pre-war officers commanding them again. Peter Reynard also joined us from Hedon but went to 'C' Company.

I felt very sorry for him as he was so obviously wholly unsuited to trench life and the command of troops, though I admired his brave and uncomplaining attitude. One night when the battalion came out of the trenches and into billets in reserve, the officers of 'C' and 'D' Companies had been allotted a reasonably well-preserved house where I had a bedroom to myself. Lingering in my room for a chat, Peter suddenly threw his arms round me and tried to kiss me, imploring me to 'go the whole hog' with him and telling me how he and 'B', a fellow officer at Hedon, had thus loved each other.

I remember my extreme repulsion at the idea and at the bristly impact of Peter's unshaven chin on my cheek. Having no possible desire to share Peter's metaphorical sty, I told him as firmly but as gently as possible that much as I liked him as a friend, I could not assume the role of a lover. Poor Peter; I think he must have suffered many rebuffs, since he took mine without umbrage and we reverted without embarrassment to our former pleasant relationship. I lost touch with him when I left the battalion but heard much later that he had been given a job at the Base, only to shoot himself when ordered back to the front. Shortly after I was demobilized his lawyers wrote that he had bequeathed me a number of his books.

The 18th Brigade had now moved a few miles north of Houplines into a much more unpleasant sector of the line, where, in its four- or five-day spells in the trenches, 'D' Company had to occupy a salient only some fifty yards distant from the German front line. The enemy's snipers and trench mortars were much too active for comfort, and every night our trenches needed repairing with fresh sand bags to strengthen weak and damaged sections of their parapet. To get back, on relief by the West Yorkshires, to our reserve billets in a ruined hamlet we had to leave a very inadequate communication trench and stumble through a ghostly cemetery pitted with fresh shell holes.

It was a macabre spot by moonlight or transitorily lit by the green of a Very light, with crosses and headstones all tumbled about and bits of coffins with exposed skeletons lying around.

We were now suffering a number of casualties. One afternoon I was chatting with Gervas Markham in our front trench, our respective heads safely below the level of the sand bag parapet, when a sniper's stray bullet penetrated a weak spot in the sand bags and, splaying out, hit Markham in the head, almost taking off his skull and splashing me with blood and brains as he collapsed dead at my feet. Apart from the shock I felt his loss keenly as did all the battalion, and it was very sadly that I resumed command of 'D' Company.

Not long after I was asleep in a downstairs room in a partially wrecked house which formed our company head-quarters in reserve, when a large German shell scored a direct hit on the upper part of the house causing its complete collapse. I remember waking to find myself buried in dark-ness beneath timbers and bricks, pinned down and half-choked by plaster dust. Soon, however, I heard the voices of Willis and Muhlig, who had been sleeping in a neighbour-ing house, summoning help to haul away rubble and find me or my corpse. I was pulled out shaken and bruised about the head, to be restored by neat whisky from Willis' flask. Our battalion M.O. found no broken bones or hurt beyond bruises, but before long I began from time to time to get severe headaches from which I suffered occasionally for many years and whose cause was unknown until a specialist diagnosed that they were due to broken bones inside my nose blocking my sinuses. Another effect of my burial which only gradually developed was the progressive loss of sight in my right eye, caused, the oculists said, by some severe blow.

Meantime, my health and spirits were not improved by the explosion of a German whizz-bang shell so close to me that it seemed a miracle that my only injury was partial deafness for nearly a week. Under Brigade orders I had taken 'D' Company to construct a new communication trench through the ruins of a small hamlet not far behind our front line. Not realizing that the spot was under obser-vation by the German gunners we were ordered to do the work by daylight. Soon after I had put the Company to work a German battery opened up on us, killing two of my men and wounding four more.

For some time I had been acting as interpreter to Colonel Clarke over billeting questions with the French civil autho-rities when we were out of the line, and he now asked me to hand over command of 'D' Company to Willis and join battalion headquarters as assistant adjutant in order to understudy Captain Anderson whose early promotion to a staff post was expected. Under Anderson I learned the techniques of writing orders and reports and enjoyed the slightly superior comforts of the battalion headquarters mess, consisting of Colonel, Adjutant, Medical Officer and myself.

Away to the north we could now hear day and night the almost continuous gunfire of the second battle of Ypres where the Germans had gained initial success in their attack through the use of gas, against which new weapon we had no protection. I seem to remember drafting orders, on Brigade instructions, for urinating on any kind of cloth and breathing through it as an emergency measure against the gas.

It was not, however, German gas, but my old enemy, hay-fever and asthma, that began to plague me on top of my headaches, and I must, I think, have been diagnosed by our kindly M.O. as being in poor physical shape when Colonel Clarke was asked by Division if he could recommend a suitable junior officer with experience of hand grenades for posting to England to train the new armies there in this branch of trench warfare. Although I protested that I would rather stay with the battalion, the Colonel told me that since nothing more had been heard of Anderson's possible promotion, there seemed to be no immediate likelihood of my becoming adjutant and that he had sent my name in to Division. A few weeks later orders came through for me to report to the headquarters of the Humber garrison in Hull for instructions as to my new assignment.

It was now late June and against the odds for infantry subalterns I had survived six months in the front line. With the warm and envious congratulations of my fellow officers to speed my departure I rode back to rail-head with the Quartermaster and battalion transport and entrained for Boulogne for a night crossing of the Channel to Folkestone. Whatever outward protests I might have made to Colonel Clarke I felt, in fact, extremely thankful for this providential and unexpected stay of execution.

After a few happy days' leave at home in London I travelled to Hull and reported to Major Maurice, the chief staff officer at Humber garrison headquarters which occupied the Station Hotel. He told me to report back to my own 3rd battalion at Hedon whence I would shortly be sent on an instructors' course at the Otley School of Military Engineering and Grenades in Wharfedale, where I would learn all about the new weapons that had been quickly produced to supersede the improvised jam tin. I have before me now my Otley passing-out certificate, reading that I had 'specially qualified as a grenadier with percentages of 95% in the written examination, knowledge of extemporary and service grenades and grenade throwing'.

Thus armed I returned to Hull to join the headquarters staff who lived and messed as well as having their offices in the Station Hotel.

After six months in the trenches I found my life at Humber garrison a most agreeable one. I was my own master, since Major Maurice gave me a completely free hand to organize and conduct my work which took me over a large area of the north-east coast and brought me into personal contact with the commanding officers and adjutants of the various battalions whose lunch-time hospitality was always at my disposal. My job was to visit each battalion, select and train bombing instructors, lecture on the use of bombs in trench warfare and draw up a training scheme under which all ranks would practise with dummies and throw at least half a dozen live grenades before proceeding overseas.

This work was soon increased by the advent of the Stokes mortar. In September I had been ordered by Northern Command in York to report to a Major Beddoes at the Grenade School on, of all unlikely places, Clapham Common. My orders were marked 'most secret'. On Clapham Common I found a large enclosure surrounded by a high fence, and Beddoes introduced the dozen or so officers on the course to the new weapon. It proved to be a very simple one, just a tube with a projecting pin inside its base. Down the tube one slid the projectile which had a cartridge-enclosed detonator. This was fired when the cap at its base struck the pin in the tube. The range, whose maximum was some 200 yards, was obtained by varying the elevation of the tube.

After a few days of instruction and practice firing with dummies, during which I lived agreeably at home in Porchester Terrace, I qualified as a Stokes Gun instructor with a certificate from Major Beddoes that 'this officer obtained 99% in his examination. Excellent, he is exceptionally capable.' I then travelled back to York in the guard's van, watching over four specimens of the new secret weapon, together with live and dummy ammunition.

General Lawson, head of Northern Command, had arranged for me to demonstrate the mortar to a gathering of his senior officers on Strensall Common. I was given a Sergeant and eight men from one of the battalions in the command and set to work to drill them. Positioning my four mortars in a line on an open space on the Common, I evolved a very smart drill whereby, on my whistle, the men, two to each mortar, ran forward; and on my second whistle one man handed the missile to his mate who inserted it into the tube and stepped back to await its exit and its explosion on the 100 yards' distant target some twelve seconds later.

Needless to say, using dummy ammunition, I had beforehand carefully marked out the target in relation to the firing point and the elevation of the mortars. Nothing could have been less like active warfare, but nothing, I thought, would be more calculated to please old General Lawson and his staff. In due course they assembled on the muddy Common, immaculate in their brass hats, red tabs and polished field boots, and took up their position well behind the firing point.

All went according to plan and three of the mortars sped their missiles towards the target but, to my horror, the missile from the fourth mortar only just trickled out of the tube and fell on the ground a foot beyond. With twelve seconds to go before it exploded I saw my squad running at full speed to the rear. Turning, I forced myself to retire at a walk, counting the seconds. At eleven I flung myself on the ground, observing as I did so a like movement on the part of the General and staff further back. I heard the first three missiles explode on the target but only silence came from the fourth lying in front of its mortar. After counting another twelve seconds for safety, I rose and marched back to my prostrate audience, saluted the General and informed him that, most unfortunately, the fourth missile must have been fitted with a defective cartridge, but that I would at once investigate it, and meantime if he moved back a short way he would be safe in any eventuality. Rising to their feet my spectators complied, but the ground was very muddy and the gloss of their appearance had departed. Feeling a complete fool, I returned in isolation to the mortar and examined the missile. As I thought, the cartridge had been a dud one, and I was able to remove the detonator without undue risk. Luckily General Lawson was in a good mood and expressed himself well pleased when I took him up to the targets which the other three missiles had well and truly destroyed.

Early in 1916, I imagined myself deeply in love with Gladys Gurdon, the Bishop of Hull's daughter. Her brother had been a friend of mine at Rugby, and I was a frequent guest at the Bishop's home at Hessel, where Gladys kept house for her widowed father. Fair and plump, she was a sunny, down-to-earth and altogether delightful character. Gladys and I became very good friends, but our relations remained wholly platonic. According to my accepted standards, relations could not be other with a girl of one's own class unless and until one proposed marriage and was accepted. Even then, pre-marital intercourse was unthinkable. I believed that, in my position, a war-time engagement or marriage would be a far too irresponsible proceeding to be considered, so I kept my pleasantly romantic feeling to myself and was much shattered when Gladys in a long letter told me of her engagement to a naval officer whom I had only casually met and had never thought of as a rival.

Towards the end of 1915, my parents had acquired a country home, with a view to my father's eventual retirement, though he was still working full time in London. It was in Surrey a few miles from Godalming. The house, Great Enton, was undistinguished in its late Victorian architecture and was rather dark as it was built below the crest of the steep slope of the garden and was overshadowed by a large Spanish chestnut tree. But the hilly, broken, surrounding countryside was pleasant and unmarred by other houses. Some fifty acres of pasture and wood went with the house, and my father was indulging a long-standing ambition by starting a small dairy farm with pedigree red-polls under the care of a working bailiff. That summer of 1916 my parents were spending all weekends at Enton and my leaves from Hull were thus made much more enjoyable than if Porchester Terrace had been our only home.

iii

In France the battle of the Somme was now raging. I had been promoted Captain and began to feel that it was time for me to get back to the front. The opportunity came when the War Office asked Humber Command for the names of officers with a good knowledge of the German language, since more Intelligence staff officers were urgently needed in France. My name was sent in by Major Maurice, and after an interview at the War Office to test my German, I attended a highly interesting course in London on the composition of the German army, the interrogation of prisoners, the interpretation of air photographs and other Intelligence skills. I passed out with flying colours and after a brief visit to Hull to pack up and sell my car, I joined the headquarters staff of the 38th (Welsh) Division in the Ypres sector of the front.

My Divisional commander was an easy-going corpulent character, fond of good food, to procure which a Divisional car paid frequent visits to Boulogne. My own work came under the G1 and G3, both competent and friendly regular officers. I was the Division's first full-time Intelligence officer and my superiors seemed to appreciate my keenness to establish the full scope and usefulness of the job. It was one, at any rate, that I greatly enjoyed and found full of interest.

Most days I spent up the line visiting our Brigades and getting to know their battalion commanders and adjutants and our front trenches which lay along the canal bank north of Ypres. With the aid of air photographs, I mapped the German lines with their concrete pill-boxes, and when night raids were ordered by Corps to take prisoners and gain information about the enemy's movements and dispositions I always made a point of going up to the Company headquarters of the raiding party in the front line so as to interrogate prisoners immediately on their capture when they were shaken and frightened and likely therefore to answer all my questions. It also meant that any important information obtained by the raid would reach Division and thence Corps at the earliest possible moment.

As a prisoner was brought in I would call him to attention in a loud voice and then, as if as a matter of routine, demand his name, number, regiment and other information. Very seldom did I find any unwillingness on the part of the well-disciplined German soldier to answer questions thus authoritatively put. In the case of non-commissioned officers, who both knew more and would be less likely to part with information, I used to bring out my air-photograph map of the German trenches with the strong points marked, and tell the prisoner that, of course, he wouldn't have any knowledge of map-reading. In order to refute this slur, he would almost invariably demonstrate his skill by pointing on the map to the position of his battalion headquarters, assembly points for reliefs, mortar and gun sites and other desirable targets for our artillery.

Back at Divisional headquarters I would write out a full report for the day's Intelligence summary before snatching some sleep during the remainder of the night. Often it was time for breakfast and the day's ordinary routine before I had finished and I found that without undue difficulty I was able to do without any sleep for forty-eight hours.

My fellow officers at 38th Division headquarters were a very pleasant and friendly lot and in their company the winter months of 1916–17 passed quickly. In the spring of 1917 we remained north of the Messines and Arras attacks which gained limited objectives, and we ourselves were only engaged in trench warfare until in June we began to prepare for the great Passchendaele offensive which was intended to achieve the final breakthrough and of which we were to be the northernmost assaulting division. Every day our artillery fire on the German lines increased as more and heavier guns were massed behind our front. It was, we were told, the greatest concentration of artillery ever known. I was very busy, in liaison with our gunners, poring over the air-photographs on which the few remaining German concrete pill-boxes and strong points showed clearly amidst the waste of pitted shell-holes into which the whole German front had been churned. Unfortunately the weather now chose to take part in the offensive with violent thunderstorms and torrential rain. Very soon every shell-hole was filled with water and the ground over which we were to attack looked from the air like one vast swamp.

The night before zero hour, dawn on the 31st July, I went up to the Canal Bank, accompanied by two runners, and joined the Commander of a company forming part of our second assault wave. Just before zero, our barrage reached a fearful pitch of intensity as we listened to our shells screaming over our heads and bursting on the German front lines. As our first assault line went over the top, the barrage lifted on to enemy gun positions further back. The Germans in the front lines offered little resistance and a message soon came back to say we had taken our first objective.

I at once went forward with my two runners. By this time the German counter-barrage was in full swing and shells were falling heavily round us, but I safely reached some cover afforded by a partially wrecked pill-box just as I met some of our men escorting back the first prisoners, a very dazed and shaken batch including an officer. To my surprise I found that they belonged to a crack Guards Division instead of the Saxon formation which had hitherto been opposite us. They had, they said, on interrogation, only come into the line the day before. This was valuable news and I at once sent back a runner with it to Brigade headquarters, requesting that it should be relayed to Division and Corps. Later I had the satisfaction of being told that my message had been received several hours before any other report was sent back in regard to the new German dispositions. I remember that I was scribbling my message when I heard the whistle of a large shell seemingly coming down on top of us. Escort, prisoners and I flung ourselves flat on the ground as the shell buried itself deep in the mud with which its explosion showered us. As we rose to our feet, I saw that the German officer, alone of our party, had remained standing.

Going forward again with our second assault wave, I crossed the debris of what had been the German front position and found some fighting going on round a concrete machine-gun post which was holding up our advance. Feeling highly elated at being in an advance at last, I took part in the post's capture which was effected by our crawling round to the rear of the pill-box and lobbing some bombs inside its back entrance. The bombs at once brought out the remaining Germans with their hands up, and entering the pill-box as the safest place I could find, I interrogated the prisoners on the spot and was able to send some more useful information back by my second runner.

By this time our second assault wave had reached all their objectives and was consolidating our new line. Our wounded were also straggling back and more prisoners, but the latter had no new information to give me. As the German shelling was now beginning to slacken I thought it was time I made my own way back to Brigade and thence to Divisional headquarters to write up my full Intelligence report.

Everyone at Division was in cheerful mood at the success

of the Division's attack, and Colonel Pryce told me that the B.G.G.S. at Corps had congratulated him on the speed with which my reports had reached him. The rain, however, be-ban to fall again, harder than ever, and news came through of the attacks on our right being held up by the combination of mud and German resistance from pill-boxes that our artillery had failed to eliminate.

This proved to be the pattern of the future course of the Passchendaele battle. Our own Division's attacks made slower and slower progress at each successive effort, though we had, I think, penetrated further than any other Division before we were relieved. Meantime the weather and the mud grew steadily worse. Such was the state of the ground that the only way of reaching our front line and bringing up ammunition and rations was along narrow wooden duck-boards laid by the sappers over the morass churned up by the incessant shell-fire. Going up the line, as I regularly did so as to be on the spot for prisoners from our further attacks, became an unforgettable nightmare.

The duckboards were under constant and much too well-aimed fire from the German artillery, but to leave the duckboard was to become hopelessly bogged down in the sticky mud and to risk drowning in a waterfilled shell-hole. Luckily most of the German high explosives falling deep into the soft slime before bursting only sent up showers of muddy earth, but there was no protection against shrapnel and casualties were heavy, the wounded often drowning in mud.

On relief the Division went into rest behind Poperinghe but had two more spells in the same section of the line, making attacks which failed to attain much success. The Passchendaele offensive finally ground to a halt in Novem-ber, its total achievement the wresting from the enemy of a few miles of completely devastated terrain at the cost of terrible casualties and the lowering of the morale of the British army.

With thankful hearts my Division left the scene and took over a quiet section of the front just south of Armentières with our headquarters in an undamaged village. There we spent a comparatively peaceful Christmas and remainder of the winter, as the trenches, both ours and those of the Germans, were in such waterlogged land that active warfare was limited to the occasional raid. Our casualties at Passchendaele had not been as heavy as those in many of the Divisions engaged in the battle and I counted myself lucky to have emerged unscathed and with the gratification of having been awarded a military cross and a mention in despatches.

At the beginning of March I left the 38th Division with regret, but Corps Headquarters, whose intelligence staff was short-handed, asked for my services and I felt that I should be of more use there than in the dull routine of a quiet Divisional sector. At Corps Headquarters I came directly under the G.S.O.2, Major Ralph Glyn, whom I greatly liked and who was to re-enter my life some years later.

I was at Corps when on March 21st the news arrived of the great German offensive on the Somme which effected the first real breakthrough by either side since 1914. To help contain the attack my old 38th Division was moved to the south. All remained quiet, however, on our Corps' Armentières front where we believed that the ground was too wet for the enemy to launch an offensive. So much so that the Portuguese Division which had recently arrived in France was made to occupy part of the line as an easy introduction to active service.

The Portuguese soldiers seemed a pathetic crowd of undersized men, shivering in the cold and wet, with singularly poor specimens of officers. I used to get the Portuguese Division's Intelligence Reports in which mild sporadic shelling would be described as a 'furious bombardment'.

March proved to be a very dry month and April set in with thick early morning mists later dispersed by warm sunshine. We now began to get reports of heavy troop movements behind the German front opposite us. The enemy's offensive on the Somme had been finally checked and we began to wonder whether the land had dried up sufficiently for the Germans to be preparing an attack on our front, though it seemed as quiet as ever.

The attack came on 9th April when at Corps Headquarters we were woken by the noise of tremendous gunfire all along the Corps front. Without the warning of any preliminary bombardment the Germans had taken advantage of the thick morning mist to launch their onslaught.

Driving up with one of my fellow corps staff after a hasty breakfast we met what seemed to be the whole Portuguese Division in disorderly rout, headed by cars and ambulances full of officers making for the coast. At our British Divisional Headquarters we learned that although our own second line was holding firmly, the Germans were pouring unchecked through the gap on the right opened by the Portuguese débâcle and were advancing towards Estaires, at the same time taking our line in the rear. Going further forward to a Brigade headquarters we found that orders had just come through for a general retreat so as to avoid our complete encirclement. We could, indeed, already hear firing going on well behind us on the right. It was in fact a week or more before the German advance was to be finally halted in front of Hazebrook by the steadfastness of a Guards Brigade and an Australian Division.

After the front had again been stabilized I was asked to run two or three short Intelligence courses for officers from the Australian Division. My first contact with soldiers from the empire overseas had been early in 1915, when a Canadian battalion, newly arrived in France, had joined the East Yorkshires in the line for a week's instruction in trench warfare. The Canadians had made an excellent impression on us, and I now met Australians for the first time. The dozen or so I had for a week at a time for the two courses I gave —on the German army, air photography, etc.—were a grand lot, all keen to learn and all, I think, commissioned from the ranks and representing a cross-section of Australian life. I was greatly taken with their independent, self-reliant outlook. For them and for me the high spot of my course was a day with a Royal Flying Corps squadron with whose Intelligence officer I had made friends. Through him, I arranged for my pupils and myself to be given short flights over the German lines in the Squadron's seemingly frail reconnaissance aircraft so as the better to be able to interpret air photographs by seeing the actual ground from the air.

Apart from my courses I saw a good deal of the Australian Division in our Corps and formed the highest regard for its fighting qualities. Then and there I began to reflect on the importance of the ties that joined Britain and the Dominions ; ties which, in our hour of need, had brought men, so like us in some ways and so different in others, of their own free will from the far corners of the earth to fight alongside us in a cause remote from their own unthreatened daily lives. We owed them a debt, I felt, which when peace came we should lose no chance of trying to repay.

Meantime I was finding Intelligence work at Corps too remote from the fighting line for my liking, and when I learned that Divisions which had ceased to exist as formations in the great retreat were being reconstituted and restaffed, I applied to join one and was posted to the 30th Division which the Corps had just taken over. The Division was commanded by a jovial, unassuming infantryman from the South Wales Borderers. On his staff were two V.C's, Neame, the G.S.O.1 and Moore, the young G.S.O.3. The headquarters' atmosphere was very pleasant and friendly and I enjoyed my immediate task of setting up the Division's Intelligence organization.

During a week's leave at home I again believed myself to have fallen in love. My parents were clearly anxious for me to meet suitable girls, and on this occasion they produced Ella Cane, one of the two daughters of old friends of my mother. Ella was small, dark and, in my eyes, very lovely. An evening together seeing the *Maid of the Mountains* and a week-end at Enton left me deeply enamoured. Again, however, I refrained from making any open avowal of my feelings, thinking it unfair to seek any formal engagement until I could offer a secure future. Back in France I started to write to Ella frequently and at length, but her replies came at longer intervals and before long Mother wrote to tell me of her engagement to a sapper officer.

We were now getting cheerful news of successful attacks by the Allied Armies to the south of us, each successive thrust making substantial gains of ground and taking numerous prisoners. At last the Germans really seemed to be weakening. Before long we on the northern wing began to take part in the general advance that by successive stages and against less and less resolute resistance was to see us deep into Belgium by 11th November. It was a novel and exciting experience to sense victory in the air after the long years of stalemate or defeat, and to be almost continually on the move forward, first crossing the waste lands of the old front and then reaching a new world of undamaged towns and villages whose inhabitants lined the streets to cheer their liberators, while Mayors in official welcomes kissed our embarrassed General on both cheeks and kindly hosts in our billets dug up precious bottles of wine, hidden for four years from the Germans, from which to drink toasts with us.

Neame and Moore felt that the place of Divisional staff was as far forward as possible with our advancing troops, and early each morning I would go with them, sometimes on horseback, sometimes by car, to be fully engaged all day in interrogating newly captured prisoners, whose low morale convinced me that the final collapse of the German army could not be long delayed, though we had been told not to expect the end of the war until 1919 and the prospect of imminent peace still seemed too far-fetched to be dwelt on.

For a few days before 11th November, however, news was coming through of approaches from Germany to end the fighting. On the night of the 10/11th, I was duty officer at Divisional headquarters.

In the very early hours of the morning I was brought a message which had just come in from Corps. 'Hostilities will cease at 11 a.m. on 11th November' it began, and went on to request that at that hour we should report the position reached by our advance.

Acting in the Haldanes' Garden at Oxford, June 1914
Top G.H. as Xanthias and Lewis Gielgud as Dyonisus in Aristophanes' 'Frogs'
Below The whole cast for the "Frogs" and Naomi Haldane's 'Prisoners of War'
(back row, fourth from left, Aldous with beard, as Charon)

Elspeth and G.H. on honeymoon in Cornwall, December 1931

I hastened to wake the General and Neame and give them the news, with which the whole headquarters was soon buzzing, and to pass the Corps message on to our Brigades. It was a clear, calm night unbroken by any sound of firing from our front. Further sleep was out of the question but I lay down on my camp bed to luxuriate in the contemplation of all that the message meant for me personally. For the first time for four years I felt free to divorce myself from the immediate present and to think of my future. It was sheer good luck, I realized, that I had a future to contemplate. Now came the question of what was I to do with it and how best to try to pick up the threads so suddenly snapped in 1914. From this my thoughts turned to friends who had not shared my good fortune. War, I reflected, made one very self-centred. Shared dangers and pleasures brought many quick and close friendships with those with whom one was brought into immediate contact. But such relationships were only ephemeral and failed to be sustained once the contact was broken and fresh contacts made in new surroundings. One's war-time friendships, at any moment, were only with those sharing one's present circumstances. Past associations, however close they had been, were soon forgotten.

By this time, Divisional headquarters was beginning to be up and about and, over an early breakfast, the General asked me to ride with him and his A.D.C. up to the front so as ourselves to be able to record on our maps the line reached at 11 o'clock by our final advance. It was a peaceful ride, though I felt uncomfortably conspicuous on top of a horse in case some straggling German sniper chose to have a parting shot at our little party. The enemy's only concern, however, seemed to be to make for the Fatherland with all possible speed and not a shot was to be heard. In fact, the only incident occurred when, precisely at 11 o'clock, we reached the right flank of our Division's advance at a village with a stream running through it.

We found the excited villagers on the bridge over the stream busy fishing up some German soldiers' corpses from the water. They told me that the Germans had been shot by an English General and his party who had passed through the village on horseback a short time before and who had then gone on ahead. This last-minute feat did not greatly surprise us, since we knew that the Brigade on our right was commanded by that famous warrior Freyberg, V.C., who must have been, I think, one of the very few people in the British army sincerely to regret the end of the fighting. Before we left the village two unfortunate girls with their heads shaved were paraded in front of us. They had, it seemed, been too friendly with the Germans.

The streets of London that night, we later read, had been jammed with wildly celebrating crowds. There were no celebrations at the front, at least in our sector; just weary men thinking of home in thankfulness that their ordeal was over. But, unfortunately, it was not yet over. Already many men had been going down with the epidemic of Spanish influenza that now strained beyond their capacity the inadequate resources available to the forward medical services so far removed from their base facilities and supplies. Half our Divisional headquarters personnel were soon stricken, including Moore. In his case, as in many others, the disease proved fatal. It was not long before I, too, became a victim, waking one morning shivering with a high fever.

I had the sense to remain firmly ensconced in my flea-bag, blankets piled over me, in my billet whence I was removed by stretcher and ambulance to a temporary hospital in a local nunnery. On being carried into bed in a large officers' ward I observed round several of the beds the screens put up to shelter the dying from their fellow inmates. There were, of course, no nurses, and though the R.A.M.C. orderlies did their hard-worked best, such luxuries as invalid food were unobtainable. I remember turning away with horror from the plate of stewed bully beef that I was offered on arrival. After some feverish and dream-like days and nights my temperature began to fall, but obstinately remained on the 100° mark, which according to the M.O. forbade me being evacuated to a base hospital. In the end I escaped by means of skilfully faking the thermometer when the orderly's back was turned, and got myself removed, first by ambulance across the old battlefields and then by hospital train, to Wimereux on the coast where I made a rapid recovery and was home before Christmas on three weeks' sick leave.

It was the first re-union of all the family since I had left for France in 1914. Marjorie had been nursing as a V.A.D., while Michael leaving Rugby at seventeen had gone to Trinity, Cambridge, for a year and then to a Guards Officers' training depot. Kit and Anne had been at their boarding schools all through the war. It was a most happy and cheerful Christmas that we all spent at Great Enton before I went back to my Division in France to await demobilization.

I found that the Division had not been among those chosen to go forward to the Rhine but had been moved right back. We were all thoroughly bored with having nothing to do but I secured a week's leave in Paris where I stayed with Lewis Gielgud in his flat. At the beginning of the war he had been commissioned in a Kitchener battalion of the Shropshire Light Infantry, but had been so badly wounded at Loos in 1915 that he had been debarred from further active service. A first-class French scholar, he was now on the staff of General Spears' Inter-allied Mission. It was delightful to be able to pick up our very long-standing friendship as if it had never been temporarily severed. General Williams was also kind enough to send me with despatches to our Corps headquarters which had been moved up to Cologne. The city's inhabitants seemed miserably shabby and wholly apathetic to the presence of their victorious enemies.

Finally, at the end of March, my demobilization papers came through and on 1st April 1919, I landed at Folkestone. I can well remember with what feelings of deep happiness and thankfulness I took a dilapidated taxi from Victoria Station to Porchester Terrace, ready to start a new life.

CHAPTER V

As I have earlier recorded, it had been decided before I left Rugby that I should make the Foreign Office my career. As the first step I had visited the Office during the Oxford summer term of 1914 for the interview with Nicholson, the permanent head, by means of which my candidature for the F.O. examination had been accepted.

On my demobilization, therefore, I at once made inquiries through my F.O. cousin, Laurence Collier, as to my prospects for entry. It transpired that the F.O. would, before long, be holding a special examination for candidates from the Forces, and that passing this should not be beyond my capacities, rusty as my brains had become. Meantime some cramming in the French language would be advisable.

An alternative would be for me to go back to Balliol, take a History honours degree and then sit for the F.O. from Oxford in a couple of years' time, if I still felt that diplomacy was my métier. But, being now twenty-five, I did not feel inclined further to postpone starting my career; nor did I like the idea of returning to a Balliol which would be haunted by the ghosts of my pre-war contemporaries who had lost their lives.

I also had an interview with Colonel Kell, head of the Secret Intelligence Service, who offered me a permanent job in his department. While I was still considering these choices, George Booth, one of my father's friends and patients, told him that he would like to take me into Alfred Booth and Company, the Booth family business, for which he was looking for a management recruit. The initial salary would be at the rate of £500 a year, rising to £750 on transfer to the Booth's shipping office at Liverpool.

At that time these were very generous starting salaries,

and when I talked over the offer with my parents, they felt, as I did, that this bird in the hand was too good to be missed. So I abandoned the ideas of diplomacy or secret service and before the end of April was learning about commerce in the agreeable surroundings of Adelphi Terrace where I received a most friendly welcome and was invited to listen in to all the partners' discussions.

I have the happiest memories of that summer of 1919. Permeating all was the glorious feeling that 'the war to end all wars' was over and that the rest of my life would be free from another such ordeal. Every day's care-free round was made more pleasurable by the contrast between my present circumstances and those of my past four years.

My work was interesting and far from exacting. Living at home I had all the money I wanted. My social life was a full one, with theatre parties and dances. All the family moved to Enton for the weekend, where Mother usually had our friends and relations to stay and organized tennis parties for our neighbours on the new hard court.

Amongst our weekend visitors was Lindsey Foot, a friend of my sister Marjorie's with whom she had nursed in a V.A.D. hospital. Her brother Dicky Foot had been my contemporary at Hillside. Lindsey and I got on well, and, seeing this, my parents and Marjorie encouraged her visits, while I spent a weekend at Lindsey's home at Berkhamsted. In the course of the August Bank Holiday weekend at Enton Lindsey and I got engaged to be married.

Looking back I now know that I was never really in love with Lindsey any more than I had been with Gladys Gurdon or Ella Cane, but now I had a secure future to offer to the object of my affections. Nor do I think that Lindsey was really in love with me. But we were both in the mood when getting married seemed to be one of the expected and desirable features of settling in to civilian life after the war.

We were both twenty-five, shared a similar class background, had many tastes in common, and both our families were warmly encouraging such a suitable match. Without any experience of passion or of the heights and depths which real love could offer, we both contentedly took the line of least resistance, and, as soon as our engagement was announced, we were both far too much involved in all the agreeable preparations for our wedding to question the strength and character of our feelings for each other. Just before Christmas we were married in Berkhamsted church.

After a fortnight's honeymoon at the Lizard we set off for Liverpool to start our married life in a charming little detached house in Greenheys Road which we rented very cheaply from one of the Booth relations, while I began a new job as personal assistant to the General Manager of the Booth Steamship Company. I found Liverpool a pleasant place both for work and socially. Shipping management proved to be full of interest, and I was keen to master every detail, creating considerable surprise by pre-breakfast visits to the docks to watch our boats unloading their cargoes of rubber, Brazil nuts and other South American produce. Being under the Booth aegis Lindsey and I were at once given entrée into top Liverpool society presided over by other leading local families such as the Holts, Rathbones and Muspratts.

It was a society wholly independent of London, both more exclusive and more formal, where powdered footmen and knee breeches were still employed for grand occasions in the wealthiest mansions. Lindsey and I were invited to dinner parties and dances and were made members of an excellent tennis club where we played on many summer evenings and Saturday afternoons. On Sundays we explored the Cheshire countryside and visited Huxley village and Huxley Old Hall, an attractive old farmhouse, which may have been the home of my ancestors.

After six months or so in the shipping office I became convinced that the Booths had made a bad mistake in placing an order for three new and very expensive passenger liners for the Amazon trade to replace two sunk in the war and one now becoming obsolescent. Once the immediate post-war rush for passages was over, even our one liner was sailing with her passenger accommodation half empty, and with cultivated Malayan rubber now largely replacing the wild Brazilian article and Amazon rubber prosperity in consequence on the wane, I believed that the three new passenger ships would prove costly white elephants and that the Booths would be well advised to cancel the order, whatever forfeit would have to be paid, and, instead, build smaller general purpose cargo ships carrying only a few passengers.

I found that my friend, the chief accountant, shared my views but had been snubbed when he put them to the management. Nothing daunted, I set out my own conclusions in a memorandum which I sent to Charles Booth. His reply was sympathetic, but I gathered that such intervention on the part of a young learner had caused considerable offence in some quarters. The fact, however, remained that the order for the three ships was cancelled shortly afterwards. My action could have done me no harm with George Booth as a few weeks later he asked me to see him in London.

There he told me that the Booths' investments in light leather and wool enterprises under the control of a Mr. Fraser had grown to such an extent that he felt that one of his own employees should be attached to Fraser to watch over the Booth interests and that Fraser had agreed to accept me in the role. This involved leaving Liverpool and moving to London to work in Fraser's office, but George offered to pay all expenses for my move and to increase my salary to £1,000 a year. Such rapid promotion seemed to confirm my hopes for a successful business career, and though I was much enjoying my time in Liverpool, I at once accepted George's proposal.

In London, feeling rich, we took a furnished flat in Queen Anne's Mansions as a temporary abode. When I succeeded with some difficulty in finding out the position of Fraser's transactions, I learned that the Booths were committed to the tune of several hundred thousand pounds in financing the building of an Abingdon and subsidiary leather factories and in the increasing scale on which Fraser was operating on their behalf in wool, with, I thought, an extremely rash confidence, since the post-war boom was proving very short-lived. It had, in fact, been caused not by any permanent increase in demand but by buyers everywhere filling up shelves that the war years had emptied.

I am not normally much of a hater, but I disliked Fraser instantly. Hook-nosed, with a pike's jaw under a bristling moustache, he was arrogant, bullying and ruthless, and seemed to have mesmerized the Booth London partners. When I first expressed my anxieties about their involvement with Fraser, they took refuge behind a barrage of words about his vision and acumen as if hard economic facts could be dispelled by verbiage. By early 1921, however, the facts had grown too serious to be talked off. Now fully disillusioned the Booths parted company with Fraser in order to try to salvage as much as possible of their investment in his collapsing house of cards. There was, of course, no longer any place for me in Fraser's office and I agreed with George Booth to move to Abingdon where I could best look after his interests in the capacity of Secretary of the Leather Company which also embraced the various subsidiary enterprises.

On starting to work at Abingdon I had taken a temporary lease of a convenient small furnished bungalow just below the south side of Boars Hill and had bought a 10 h.p. Standard car for my transport to Abingdon. Now that my work at Abingdon seemed likely to be indefinitely prolonged, and since no small houses in the country round were available for purchase or unfurnished lease, I determined to build, financed by a loan from my father, and found for sale a two-acre field on Boars Hill above the village of Sunningwell in then entirely unbuilt-over country with a wide southern view across the Vale of White Horse to the distant Berkshire Downs.

I was lucky enough to take on nineteen-year-old Harry Webb, the son of a gardener at Cumnor, to help make the garden which became my immediate main spare-time occupation. The Boars Hill soil was very light and sandy, so we concentrated largely on flowering shrubs and on one large herbaceous border, in which lupins and irises especially flourished. We made, too, a small square rose-garden with a sundial in its centre. Harry Webb supplied the professional knowledge which both Lindsey and I entirely lacked. It was then that I acquired the love of gardening that has ever since provided me with so much interest and pleasure and has proved the most rewarding of hobbies. I have been lucky enough twice in my lifetime to have had the opportunity of creating from nothing the order and beauty of a garden. I know of no more deeply satisfying pursuit, and as Bacon wrote, a garden is 'the Purest of Humane pleasures'.

At Greenheys, as we named our house, Lindsey and I settled down to an uneventful married life. We made a number of friends from among our neighbours with whom we played a lot of tennis. We also took up golf at Frilford Heath, while Lindsey soon found a very rewarding interest in the Women's Institutes. Joining the newly formed Sunningwell Institute she became its President and before long was elected a member and treasurer of the Berkshire County Committee, displaying considerable aptitude as a platform speaker. Most of our evenings were devoted to reading. It was Aldous' essays, short stories and novels that I enjoyed above any other current books. Apart from my personal interest, I found his writings outstandingly original and stimulating, and I rejoiced in the very high reputation that he was building up.

Alas, I had little opportunity to see him and his delightful Belgian wife, Maria. They were living in London, Aldous working at great pressure on journalism as well as book-writing. It was only occasionally, when I stayed the night at home in Porchester Terrace, that I was able to visit them.

By now Lindsey and I had become deeply concerned at our failure to produce a family. Medical tests failed to reveal any reasons or remedy and our marriage continued to lack this vital bond which might have held it together. It was not until long after we had parted that I learned that a growth had prevented Lindsey from child-bearing.

Meantime my mother's physical and mental health had been steadily deteriorating. During her over-worked war years she had developed gall bladder trouble, but both then and later refused to have the operation that might have cured her. Thus physically poisoned and weakened she had become mentally ill—subsequently it was found that she was suffering from encephalitis—refusing to meet anyone or to leave the house or take food, so that resident nurses had to be engaged to look after her. It was desperately trying for my father who had already given up his London practice and had sold the lease of Porchester Terrace, making Enton his only home.

In 1925, in the hope that a complete change of atmosphere might help Mother and also to be near a psychiatrist at Oxford in whom he had faith to treat her, he sold Enton and bought a dairy farm on the southern slope of Boars Hill in the parish of Wootton, the next parish to my Sunningwell. The farm house, known as Vale House, lay just back from the road through the scattered houses of Wootton village leading up to Boars Hill. It was an attractive old red brick house, but it lacked the room and convenience that my father needed for Mother and as the family home. He and I therefore arranged that I should sell Greenheys and buy Vale House from him, while he built a new house for himself on a site up the hill at the top end of the farm with a panoramic view to the south over the White Horse Vale. He also entirely remodelled the farm buildings so as to provide a really up-to-date home for his Red Polls and for the production of the purest Tuberculin Tested milk which he sold retail in the neighbourhood. All of this gave him fresh interest and some much-needed relief from his anxieties about Mother.

It was very pleasant for me to have my parents so close at hand, and Lindsey was a great help with Mother, whose physical and mental health failed, alas, to respond to the change.

Lindsey and I had been sorry to leave Greenheys and the garden that we had made, but Vale House, though less convenient, had much more character. Its small flower garden, lying between the house and the road and protected from passing traffic by a high brick wall, had been neglected by its former farmer owner, but its heavy soil and shelter were excellent for roses which now became my major gardening interest to such good effect that I was soon winning prizes for specimen blooms at local flower shows.

By the spring of 1926, however, my job at Abingdon had virtually worked itself out, the major sources of loss having been one by one eliminated. Discussing my future with George Booth he told me that all he could offer me was the management of a glue factory in Lincoln, which I knew was a moribund business. We therefore agreed that in my own interests I should look elsewhere for my future. With a generous cheque for a year's salary in my pocket, I found myself adrift at the age of 32 and at a time when jobs were increasingly hard to come by, especially for people like myself without any professional qualifications.

The locusts had, I reflected, eaten my seven years with the Booths. I had, I supposed, learned in the hard way the lesson of how business should not be conducted by its management, and I had gained useful first-hand experience of marketing at different levels, but my association with the Booths' dismal post-war commercial record would be unlikely to commend itself to prospective business employers. I felt, too, that my work had never called for any sustained mental effort. It had all been too easy-going and casual, and I feared that such untested brain power as I possessed might have become atrophied. These years had done little, too, to foster intellectual interests. Although ample leisure had enabled me to keep up with contemporary writing mainly in the field of fiction ; living and working in the country had afforded few opportunities for taking an interest in music, drama or art or for sharpening my wits in the company of my betters. What I wanted to find was work that would really stretch all my capacities.

It was at this point that a fortuitous encounter changed the whole course of my life. My sister Marjorie happened to meet her old school friend Bridget Tallents and her civil-service husband Stephen at a London dinner party. I had known Bridget as a schoolgirl but had never met Stephen. In the course of the evening he asked Marjorie what I was doing. On hearing of my experience with the Booths and that I was now looking for a job, he suggested that I might like to come to see him as he had just taken on a novel and interesting government assignment in which he thought he might find me a place.

CHAPTER VI

i

I LOST no time in following up Stephen Tallents' invitation. When I saw him at his office in Queen Anne's Gate he told me that he had been appointed Secretary of the newly formed Empire Marketing Board.

The Board's origin stemmed from the rejection by the electorate in the 1923 General Election of the proposal to impose certain food taxes which would enable preference to be given to Empire produce. When the Conservatives returned to power in 1924, Baldwin had regarded himself as pledged not to introduce such taxes, but proposed that, in lieu, the British Government should spend a million pounds a year to foster trade within the Empire so that the Dominions should secure a larger share of that part of the United Kingdom market which could not be supplied by the home producer. The million pounds a year was to be spent on a publicity campaign addressed to the United Kingdom consumer on behalf of Empire foodstuffs, and on co-ordinated research to improve their production, preservation and marketing. Finally, and only three months ago, Amery, the Secretary of State for Dominion Affairs, had announced in the House of Commons that £500,000 was being set aside for the fiscal year 1926–27, with the full amount of a million for 1927–28, and that he was to administer this vote assisted by a Board under his Chairmanship on which home agriculture and the Dominions would be represented.

It was to organize this Board—named the Empire Marketing Board—that Tallents had been appointed as its civil service head. Such a move by a British Government was a completely novel and exciting venture and there were no precedents for its guidance. Tallents intended, he said, to set up two main Committees under the Board, one for Publicity and one for Research, each with a Secretary in charge of its work. A civil servant, Lloyd, had been appointed Secretary of the Research Committee. Would I, he asked, like to be considered for the Secretaryship of the Publicity Committee, as he felt that this post would best be filled from outside the permanent civil service?

I had listened to Tallents with ever-growing interest. Here was, indeed, a job which, if I could measure up to it, would stretch my powers to the full, and they would be exercised in a cause which made the strongest appeal to me, since I had never forgotten the impression that the men of Canada and Australia had made on me during the war and the wish I had then formed to do something to repay the debt that I felt we owed them. Besides, I had at once taken to Tallents. He was in his early forties, a trim military figure, spare, balding and moving briskly with a limp, the legacy of a severe wound at Festubert in 1915. Radiating confidence and energy, he spoke of his new job with contagious enthusiasm. Unhesitatingly I told him that there was nothing I should like more than to join his team. Nor did it seriously weigh with me that the salary authorized by the Treasury for the post was substantially lower than the one the Booths had paid me. Although my appointment as a temporary civil servant would need official confirmation, Tallents asked me to start work next day.

His offer and my acceptance of it marked a turning point in my life. To this chance encounter of Marjorie's I owe all the good fortune both in my work and in my private life that I have ever since enjoyed.

Getting the Board's publicity campaign started occupied every moment of my time and all my thoughts. It was seldom before eight in the evening that I left the office and I was lucky to catch the one forty-five on Saturday afternoons for Oxford and Wootton, taking a brief-case of homework with me. During the week I shared Marjorie's London flat.

No British Government in peace time had ever embarked on so large a publicity campaign and its aims were such that ordinary commercial advertising afforded us little guidance.

The Board's Publicity Committee numbered twelve members, with Ormsby-Gore, the Parliamentary Under Secretary of State for the Colonies, as its Chairman. His rather vacant looks and receding chin gave no clue to his very real ability and his wide range of interests. His parliamentary duties, however, occupied too much of his time to enable him to give any close personal attention to his Committee's problems which, in any case, lay quite outside his experience. It was, in fact, with three of the Committee's members that Tallents and I worked out the policy and methods that the Board's publicity should adopt. They were William Crawford, founder and head of the Crawford advertising agency and Vice-Chairman of the Committee, Frank McDougall and Frank Pick. Corpulent and rubicund, Crawford was the complete extrovert. His approach to advertising was inspirational rather than logical. 'We must reach for the Empire,' he would remind us. But he possessed a flair for good advertising, and in copy, lay-out and design his agency's techniques were in advance of those of most of his competitors. McDougall, short and stocky with a pipe always in his mouth, was the son of a Chairman of London County Council. With his brother he had emigrated to Australia to grow fruit on the Murray River. There he had made a special study of marketing and had been sent to London by the Australian Dried Fruits' Board and appointed Australia's representative on the Imperial Economic Committee and Empire Marketing Board. Immensely industrious as well as enthusiastic in the Empire cause, he cherished the belief that almost any problem could be solved by his writing a memorandum on it. It was, however, Frank Pick's experience and expertise that was of most help to us. A large, reserved Yorkshireman of uncompromising integrity, Pick's ability and force of character had brought him from the ticket office in a Yorkshire railway station to the Managing Directorship of London's Underground Railways and Buses. Outstanding as his administrative qualities must have been, they were combined with a remarkable love and knowledge of the arts, and it was this that he had made use of in helping to create a new and up-to-date image for London's transport, personally commissioning the posters by well-known and coming artists to advertise the attractions of London and its environments. In order that Londoners should, albeit subconsciously, recognize something distinctive about all their transport's publicity, Pick had got Eric Gill to design a special type-face for use in all his printed material and notices. He had also been responsible for commissioning Epstein's controversial statuary group which adorned the new Underground Head-quarters building at St. James's Park, and he had threatened to resign rather than agree to his Board giving way to the philistine public outcry for the removal of Epstein's work.

The other most useful members of my Publicity Committee were Lord Burnham, the owner of the *Daily Telegraph*, and Sir Woodman Burbidge, the Chairman of Harrods Department Store. Lord Burnham encouraged me to consult him over any question of our Press relations and gave me much good advice as to how the Press should be handled, but at the monthly meetings of the full Publicity Committee he would usually arrive late, shuffle through his papers which he clearly had not previously looked at, interject some remarks quite irrelevant to the subject being discussed and then depart, leaving me with the difficult problem of how subsequently to work his remarks into the Minutes, for whose form and accuracy Tallents was a stickler and on drafting which I spent many a weary late hour at home. Burbidge caused me no such difficulty. His remarks were always very much to the point, though it seemed that the sole criterion by which he judged the importance of any subject was whether it was of interest to Harrods. No doubt such single-mindedness was the secret of his success, and his advice on merchandising matters was invaluable.

Important as was all this outside assistance, it was Tallents who provided the central inspiration and driving force in the development of this gallant venture which, though much disliked and distrusted by bureaucracy, was in its seven years of life to render lasting service to Commonwealth

Elspeth and G.H. with Charles
at his christening, 1944

G.H. and Charles age 3
Bill Esty and daughter Jane at New Canaan, 1939

Agricultural research and to pioneer the entry by Government into the publicity field, employing methods and setting patterns that have subsequently been followed by so many branches of Government.

The longer I worked for Tallents the greater grew my admiration for him as my chief. He was, on the one hand, a most capable administrator; a hard taskmaster who, never sparing himself, expected a like devotion to their work from his subordinates, leaving them free to get on with their job but always ready to give them help and backing. Such qualities were common in the higher ranks of the civil service, but where Tallents was exceptional was that he was a civil servant with an imagination completely unfettered by red tape. Outwardly he was a shy man whose aloofness and reserve of manner discouraged intimacy and made many people find him cold and awe-inspiring. Nor did a lack of a sense of humour or of any interest in the small change of conversation make for ease or light-heartedness in his company. This outward reticence hid, however, a highly romantic side to his complex nature, which had found expression in writing over-stylized prose articles for the back page of the *Manchester Guardian*. It was, too, this other side of his character that gave him his interest in all the arts and that caused him to adopt as his hobby the skills of idealized bygone countrymen such as the use of the scythe, the growing of cricket-bat willows, the making of pocket-book bindings from rat skins and the methods of cooking grey squirrels for the table.

A product of Harrow and Balliol, Tallents had entered the pre-war civil service in the Ministry of Labour and after his war-wound had invalided him out of the Guards, he had enjoyed a varied and unusual career, in the war-time Ministry of Food, as British Commissioner in the Baltic Provinces at the war's end and finally as Imperial Secretary for Northern Ireland, whence Amery had picked him out, as an exception to prevailing Whitehall orthodoxy, to take charge of the Empire Marketing Board. It was an inspired choice; and in the Board's development Tallents was free to give full rein to his active and cultured mind, to the catholicity of his interests and to a flair for publicity which by no means commended itself to his civil service seniors. As a sharer in his enthusiasm for the Board's objects I was given his full confidence; our personal and official relationships were always of the happiest and I was admitted to as close a friendship as his nature allowed.

As the result of our discussions with Crawford, McDougall and Pick we recommended to the Publicity Committee that the Board's appeal to the public should be to buy first the produce of their own country and next the produce of overseas Empire countries, summed up in the phrase 'Buy Empire goods from Home and Overseas', a formula which we felt to be applicable to all parts of the Empire—and that the function of our publicity should be to create a general background of interest in the Empire and its products against which individual Empire countries, producers' associations and private firms might throw into relief their own special claims.

We recommended newspaper and poster advertising as the principal media to carry our appeal, but for our main poster effort, we adopted Frank Pick's idea to take advantage of our Governmental status and national aims in order to create a wholly distinctive campaign which would not have to compete with the advertisements on the commercial hoardings but would have its own hoardings in the form of specially designed frames on sites given free of charge by Government Departments, Municipalities and private owners on which no commercial display would ever have been allowed. Our poster frames would be made of English oak and British Columbian Douglas fir and would each hold a set of three pictorial posters separated from each other by two letterpress posters, with a top strip. As subsidiary media we proposed to employ films, to provide lectures, to participate in major Exhibitions, to issue shop display material, to encourage local Empire shopping weeks and to distribute booklets and leaflets.

Our proposals were all warmly endorsed by the Publicity

Committee and the Board, and for the rest of 1926 I was very hard at work on preparing the campaign material.

By the end of the year we were able to start our poster campaign and our first poster frame was in position on the railings of Montagu House in the centre of Whitehall to be unveiled to the public view by the Prince of Wales. As more frames were put up all over the country, their novel form and contents created much public attention and large numbers of spontaneous requests began to arrive on my desk from headmasters and mistresses of schools for the supply of copies for classroom teaching about the Empire. To meet this demand we decided to reproduce the most suitable sets of posters in smaller size for free issue to schools, each set being accompanied by a leaflet descriptive of the subject for the teacher's use. I much enjoyed being allowed to persuade well-known authors such as John Buchan, Sir Henry Newbolt, David Bone, Ivor Brown, Robert Lynd and Ian Colvin to write our leaflets. Eventually no less than 26,000 schools in the United Kingdom were receiving our poster reproductions and leaflets, while the number of poster frames finally reached nearly 1,800 on their special sites in 500 different cities and towns and we had commissioned and displayed over 100 sets of posters.

Our poster campaign on the public hoardings began with the display of a most arresting highly-coloured map of the world in 48 sheet (20' × 10') size designed by MacDonald Gill on an unusual projection and fancifully decorated with little drawings. It was entitled 'Highways of Empire' and showed ships carrying Empire produce to and fro along the trade routes. I remember the pride with which I watched little crowds of passers-by stopping more closely to examine all the interesting details and quotations that Gill had embodied in his superbly executed line drawings. It was, I think, something unparalleled in poster history.

My responsibility for our posters was not without its trouble and frustrations. I well remember three particular episodes, all of which had their comic side. The first concerned a set of posters for our frames to advertise the produce

BUY EMPIRE GOODS FROM
HOME AND OVERSEAS

of Eire. Initially, though represented on the Board from the start, the Free State Government had been unco-operative about our work, and Dulanty, its representative on the Board, had made no response to my proposal for a set of posters. Later he came to me to say that his Government were complaining about our neglect. I was, of course, delighted to agree to start work on a set at once, and in consultation with Pick, Dulanty and I chose as our artist Paul Henry, well known for his attractive travel posters of Ireland. In due course he produced three very pleasant pictures. Dulanty professed himself well pleased with them but insisted on taking them to Dublin to show to his Prime Minister, de Valera. On his return he regretfully reported to me that they had been rejected on the grounds that, in one of the posters, an ass-cart being driven along a road was portrayed and that this would make people think that Irish agriculture was out of date. So we said we would try again, only, with Pick's assent, asking Dulanty and his Prime Minister to select their own artist and subjects. After further consultation with Dublin they chose a local painter whom I duly commissioned. When the paintings arrived I was horrified to see that in the centre poster, representing a bacon factory, the men portrayed were of the most villainous cast of countenance I had ever seen. Expressing my apprehensions to Dulanty he said he would at once take the paintings to Dublin to be examined by a special committee of de Valera, Yeats and other important personages. He returned with rather a long face. The centre painting, he told me not to my surprise, must be amended. It was, however, he said, a simple matter. All that was wrong was that some of the pigs' tails curled the wrong way. Suitably amended, the posters were printed and displayed.

The second episode concerned the Falkland Islands. One day their fiery colonial Governor came to see me, and thumping my desk said that we had insulted the Empire by failing to include them in our campaign. When I asked what product he wanted portraying he replied, 'Whales, of course.' It so happened that I was about to commission my war-time friend Keith Henderson to paint a set showing some outlying colonies and their products and I therefore arranged for Keith's centre-piece to be a whaling scene off the Falkland Islands in which a whaling ship and a couple of whales spouting were shown. Realizing that the slightest inaccuracy would bring down the wrath of the Governor I sent one of my assistants, Basil Marriott, to the Natural History Museum to get their experts to make sure that the two whales shown in the picture were of the right type for those waters. Some weeks later I inquired from Marriott what had happened to the poster and, being told that it was still at the museum, asked him to fetch it back. He returned white-faced to show me the poster in which the sea was now swarming with whales of every known kind. It appeared that the ancient head of the museum's whale department, in an excess of excitement at this unique chance of showing to the public the objects of his life-long devotion and expertise, had himself painted in a whole repertory of whales, completely, of course, defacing Keith Henderson's attractive poster. Luckily, Keith, being a friend, took this astonishing addition to his work with great good humour and agreed to repaint the picture. There remained, however, the question of who should be responsible for paying his additional fee. Our finance officer insisted that the museum should pay, but their finance officer repudiated this on the grounds that it was we who had called on them for assistance. I believe that the file was still passing to and fro some years later.

The third episode took place towards the end of my time with the Board. Daringly, Pick and I had agreed that one or two of our posters should be really modern in treatment, and we commissioned Stanley Spencer for a set portraying British factory workers fulfilling contracts from the Empire overseas. Knowing that my Board would be unlikely to be favourably impressed by Stanley Spencer's style, I awaited his pictures with some anxiety. Sure enough they were very Stanley-Spencerish in treatment, thick-legged lumpish workmen in wooden-like trousers, but nonetheless striking paintings. Tallents and the other members of our poster sub-committee shared my anxiety as to the Board's reactions and insisted that the Board must see the paintings before they were printed. As I feared, our Board members would have none of them and they were put into store. Not long after we got an unpleasant letter from the Treasury asking why public money had been wasted on paintings which were not to be used. Pick was furious. Announcing that he would show the Board what hide-bound philistines they were, he arranged for the sale of the paintings to an art dealer for considerably more than we had paid for them.

As it developed, our publicity campaign embraced many other media. Already in the autumn of 1926 we were taking part in major exhibitions, using a special pavilion designed for us by Professor Richardson, which allowed us to offer free space to the home Ministry of Agriculture and to Dominion and Colonial Governments to display their produce in a unified Empire setting. This, of course, involved me in close and very pleasant co-operation with their marketing and publicity officers who were quick to take full advantage of the background provided by our campaign by substantially increasing their own promotion efforts.

It used to be one of my annual assignments to escort King George and Queen Mary round our Empire section of the British Industries Fair. The Queen would closely inspect every exhibit, waiting to be offered and graciously to accept a large sample of the produce on display. This, of course, was gratifying to the exhibitors who promptly put a card on the exhibit saying, 'as chosen by Her Majesty, the Queen', but I often wondered how the household staff at Buckingham Palace welcomed the large consignments of tinned jams, etc., on which they presumably had to subsist.

Local Empire shopping weeks were another activity which we encouraged, providing challenge cups for window dressing competitions.

Another of my early tasks was the organization of lectures and talks on Empire subjects. A scheme for subsidizing popular lectures illustrated with slides was worked out with the recognized lecture agencies, while I also began to form a panel of our own speakers, but the demands grew to such an extent that before long we had to engage a special officer from the Board of Education to look after this branch of our publicity. There were, too, leaflets and pamphlets to be thought of and produced. An unusual one, I remember, was a set of menus and recipes for banquets at which only Empire produce would be served.

After a few months it had become clear that we must form a Press section to help interpret the Board's work to the press at home and overseas. As the section's head Tallents and I chose A. P. Ryan from the *Daily Telegraph*. No choice could have been more fortunate. Apart from his skill as a writer and in handling every side of press relations, Pat Ryan proved to be a most entertaining, stimulating and delightful colleague, whose advent greatly added to my enjoyment of office hours, and I was soon on terms of close friendship with him and his wife Rachel, a daughter of C. E. Montague and a granddaughter of Scott of the *Manchester Guardian*.

What, meantime, of my home life, limited to Saturday afternoons and Sundays at Wootton? Lindsey had no part in my London life and work in which I was so wholly and so self-centredly absorbed that I paid small attention to her and her doings. Luckily she was finding an increasing interest of her own in the Women's Institute movement and had been elected to its National Executive where she had become the Honorary Treasurer, a post which she filled with great success; but the diversity of our interests was further weakening the ties between us. In any case my weekends were largely spent at my parents' new home just up the hill from our Vale House in Wootton.

Mother had grown steadily weaker and was now a pathetic figure, terribly thin, pale and worn, and far removed from the vital force I had always known. Nevertheless she took great interest in all my doings and seemed to want me to be with her as much as possible. She died early in 1927, and I felt glad for her sake to see the end of her suffering. We had always been especially devoted to each other and my still unfading memories of her are happily unmarred by any useless regrets for coldness or lack of understanding and affection, but her death removed the potent influence which throughout my life had been my constant guide and support. My preoccupation with my work served, however, to lessen the immediate impact of my loss and before long my thoughts were dominated by anticipation of a most exciting experience that was to befall me.

Early in the summer of 1927 Tallents broke it to me that Amery intended, while in Office as Secretary of State for the Dominions, to make an eight-months' tour of South Africa, Australia, New Zealand and Canada in order to expound as widely as possible by personal contacts and by public speeches the significance of their new constitutional status as defined at the 1926 Imperial Conference and as subsequently embodied in the Statute of Westminster.

It had been Amery's own imaginative concept, for whose fulfilment he had long worked, that the Imperial Conference had adopted, and he was anxious to make it clear that the complete independence of the Dominions and their full constitutional equality with the United Kingdom as nations in their own right did not involve isolation from their former mother country or from each other or any weakening of imperial ties, but rather that each, in its own nationhood and in free co-operation with the United Kingdom and the other Dominions, accepted responsibility for the welfare and security of the Commonwealth as a whole. Amery wished to be accompanied by an officer from the Dominions Office and an officer from the Empire Marketing Board, and Tallents had recommended to him that I should fill the latter role. We were to start our tour at the end of July.

ii

The little party that assembled at Waterloo Station to catch the boat train to Southampton consisted of Mr. and

Mrs. Amery, William Brass, M.P., Amery's Parliamentary Private Secretary, Geoffrey Whiskard of the Dominions Office and myself.

I had, of course, had contact with Amery in his official capacity as the Board's Chairman during the past fourteen months and recently I had dined with him and Mrs. Amery at their home in Eaton Square. I had greatly admired what I had seen of the Secretary of State, then in his middle fifties. Very short, indeed almost square in build, clean shaven and bespectacled, he seemed to radiate physical strength and vitality. I also believed passionately in the Imperial cause for which he stood and worked, but until I dined with him I had not realized the breadth of his cultured mind or the diversity of his interests, although I knew that he had been a Balliol scholar and a Fellow of All Souls.

My impression of Mrs. Amery was of a most friendly, warm-hearted personality, and I had felt happy in the thought of sharing close companionship with them in the coming months. I had already made friends with Geoffrey Whiskard. Here, again, I was lucky in having him as my fellow civil servant. I found him a most kindly man, some ten years my senior, who shared my enthusiasm for the tour and with whom I had most likes and dislikes in common. He and I both felt that 'Billy' Brass was rather a joke—a wealthy bachelor, stout, red-moustached and rubicund, who was, we had heard, famous for his expensive presents to his lady friends. He had no intellectual pretensions, and we imagined that his election to Parliament for a Lancashire constituency must have been due to his asking the electors to 'vote for brass', an appeal to the pocket to which few Lancastrians would fail to respond. But he breathed bonhomie and he and I got on very well.

In the upshot, Amery proved to be not only the most thoughtful and generous of chiefs, but also the most agreeable and intellectually stimulating of companions, while Mrs. Amery, who won all hearts wherever she went, took the most sympathetic interest in the welfare of our little band. All through our long tour, in spite of the strains imposed by endless speech-making and receptions from hosts of strangers and of the minor rubs of continuous travel, Amery, supported by his wife, was never anything but cheerfully unruffled, sweet-tempered, considerate and undemanding. Indeed, I cannot remember a single note of complaint or acrimony disturbing the harmony of our relations.

We were first to visit South Africa, then Australia, New Zealand and Canada, the whole tour extending over eight months. These months constituted the high spot in my own life. The desire to get to know more of my fellow citizens in the Empire and of the lands where they lived that I had formed when I fought alongside Canadians and Australians in the war was now fulfilled in a manner beyond any possible expectations. Never before could travellers have gone so far, seen so much and met so many people as did the members of Amery's party. In no other circumstances could I have had the chance of hearing, at first hand, the views of all the men who guided the Empire overseas and of making personal contact with all sorts and conditions of people representing so many aspects of Dominion life.

Throughout our whole tour my own assignment was to meet the agricultural communities and the Government agricultural and research officers, to tell them about the Empire Marketing Board and the assistance it could afford them, to discuss their problems and needs, and to send back reports and recommendations to Tallents for the Board's consideration. I was fortunate in that the fulfilment of my mission involved my frequent detachment from our party in order to visit places, meet people and address audiences outside Amery's own more political orbit. It involved, too, my gaining a wide if superficial knowledge of methods of production, marketing and research in respect of farm produce in all the Dominions. Everywhere I was absorbed by the sheer romance of all the pioneering efforts that, in the face of all obstacles and by courage, enterprise, skill and hard work had built up these great agricultural industries. It represented the triumph of man and his works, the victory of

field and furrow, fence and plough over the wild and bound-
less disorder of nature; and it was a victory that brought
prosperity and a healthy, independent life to many thousands of British emigrants, as well as supplying Britain's
industrial population with good and cheap food.

In many respects I found Dominion agriculture to be
well in advance of British practice. It was, for instance, in
Western Australia that I first saw a combine harvester at
work in the wheat belt, and in dairying there was nothing at
home to match New Zealand's intensive use of grassland for
butter and cheese production. In marketing, the care taken
in grading for quality far surpassed anything in Britain,
while everywhere I found the co-operative movement gathering force, whether for citrus, grapes and wine in South
Africa, dried fruit in Australia, butter, cheese and lamb in
New Zealand, or in the wheat pools of Canada's prairie
provinces. It was a movement which won for the individual
farmer a power to match that of the buyer of his products,
and I found it a sad reflection that, alone in the Empire, the
British farmer was playing no part in it. Very impressive,
too, was the amount and quality of the scientific research
being undertaken in all the Dominions for land and crop
improvement and for the control of pests and diseases; and
I felt that the British taxpayer's money was being very well
spent, through the Empire Marketing Board, in making
grants to such outstanding research institutes I visited as
Ondostepoort in South Africa, the Waite in Adelaide, the
Cawthron in New Zealand and Guelph in Ontario, the bene-
fits of whose work would be felt by farmers all over the
Empire.

Apart from its intrinsic interest my assignment was a very
easy and pleasant one, reporting as I was on a novel effort
on the part of Britain to give practical help to Dominion
agriculture. All the many talks I gave on the work and objects of the Empire Marketing Board were greeted by my
audiences with warm appreciation, and often evoked the
response that my hearers would reciprocate by buying more
from Britain.

In 1927 it was their primary agricultural products that formed the basis of the economy of Australia, New Zealand and Canada, and though gold was South Africa's most important economic asset, hers was primarily also an agricultural economy. Moreover it was to the British market that all the Dominions then looked almost exclusively for the sale of their agricultural exports. Hence arose the value of the Empire Marketing Board. The vast mineral resources which were to contribute so much to the economic growth of Australia, Canada and South Africa and to industrial development in those countries were still largely unknown and untapped. Throughout our tour, therefore, we remained in ignorance of these potentialities, and we thought in terms of the sale of primary agricultural products to Britain and the purchase in return of British manufactured goods.

The main purpose of Amery's tour lay, of course, in the political sphere, and it was in South Africa, at the outset of our tour, that the political element was both most important and most tricky.

Our African itinerary started, however, in Southern Rhodesia which presented no political problems. Only thirty-seven years had passed since the first settlers had entered Mashonaland, and memories of those pioneers and of Cecil Rhodes, the country's founder, were still green among the white inhabitants, already numbering 40,000, almost all of British stock and passionately loyal to Britain. In 1923 Southern Rhodesia had left its purely colonial status behind when the white settlers had chosen the path of virtual self-government instead of voting to join the Union of South Africa. Four years later it was everywhere confidently expected that Southern Rhodesia would shortly attain full Dominion status, an end which Amery intended to foster. We left Southern Rhodesia deeply impressed with what the white settlers had achieved in so short a time. Apart from agriculture, mineral resources in coal, chrome, gold and silver had been developed, while Salisbury and Bulawayo were no rough bush dorps, but well laid out towns already offering every urban amenity, with electricity, good hotels, large offices and well-stocked shops. It was evident, too, that white settlement had already brought a much higher standard of life as well as unaccustomed peace to the native Africans. A spirit of optimism dominated the country. Party politics seemed to be non-existent. Everyone seemed to be for the State, with all energies concentrated on its development. No one then appeared to be concerned about the problem of a black African population far outnumbering the whites and sure to increase the disparity in numbers with improved hygiene, nutrition and law and order under white rule. Rhodes, it was believed, had laid down the answer by his dictum of equal rights for all civilized men, irrespective of colour, and the white Rhodesians seemed to be agreed in fulfilling this by fostering the gradual mental and economic progress of their African fellow-countrymen.

In South Africa the political scene was dominated by the ill-feeling between the two white races, the Afrikaners of Dutch descent and the South Africans of English origin. In a general election in 1924 General Smuts and his South African Party, supported by almost all English South-Africans, had been defeated, and General Hertzog had taken office as the head of a Nationalist–Labour coalition, the so-called Labour party consisting of white trade unionists whose aim was to preserve the privileged position of white versus black labour.

Although both Hertzog and Smuts had voiced their support of the Balfour declaration at the 1926 Imperial Conference as granting South Africa the independent Dominion status that they desired, Hertzog was not yet wholly convinced of the genuineness of the United Kingdom's new imperial policy and was being attacked by some of his Afrikaner supporters as having been hoodwinked into betraying their republican aspirations, while Smuts' imperialist English-South African followers feared that the Balfour declaration would soon lead to South Africa becoming wholly separated from Britain and the rest of the Empire.

At the time of our visit ill-feeling had been further enhanced by a Bill brought in by the Nationalists to provide South Africa with its own national flag in place of the Union Jack. Bitterly opposed by the English-South Africans this Flag Bill threatened to destroy any hope of national unity. I realized that Amery could not ignore the controversy, but that each side would be alert to take offence at any public reference he made to it and would try to interpret or rather misinterpret his words to suit their cause.

It was in Natal, the stronghold of the English-South Africans, that the atmosphere over the Flag Bill was the tensest. There also the feeling was strongest that there was no future for the English in South Africa under a Nationalist Government that had already begun to fill all official posts with Afrikaners; racial origin and language rather than merit being the criteria for appointments and promotion. South Africa, people in Natal were saying, would soon become an Afrikaner-dominated country with the British denied any share in directing its affairs. It was therefore with considerable apprehension that Whiskard, Brass and I took our seats at the crowded tables in the Marine Hotel in Durban where a civic banquet in Amery's honour was being given. Amery, however, appeared as unruffled as ever, nor had he given us any indication of the line he proposed to take in his speech. Our worst fears seemed to be realized when Durban's Mayor delivered a most foolish and inflammatory oration, referring to 'scab' flags and declaring that Natal would take up arms and secede from the Union rather than abandon the Union Jack. His words were calculated to arouse all the worst anti-British feelings of Afrikaners, especially as they were punctuated by loud cheers from most of the audience. It was in this tense atmosphere that Amery rose to make the finest speech on the Empire that I had ever heard. At once lifting the whole subject out of the dissensions of racial politics, he proclaimed that there should be no conflict between the concepts of South Africa first or Empire first, but that the best imperialist was also the best South African, since no finer work could be achieved for the Empire than in helping to build a great and united South

African nation. The Empire, he pointed out, was not something imposed on its members from without, but something springing from within each of its partner nations. Taking as his text, 'if I were a South African', he showed that politically, spiritually and economically it was within the Empire that South African nationality would attain its fullest development and that, as an equal partner with Britain and the other Dominions, South Africa would command a far greater influence in the world than she could ever win in isolation.

The Durban audience listened spellbound to this rebuke to the extremists of both sides, and I was convinced that, fully reported as it would be all over the country, Amery's speech might well mark a turning point in the attitude of all but the most bigoted Afrikaners or British towards South Africa's role in the Empire. Forty years later I was dining in the Mount Nelson Hotel in Cape Town with a party of South Africans, amongst whom was Laurens Van der Post, and when I recounted the episode and expressed my belief in its importance, 'Yes, indeed,' said Laurens, 'I can endorse that. I was present at the banquet as a very young reporter on a Natal newspaper and I remember to this day the tremendous impact that Amery's words made on me and on the whole audience.'

What, however, all the Amery party felt to be fraught with most trouble for the future was that the division between the two white races seemed to be blinding both to a far graver question, which, when it had been mentioned in our official or private discussions, had, to our surprise, been dismissed by English-South Africans and Afrikaners alike as no problem at all. This was the political, social and economic relationship between one and a half million whites sharing South Africa with a black population that already numbered five and a half million and that was very rapidly increasing.

After long travels through Australia, New Zealand and Canada, we were back in the gloom of London in February. I was very sad to think that our little party which had so happily weathered all the storms of eight months' constant association had been broken up, and that all the romance and excitement that every day had held out had been replaced by my former office routine.

I thought that in this unique tour Amery's political career had reached a new peak. At home, despite his integrity and great ability, he had never seemed to inspire public enthusiasm, but in the Empire overseas he had acquired new dimensions. All the three hundred speeches he had made had been listened to by enthusiastic audiences. In none of them had he failed to introduce local colour and understanding, and on the big occasions he had risen to great heights, both in matter and in eloquence. Besides this, his humour, friendliness and utter lack of pomposity had endeared him as a person and as Britain's representative to the thousands who had met or heard him. I only hoped that his countrymen at home would appreciate how much he had done to strengthen the ties not only between Britain and the Empire overseas but also between the Dominions themselves.

As for myself, I had never felt as full of energy and confidence. Contact with all the freshness of outlook and optimism of the new nations had had a tonic effect. Precedent and custom seemed to have lost importance after visiting lands where they necessarily counted for so little, where no one was afraid of bold experiments and where there were no cobwebs of the past to hamper action. Difficulties, like distances, seemed to have assumed a new perspective. I had gained, too, a new understanding of the significance of the Empire to its citizens. I not only appreciated the world-wide material opportunities that our Empire partnership offered for a better life for my own fellow-countrymen who had the ambition and courage to grasp them, but I also realized how the Empire brought an enhancement to the cultural life of all its partners who shared enough in common for each to gain directly from each other's advances in the arts and science. Whether it was political experiment such as compulsory voting in Australia, or social progress such as child welfare in New Zealand and rural education and the Women's Institute movement in Canada, or economic development such as co-operative marketing, the example had a greatly added force because it came from within the partnership.

My mind had been enriched, too, by the wonderful variety of scenic beauty that I had encountered on my travels. Geographically the Empire overseas no longer consisted of names on a map, but had become familiar country with each name evoking its picture. There were pictures of the seas that joined the Empire together; the South Atlantic to the Cape with the sun glittering on the flying fish as they skimmed over the deep blue of the quiet waves; the lonely wildness of the southern Indian Ocean between the Cape and Australia where day after day showed the same grey emptiness of heaving waters with the albatross as the ship's only companion; the misty heat of the South Pacific; the steep foam-streaked walls of the winter North Atlantic.

There were pictures of the harbours into which we had steamed; Cape Town under the blue shadow of its mountain; Albany lonely amongst its forests; Melbourne spreading wide over the low shores of Port Philip; Hobart asleep under Mount Wellington; the flashing blue waters of Sydney's inlets; Brisbane's broad river; Auckland with its islands; the mountain-locked waters of Wellington; the steep pine-clad shores of Victoria and Vancouver; Montreal and Quebec on their river in the heart of a continent; Halifax and St. John in their mists.

There were pictures of the great rivers we had crossed; the Limpopo, a trickle of water in its broad sand bed; the Zambezi leaping mile-wide into the chasm of the Victoria Falls; the dun-coloured Murray running slow between its sage-green, gum-fringed banks; the tangled tree-ferns of the Waikato; the Fraser hurrying down its canyon under the tall snow peaks of the Rockies; the jostling ice-blocks of the St. Lawrence.

There were pictures of mountains; the Drakensberg's wide-flung line of rocky walls and below them the fresh spring green of the veld after burning, with the clustered huts of the kraals surrounded by hedges of golden mimosa and wild peach trees, their pink blossom translucent against the pale blue sky; the Alps of New Zealand in all the dazzling glory of white peak after peak bounding the horizon of the plains; Egmont rising in solitary grandeur from the green Taranaki pastures; the Rockies in the silence of their winter snows.

There were pictures of journeys by train; that first ride up the Hex River valley when all the mountain ramparts were clothed in the changing pageantry and the unimaginable splendour of the South African sunset; the line stretching endlessly straight across the white-hot Nullarbor desert on the trans-Australian railway; the train from Oamaru to Dunedin in New Zealand clinging to the side of sheep-grazed downs on the edge of a jade-green sea; the long and tortuous climb through the snows of the Canadian Rockies with the dark pines struggling up the sides of the mountains on either hand to be lost in the clouds above; the snow-bound prairies rolling away for mile after mile and hour after hour as we crossed Canada's western provinces.

There were pictures of journeys by road; the sandy track winding through the Rhodesian bush with the sudden sunrise firing the green and gold of the mopani trees; the descent from White River into the Crocodile Valley in South Africa's low-veldt, where the scent of the orange blossom lay like a mist along the flats; the drive through the wheat belt of Western Australia with its undulating miles of green corn and brown fallow; the lovely river country of northern New South Wales where our road ran through rich emerald pastures with forest-clad mountains on one side and on the other the white surf line of the blue ocean; in New Zealand's Southland the road cresting a rise to open out all the loveliness of Lake Wakatipu under its sheltering snow-topped mountains.

All my experiences and contacts were to be of future value to me, but meantime, as our train brought us from Liverpool to London on the last lap of our journey, the words of Kipling's 'Chant Pagan' had kept running through my mind. I wondered, indeed,

'If it's only my fancy or not
that the sunshine of England is pale,
And the breezes of England are stale
an' there's something gone small with the lot.'

iii

A warm welcome from Stephen Tallents, my colleagues
and the members of the Board awaited me on my return to
the office. A civil servant from the Treasury had filled my
place during my absence, and I gathered that he had lacked
any special interest in the work. It was, however, with more
enthusiasm than ever that I took over the reins to try to
make the fullest use of all my new experiences and contacts.

The Board itself was flourishing and already proving the
worth of its novel role, both imports from Empire countries
and exports to them showing a steady rise, while reports
from the retail trade showed that consumers were increasingly demanding Empire products in the shops. In my own
publicity field it was to the use of films that Tallents had
been devoting most of his attention. He had added a new
recruit to the Board's staff in the person of John Grierson,
a thirty-year-old Scot with the air of a tough little terrier,
under whose dynamic spell Tallents had so completely fallen
that it seemed that films should form the most valuable
single medium for the attainment of the Board's objects.

Grierson's advent was, indeed, to lead to important
developments in the film world. I found that he was already
engaged in producing for the Board a silent film called
Drifters on the subject of the home herring industry. When
completed in 1929, it won immediate recognition as marking a new era in documentary films, gaining a wide and
profitable theatrical distribution, while a shorter version
was much in demand for showing to school and many other
non-theatrical audiences. Under Grierson's leadership,
backed by Tallents, the Board's film activities soon assumed
such importance that Tallents constituted a special film

committee with myself as its Secretary. The committee's scope came to include the maintenance of a unit for the production and editing of films for both theatrical and non-theatrical use, the setting up of a Library of films for schools and the maintenance of a cinema at the Imperial Institute, the Board's activities in this field being the subject of special commendation by the Imperial Conference of 1930. The Board was, indeed, the first patron of documentary films, and only recently *The Times* justly referred to Grierson as their grandfather.

One result of the Board's work was that newspapers and other journals both at home and overseas were increasingly glad to devote space to the material issued by the Board's Press section. Pat Ryan, its head, now found himself in need of a capable assistant Press Officer, particularly for writing about the Board's ever-widening range of grants for scientific research and the problems they were helping to solve. I well remember Tallents asking me at the beginning of 1929 to join him in interviewing for the post a twenty-two-year-old Miss Elspeth Grant who had been recommended to him by Frank McDougall. Largely brought up in Kenya, she had taken a diploma in agriculture at Reading University followed by a year on the same subject at Cornell University in America where she had also worked on the *New York State Agricultural Journal*. McDougall had met her recently at Aberystwyth when she had been doing some work for Professor Stapledon, and had urged her not to go back to the U.S.A. as had been her intention. Tallents, Ryan and I, all thought that she was well worth taking a chance on despite her lack of experience of English journalism. She proved an immediate success, having the great gift of making articles on scientific research subjects both easily comprehensible and highly readable to the layman. I had no premonition of how this appointment was to affect my future life and happiness.

At the moment I was busy getting ready for another overseas visit, having been lucky enough to be chosen to represent the Board at a Conference in Barbados of all the British

West Indian islands and territories. It was to open at the end of January under the chairmanship of Sir Edward Davson who represented the Colonies on the Board.

Trinidad was extremely hot and humid, but our party stayed very comfortably for a few days at Government House before we sailed on to Barbados. The Conference met at the old rambling wooden Marine Hotel in Georgetown where all the delegates also stayed. They were a very friendly bunch of men, mostly white. We all consumed large quantities of rum drinks, but a dip in the sea at once dispelled any hang-over next morning. So poor were the inter-island communications that most of the delegates had never left the shores of their own islands except for a rare visit to Britain. It was the purpose of the Conference to try to persuade the representatives of the various island legislatures to unite in common action over such matters as transport and crop production and marketing. Although Davson was an excellent Chairman who knew the West Indies well and was one of the leading sugar producers, insular parochialism triumphed over common sense and most of the speakers devoted themselves to the assertion of their own island's claim to priority on historical grounds. I did succeed in getting the delegates to agree to my recommendation that they should establish a joint Trade office in London which the Empire Marketing Board would assist. On my return to England I wrote and sent back detailed proposals for such a service but nothing ever came of my efforts.

I had not been back at work long before, to my great regret, the Board changed its political masters. Baldwin's Conservative administration of 1924, under which the Board had been started, was approaching the term of its natural life, and the General Election which took place in the spring of 1929 resulted in a Labour victory. Baldwin at once resigned and Ramsay MacDonald formed a Labour administration.

From its start the Empire Marketing Board had included representatives from all three political parties, but Sydney Webb, created Lord Passfield, the new Secretary of State for the Dominions, now replaced Amery as the Board's Chairman, while I had his Under Secretary, William Lunn, as Chairman of my publicity and film committees in place of Ormsby-Gore.

Although the new Government announced that they proposed to continue the Board, its inspiration from now on began to fade and its fortunes to decline. Passfield, looking exactly like an elderly billy-goat, was the dullest of chairmen, and the Board's meetings were not enlivened by the presence as new members of the two prosy, dreary ex-medical Labour Ministers, Doctors Addison and Drummond-Shiels. I found that Lunn, a Trade Union Member of Parliament, lacked any spark and seemed to be chiefly interested in ensuring that I obtained for him the maximum travel and maintenance allowances when I accompanied him to Empire shopping weeks or other events.

Moreover, before 1929 was out, the world economic crisis was beginning to affect the Board's present and future position. Hampered by the fact that at any moment the Government could be overthrown by the combined Conservative and Liberal votes, MacDonald and his colleagues contented themselves with optimistic words and did nothing to stem the growth of unemployment. J. H. Thomas had been appointed Lord Privy Seal specifically to deal with this, but after his failure to produce any policy and Oswald Moseley's despairing resignation over the Government's refusal to consider any programme of public works, Thomas preferred to change his post to that of Dominions Secretary and replaced Passfield as the Board's Chairman. He was certainly a livelier one and I was often astonished at his quickness in apparently mastering a brief which I knew he had not read, but the contrast between his superficiality and Amery's sincerity and knowledge was a painful one. The Imperial Conference of 1930 did, it is true, warmly endorse the Board's activities and recommended their continuance, and the Labour Government agreed to furnish the Board with a fixed minimum annual income. But the worsening of the general economic situation made drastic reductions in public expenditure the main plank of the Government's policy, and in July 1931 the Committee on National Expenditure recommended the Board's abolition.

Although the Government refused to accept this recommendation, the funds promised to the Board were substantially cut. Our annual expenditure on publicity had averaged well over £200,000 with a peak of close on £300,000 in 1928, but our vote sank to £97,000 for 1931 and to only £63,000 for 1932. The economic crisis reached its climax in August 1931 when MacDonald, followed only by Snowden and Thomas among his Cabinet colleagues, agreed to head a National Government with the Conservatives and Liberals in order to impose the economies deemed necessary to avert national bankruptcy. The General Election which followed in October saw the return of 558 supporters of the National Government, mostly Conservatives, while the Labour opposition could only win 56 seats. Thomas remained Chairman of the Board, but I was lucky enough to have Lunn replaced by Malcolm MacDonald as Chairman of my Publicity and Film Committees. Young, highly intelligent and keen, I found Malcolm the most sympathetic of all my political masters, Amery always excepted, and I was very soon on the friendliest of terms with him. Shortly after he became my Chairman I was able to help muster for one dramatic effort all the publicity resources that the Board had built up over the past five years, when the Government asked us to mount a 'Buy British' campaign with all the power that our funds would allow. Since these had been so heavily reduced I realized that while we could provide actual material such as designs, print and paper, it would be impossible for us to buy the space on the hoardings or in newspapers or other media needed to arrest the public attention on a national scale. Instead we should have to ask the owners of these media to give us their facilities without charge. This Tallents and I set out to obtain, and such was the general mood of patriotism engendered by the National Government that we got willing co-operation from every quarter. All was carefully timed, and one morning the whole country woke up to see our slogan 'Buy British from the Empire at Home and Overseas' carried in striking design and colour in different forms and sizes on the poster hoardings, on the sides of buses, in railway stations, in shop windows, post offices, banks, in every possible place of display, as well as being printed in newpapers and magazines.

All the space had been provided free, and never before had there been seen such a simultaneous concentration of national publicity on one single theme. But it had become clear to me that this might well be a dying effort and that the omens for the long-term continuance of the Board were becoming more and more unfavourable. My belief was reinforced in the spring of 1932 when the Select Committee on Estimates stated in their report on the Board that its *raison d'être* had disappeared with the adoption by the British Government of a general tariff coupled with Imperial Preferences. It had become time, I felt, to look elsewhere for employment.

iv

The years following my return from the Amery tour did not only see the decline of the Empire Marketing Board. They also witnessed the collapse of my marriage.

My six months abroad had further weakened the ties between Lindsey and myself. She had, I think, enjoyed her freedom to pursue her Women's Institute activities without being hampered by any domestic cares and we were both more than ever absorbed in our own separate interests. Nor was there any likelihood of children forming a common bond. With the marriage of my elder sister Marjorie to Sir Edward Harding, the permanent head of the Dominions Office, I had ceased to share her flat in St. George's Square and had rented a much smaller one in Vincent Square, keeping on her old housekeeper, Minette, to look after me. Lindsey was seldom there, though we spent Saturday afternoons and Sundays together at our house below Boars Hill.

Looking back, I realize that we had both become more

critical of each other. Nor did either of us derive much pleasure from the other's company. Matters came to a head on one of the rare nights that Lindsey spent in Vincent Square. Coming back from the office I found that she had gone out for the evening, and on her return she declined to tell me with whom she had been. A day or two later I saw a letter lying open. It began 'Lindsey, my tall Darling' and was from Walter Elliot. He was one of the very few original Board members whom I had never liked, thinking him far too volubly pleased with himself and his compendious, if sometimes superficial, range of knowledge, but I knew that Lindsey much admired him and had frequently consulted him over Women's Institute matters. Now, all my possessive instincts rose in jealous rage and I felt specially aggrieved because it was on my birthday, which Lindsey had forgotten, that I found the letter. Over the weekend we had a long-drawn-out quarrel which ended in Lindsey's declaring that she intended to leave me and would gladly divorce me if I gave her grounds. Before long she was sharing a flat in London with one of her colleagues from the Women's Institute headquarters. Thus matters remained for the time being, since I saw no purpose in committing an unwanted adultery with some persons unknown in order that Lindsey should divorce me.

It was when I was in this state of semi-widowerhood that I began to find myself strongly attracted to Elspeth Grant, the Board's assistant Press Officer, who was making a brilliant success of her writing for the Board. I saw a good deal of her in the course of my work, and the more I saw the more I liked her gaiety, her intelligence and her looks. In spite of the thirteen years' difference in our ages we seemed to have most of our interests in common and on the occasions I took her out to dinner in Soho the evenings passed all too quickly. Before long I realized that, for the first time in my life, I had fallen madly and desperately in love and knew what it was to have my whole being filled with a sense of happiness so deep that it coloured every moment of my days. It seemed, too, that Elspeth was entering this same enchanted world and would marry me when I was **free**.

What, however, were the steps that I should take to set in motion the divorce proceedings which Lindsey was so willing to take against me? On two points I was determined. One was that Elspeth should in no way be involved; the other that nothing would induce me to commit adultery, the very thought of which was the more abhorrent now that I had fallen in love, in order to comply with the letter of the law. With these restrictions, the path to getting divorced seemed likely to be a thorny one.

I first sought the advice of my solicitor cousin-by-marriage, E. S. P. Haynes. He proved to be fully prepared to help me and advised that I should make the Charing Cross Hotel the scene of my marital offence, but he was unable to suggest any suitable partner who would be willing to have her name cited in the divorce court. I had heard that such persons could be hired but had no idea of how to get in touch with them. After pursuing various lines which led nowhere, I had the idea that the answer might be found in France. Lewis Gielgud was still with the International Red Cross in Paris and, at the moment, was wifeless, so I went over to Paris to see him. Not only did I much enjoy his company, but, sure enough, he had the answer for me. Taking me to a Lesbian night-club where a number of the women were wearing plus fours and smoking pipes, he introduced me to Germaine, a lady of uncertain age whose hair was dyed a startling shade of orange. She had, Lewis assured me, no wish for intimacy with a member of the male sex, but would be glad to visit England for a weekend and lend her name as my bedfellow, though in fact a chaste one, in return for her expenses and a suitable fee. At least, I thought, the chambermaid at the Charing Cross Hotel when she came to testify in court would be sure to remember the sight of Germaine's remarkable head of hair on the pillow of the double bed when she brought in the early morning tea.

I duly met Germaine at Folkestone one Saturday afternoon and brought her to the Charing Cross Hotel for two nights. There proved to be no difficulty about the chaste nature of our shared bed, but I was almost asphyxiated by the overpowering odour of the chypre scent which she used so liberally. On Sunday I drove her in my car to Brighton where I thought that the sea-breezes might make the chypre less all-pervasive, and next morning thankfully put her on the boat for France and went to tell Ted Haynes that my 'adultery' had been successfully accomplished.

Lindsey was duly granted a decree nisi, made absolute six months later so that she and I were both free. She never remarried and I only once saw her again. It was at a Victory service in Westminster Abbey in 1945 when she was in command of the contingent of members of the Women's Voluntary Services which she had joined in 1939 and where her work had been so outstanding that she had been awarded the C.B.E. Not long afterwards I had news of her death from cancer and I then learned that a growth on the womb had prevented her ever having a child.

Once the divorce evidence had been produced and the proceedings started, Elspeth and I felt free to see much more of each other, but our meetings were so conducted that none of our Empire Marketing Board colleagues had any inkling of our attachment. Only Elspeth's and my immediate families were told of our intention to get married.

Our marriage took place in December 1931 at the Kensington Registry Office, the witnesses being my father and Lady Denman, one of Elspeth's mother's oldest friends, and we went to Cornwall for a short honeymoon. Elspeth's parents were in Kenya, but I had met them both when they had recently visited England. Her father, 'Jos' Grant, the eldest son of Sir Charles Grant who had been Foreign Secretary to the Government of India, was a man of much charm but of singular incompetence in business affairs. After he had succeeded in losing almost all of his quite substantial inherited capital in futile business enterprises, he and his wife had started coffee-farming in Kenya, taking their four-year-old daughter Elspeth with them. My new mother-in-law, Nellie, was a tremendous personality. Born Eleanor Grosvenor, the daughter of the First Lord Stalbridge, the

First Duke of Westminster's younger brother, she was very much the dominating partner in her marriage. At the outbreak of the war they had returned with Elspeth to England, Jos to rejoin his regiment and Nellie to find an outlet for her great energy and organizing talents in running the Women's Land Army in Wessex. Elspeth had been sent to a fashionable boarding school in Suffolk which she so cordially disliked that when, at the war's end, her parents went back to Kenya, she contrived to get herself expelled so as to rejoin them and complete a somewhat sketchy education at the Nairobi Girls' High School before going to Reading and Cornell.

Only Tallents and Pat Ryan at the Empire Marketing Board had been told of our approaching marriage and they had been as surprised as they were pleased. Now on our return to the office from our honeymoon our well-kept secret was out. One serious consequence of our marriage was that either she or I would have to leave the Board since it was against civil service rules for a married couple to be employed in the same Department. Most uncharacteristically, however, on Tallents' plea of the value of Elspeth's work, my brother-in-law, E. J. Harding, agreed that the rule should be waived for six months. But Elspeth and I decided that we should both aim at getting new jobs during 1932 and that, if possible, they should be out of England, preferably in Africa. Elspeth's opportunity came when the widow of Lord Delamere, the father of white settlement in Kenya, passed over a number of established English writers who would have been glad to write Delamere's biography, in favour of someone with a full Kenya background, and asked Elspeth if she would undertake the work. It was a brave and generous offer to someone who had never written a book, and Lady Delamere could have had no premonition of how brilliantly the task would be fulfilled.

I myself had been making tentative inquiries as to jobs with the Trade Commissioner Service of the Department of Overseas Trade, when John Still, the Secretary of the Ceylon Association in London which represented the major tea and other plantation companies in Ceylon, asked to come and see me. I had helped him with the staging of the Ceylon exhibit at the British Industries and other Fairs and had found him a most sympathetic and intelligent man, who was the author of *The Jungle Tide*, a classic book about Ceylon. Now, he wanted to know if I could recommend anybody who would be qualified to head a new publicity and marketing body that the Ceylon tea interests, backed by Government, were setting up.

It appeared that, owing to overproduction in Ceylon, India and the Netherlands East Indies, tea prices were falling disastrously and urgent steps had to be taken to try to remedy the situation. The planting interests in all three countries and their Governments were trying to work out some joint method of restricting production, but in the meantime Ceylon—whose tea was the mainstay of the island's economy—intended to start strong promotion work in the chief consuming markets for her teas, and the Government had levied a cess on all Ceylon producers which would furnish very substantial sums for the purpose.

The more I thought about John Still's inquiry, the more I felt that it was a post which I myself would like to fill. It seemed to be very much in the line of country in which I had been working for the last six years and in which my experience and contacts would be of value. Moreover, the challenge of starting up a new organization from scratch held a strong appeal, especially as I should be my own master with a free hand to make what I could of the job. John Still seemed to be delighted when I told him that, if he wished, he could put my name forward to Ceylon, and said that he would do so with the strongest possible recommendation, suggesting a salary very much higher than my civil service pay, together with most generous expenses and other conditions. The authorities in Ceylon proved to be equally welcoming and in due course appointed me Chief Commissioner of their newly formed Board as from the 1st January 1933, my initial assignment being to visit Ceylon to meet the Board, acquaint myself with the workings of the planting industry and draw up policy and plans for the promotion work.

Meantime Elspeth and I had a glorious and care-free summer holiday on the Riviera. Aldous and Maria were living not far away at Bandol and we spent some very happy days with them. It had been some years since I had seen Aldous, but, as always, our old ties were so close that no interval could weaken them.

At the end of June Elspeth had left the Board and started gathering material for her life of Delamere. Most of it would have, of course, to be obtained in Kenya, and when the confirmation of my appointment arrived from Ceylon we arranged that we should both leave England early in January, and booked our passages on ships that conveniently left Marseilles at about the same time, hers to Mombasa and mine to Colombo. Pleased as I was at the idea of my new assignment it was sad to have to break the news to Tallents. My admiration and affection for him had never ceased to grow and I well knew how much I owed to the opportunities he had given me and how much I had learned from his wisdom and his methods. He wrote to me in typically generous terms saying, 'I don't like to imagine what the E.M.B. publicity would have been without you. You can look back on it, I feel, as a brilliant job in a new field.' Although I only officially left the Board at the end of the year, Tallents arranged to release me a month earlier; a month which I mostly spent in Mincing Lane learning all I could about how tea was marketed and the arts of tea tasting and blending. I availed myself, too, of the opportunity to have a sinus operation performed which removed a quantity of bone that had been broken when the shell had buried me under rubble in 1915 and that had ever since been the cause of recurring headaches.

A farewell lunch given by the Board and presided over by Malcolm MacDonald at the beginning of January gave Elspeth and me a very warm send-off, but we were an utterly miserable couple who parted a day or two later at Marseilles, each to board their own ship, uncertain as to how soon we could hope to be reunited. Not until our parting did either of us, I think, fully appreciate how much we had already come to mean to each other. Nor could I have imagined as I boarded my ship that I was taking my first step along a road that would give me happy and rewarding employment for the next thirty-five years.

CHAPTER VII

i

A N uneventful voyage, brought me to Colombo at the
beginning of February. I was met on board by the
Ceylon Tea Board's Secretary, a disillusioned and pessi-
mistic ex-employee of one of Colombo's Tea Agency
houses, with the look of a melancholy bloodhound. Colombo,
its harbour crowded with ships, seemed a cheerful, busy,
clean city, the inhabitants, both Sinhalese and the darker
Tamils, well clad and smiling, and the women's bright-
coloured saris adding a pleasing note of colour. The climate
was, of course, hot and humid but tempered by the breeze
that blew in from the sea over the wide green space of the
Galle Face that lay between the shore and the nearest line
of buildings, which included a handsome new Parliament
House and Government Offices. My destination, the Galle
Face Hotel right on the sea, closed the Galle Face at the
far end. Over lunch I had a long talk with Stewart, the
Chairman of my new Board. A partner in an Agency House,
I found him much to my liking, decisive, quick-minded,
intelligent and cultured. I was subsequently to discover that
it was these very qualities that made him unpopular with
some of his fellow Britishers who ran Ceylon's planting
industry. To them 'cleverness' seemed to be an object of
suspicion. Indeed, as I got to know them, it appeared that
an education at a leading public school and a good war
record were the criteria for their approbation. Fortunately I
passed on both counts. It seemed, too, that *camellia theensis*,
the tea bush, shared their prejudices and would presumably
give its biggest yield under the supervision of an old Etonian
V.C. The reasons for their attitude were not far to seek. In
order to become a tea planter in Ceylon you had to pay a
quite substantial apprenticeship premium, so as to be taken

L   161

on as a 'creeper' on an estate, whereas in India no such premium was required. This more or less confined Ceylon planters to public school products. Tea planting was, however, a career that only the least academically successful would be likely to fall back on. Not that I ever had any reason for anything but the kindliest feelings towards the British planting community. They never failed to give me their friendship and trust and a completely free hand to direct the market promotion work for their product.

My relations with my Ceylonese employers were equally pleasant. Some were Sinhalese, descendants of the original rulers of the island; others were Tamils whose ancestors had invaded Ceylon from South India, and others were of mixed Sinhalese-Portuguese or Sinhalese-Dutch descent. Many of those I met had been at Oxford or Cambridge, all spoke perfect English and were certainly not inferior in intelligence or culture to the British in Ceylon. One was reminded that Sinhalese kings ruled Ceylon long before the Romans came to Britain and that, while Europe was plunged in the dark ages, great cities were being built in Ceylon and vast irrigation works constructed for growing rice. The upper class Sinhalese were even now a land-owning aristocracy, deriving their wealth mainly from their coconut plantations, an industry requiring little effort or skill. The chief fault in the Ceylonese, whether Sinhalese or Tamils, seemed to be that no man trusted his fellow, though they gave me, an outsider, their full confidence. My Board was half-in-half British and Ceylonese. Government was represented on it by the British Financial Secretary and the Ceylonese Minister of Commerce (although Ceylon was still a Crown colony it had recently been given a constitution that set it well along the road to the independence it achieved in 1948). Other Ceylonese represented the Chamber of Commerce, the smallholders and low-country planters, while British members represented the main body of the mid- and up-country planters and the Colombo Agency houses. As a Board, these diverse elements seemed to work without any friction.

On arrival in Ceylon I had been solemnly warned that for a European to go out of doors at any time between 10 a.m. and 4 p.m. without being fully clothed and wearing a topee was to invite an early death from sunstroke, whether the sun was shining or not. This myth was not to be dispelled until the Second World War when British troops worked bareheaded and clad only in singlet and shorts without any illeffect. As a result topees ceased to be worn by the British, but then became the fashionable head-gear for the Ceylonese. Actually I found my topee very comfortable and I rather fancied myself in it. Anyhow I never failed to wear it as I rode to and from the office in Colombo in a rickshaw or went visiting tea estates up-country, which I shortly did, as I felt that my first task was to try to learn all about tea at the production end. The industry's structure appeared to me to be carrying an unnecessary burden of overheads. In London I had met Directors of the Tea Plantation companies, mostly elderly gentlemen retired from Ceylon, all drawing fees to attend, often from Scotland, a monthly Board Meeting in London and to pay an annual or biennial visit to Ceylon in the cold weather to go round the Estate at the Company's expense. It was, however, the Agency Houses in Colombo who, on behalf of the London companies, performed the real managerial role and the Superintendents on the Estates were under their close control. A visiting agent from Colombo carried out regular supervision of their work, and everything needed for the estate was bought by the Agency House, which also arranged for the tasting and valuing of the estate's teas and for their shipment to London or their sale by auction in Colombo. Altogether the Agency business seemed to be a most profitable one.

After some days in Colombo I drove up-country with one of the visiting agents to visit typical estates and to meet their superintendents. First through flat country, densely populated and every acre cultivated, where vivid green rice stood immersed in water, and coconut gardens and fruit trees hid little palm-thatched villages. As the land began to rise our road passed many rubber plantations, the bare stems of the trees standing like pillars in a dark cathedral aisle. Here, too, were the low-country tea estates. Climbing higher, we entered the foothills leading to Kandy, the last capital of the Sinhalese kings, with its lake and temples, and round it some of Ceylon's richest country. Tea was grown here and cocoa, breadfruit and bananas, coconuts and pineapples. Two-wheeled carts, thatched with palm leaves and drawn by little bulls lumbered along the road, tame buffaloes wallowed in the mud of the fields and elephants were being driven by their keepers to bathe in river pools. Beyond Kandy the mountains rose up to four, five and six thousand feet and the road climbed steadily by hairpin bends and through narrow passes until it reached the open uplands where the lower slopes of the forest-covered peaks were carpeted thick with dark green tea bushes and where the rushing mountain streams that we crossed and recrossed ran brown with eroded soil.

This mountain land was the home of Ceylon's world-famous quality teas. It was there in the sparkling sunshine and cool crystal-clear air that the tea bushes matured slowly to develop the finest flavour in their leaves. I much enjoyed my first and many subsequent visits to the tea estates, each with its three- or four-storey factory to which the green leaf was brought for the withering, rolling, fermenting and firing that turned it into carefully sorted grades of made tea. In the fields I watched the endless cycle of growth, the cultivation of the soil, the planting out of the seedling bushes from the nurseries to make bushes fit to pluck in five or more years, the pruning of the bushes at regular intervals and finally the plucking of the leaf that went on all the year round with the lines of women pluckers, their bright-coloured clothes showing vividly against the dark green bushes, moving up and down the hilly slopes, the women's dark hands flickering like moths over the tea bushes as with incredible speed and dexterity they plucked only the tender buds and young leaves and flung them into the baskets they carried on their backs secured by a brow band. Each estate formed a little world of its own, with its school, its shop, its dispensing and first-aid unit, and since all the workers were Tamils from South India, its Hindu shrine. The workers were well housed in their lines of huts; women washed their clothes by a stream and children played all round. The superintendent and his white assistants and their wives had their comfortable bungalows, with gardens ablaze with flowers, and somewhere in the neighbourhood would be the Club with its tennis courts, the centre of the planters' social life, where they spent Saturday evenings and Sundays. A member of my Board, Robert Scott, had invited me to stay with him. He was one of the very few remaining planters who still owned and lived on his own estate. Robert Scott was the kindest of hosts, immensely keen on improving his family estate and a leader in all matters affecting the planting community. With him I visited the industry's highly efficient research station of which he was one of the strongest supporters and which was proving of great assistance in combating diseases and improving methods of cultivation.

Back in Colombo I set to work to draw up my proposals for the Board's policies and for the methods of carrying out its promotion work. Since joint regulation of production on the part of India, Ceylon and the Dutch East Indies would soon be coming into force, it seemed obvious that efforts merely to divert trade from one restricted source to another would do nothing to achieve the increase in total world consumption that alone would relieve the consequences of overproduction. My aim was therefore to persuade India and the Dutch to join Ceylon in joint market promotion for all tea. As an immediate policy I therefore recommended a triple formula—to increase the world consumption of tea; to increase the demand for quality tea; and to associate the name of Ceylon with quality tea. The Board unanimously welcomed my proposals and at the end of March I set forth on the first leg of travels that until the outbreak of the Second World War were to be almost non-stop and were to take me and Elspeth all over the world.

From Colombo I sailed to Bombay and endured the long and weary train journey to Calcutta in order to meet there the heads of the Indian tea industry and discuss with them my proposals for joint promotion work. What a contrast I found between Ceylon with its green country and the smiling faces of its people and the brown bare vastness of India with its swarms of miserable-looking inhabitants. My discussions in Calcutta went well, and finding that a British India boat went from Bombay to South Africa via Mombasa I thought that a report to Ceylon on the small but expanding tea growing industry in East Africa would give me a good excuse for visiting Kenya and seeing Elspeth on my way to South Africa. It was a great moment when I saw her and her mother on the platform at Nairobi station and, for the first time, drove to Nakuru and Njoro with breath-taking views over the Rift Valley from the road. Like all visitors I fell under Kenya's spell, the bracing air of the highlands, the sunshine, the enormous vistas of sky, plain and mountain, and the friendly cheerfulness of the Africans. My in-laws' little house above Njoro was a ramshackle affair but very comfortable. The garden was full of the colours of flowers and birds, and the site commanded a superb view to distant mountains. With Elspeth I visited the tea estates at Kericho, and a fortnight passed all too quickly before I was back at Mombasa and on the ship for South Africa to meet the tea trade and prepare the way for Ceylon's first tea promotion campaign. This successfully accomplished, I found that Imperial Airways had just started a weekly flight from Cape Town to London and I thought it would be a good idea to try the new method of transport which would give me another week in Kenya where I would pick up Elspeth to travel on home with me by air. We left Cape Town at dawn in thick wet cloud, but once over the mountains we flew into the bright sunshine of the Karoo and the high veldt and reached Johannesburg in the late afternoon for a night stop. Next day we had an uneventful flight to Salisbury, our next overnight stop. On the third day we picked up at Broken Hill Sir Hubert Young, the Governor of Nyasaland, who was being hurried home for medical treatment. On board we also had Sir Basil Blackett and his female secretary and a young South African. From Broken Hill our next stop should have been Mpika, a two-hours' flight over a desolate country of rocky bush, the ground obscured by the smoke of small bush fires. More than two hours passed with no sign of Mpika. We now seemed to be continually changing direction, and before long we realized that the pilot was hopelessly lost, though he prevented any communication with his five passengers by keeping the cabin door locked. We knew, however, that we should soon be running out of fuel. Sure enough the pilot kept on swooping down low obviously in search of a piece of level and open ground on which to make a forced landing, only to find nothing but rocks and thick bush. We passengers sat in silence cogitating on what the odds were against a safe landing in such inhospitable country. My own reaction was one of mounting anger at the pilot's incompetence in losing his way rather than one of fear. Another half hour must have passed before the pilot, his fuel tank now almost empty, spotted a small patch of cleared ground where a crop of thin millet had been grown. Circling low over it we could see that unfortunately the cultivation had left a number of charred tree stumps still standing. But it seemed our only chance of survival, and our pilot, whatever his defects as a navigator, proved to be a superb handler of aircraft. Somehow he managed to bring the plane down in a series of bumps, turns and skids, undamaged except for a ripped tyre. Giving devout thanks to Providence we passengers climbed out on to terra firma. 'Tich' Attwood, the pilot, then apologetically explained that on leaving Broken Hill he must have taken a wrong map-bearing and the radio operator had been unable to make any contacts. Now Attwood did not even know which country we were in, and the radio operator reported that his apparatus had got damaged in the forced landing and wasn't working. What to do next? Attwood and I set out on foot to explore our immediate neighbourhood. Walking along a path through the bush we almost fell into a concealed pit full of sharp stakes, obviously a lion trap. But we saw no other sign of human activity. Returning to the aeroplane we found that the second officer had discovered that the contents of the emergency box of food had gone bad, never having been inspected, though some mouldy tea and sugar was still usable. He had, however, found a nearby stream and plenty of old wood lying about. So we lit a roaring bonfire, on which I made tea using a handkerchief as a tea bag and a large tin as a kettle and tea-pot combined in Australian 'billy' fashion. We also removed some of the seats from the passengers' cabin on which we sat round the fire. Presently we were cheered to hear from the radio operator that although he couldn't send signals, he had succeeded in repairing the receiving end of his set and had picked up messages from planes that had been sent out to look for us. It was, I thought, a useful thing to have a Governor on board, as the Governors of neighbouring colonies would be losing no time in trying to locate their missing colleague.

As the light began to fade we saw dark faces peering at us from the edge of the trees beyond the millet clearing and presently shy men and women cautiously approached us. They knew no English but seemed well aware of the value of the shillings that we held up, and by dint of our gestures understood our wish to buy food. Some small skinny fowls were soon produced which we plucked and roasted on sticks over our fire for our supper, after which we settled ourselves for the night in our seats, confident that the fire would keep lions and other animals away. I was sharing a double seat with Hubert Young and in spite of his snores soon dozed off. I woke with a start thinking how loud my bench companion was snoring, but he was no longer there, and in the light of the fire I saw all our party making at full speed for the shelter of the bushes while a herd of elephants, whose noise I had taken for Hubert Young's snores, was tramping through our camp, pausing to inspect the aeroplane. After their departure we returned to the fire, and sat around it till dawn, listening to various noises 'off', some of which we thought were the grunts of lions.

A council of war next morning decided that our best plan was to stay by the plane rather than try to find our way through thick bush and unknown country to some settlement. Moreover the radio operator reported that he was picking up messages from light planes that were continuing to search for us. The local Africans also returned with eggs and more chickens, and with the aid of our proffered shillings we got them to start clearing our millet patch of the tree stumps in order that our rescuers, especially if in a light plane, could make a safe landing. Another day and a night passed, however, without a sight or sound of rescue. Nor was it any use trying to send up a smoke signal, as the country was full of the smoke of little bush fires. We did, however, decide that if no rescuing plane appeared next day, the second officer and I should go off to try to find help on the ground. Fortunately this necessity did not arise, as early next morning we had the welcome sight of a small plane flying low to land safely in our clearing. The pilot was a young Rhodesian Air Force officer, who jumped out to greet us with a bottle of whisky in his hand. He told us that he had luckily caught sight of the shine of the metal of our plane in the glancing light of the early morning sun, otherwise he would never have spotted us with all the smoke about. We were, he said, on the Northern Rhodesian and Tanganyikan border and some fifty miles east of the airfield at Mpika for which we had been making. He could only fly us out one at a time, and although Attwood thought he could get the Artemis away with some petrol and a new tyre, the plane would have to be free from the weight of passengers. So our Rhodesian flew off to Mpika taking Hubert Young with him to return with cans of petrol, a new tyre, food and more whisky. The whisky was especially welcome as I had not realized what a long and sweaty task it was to blow up aeroplane tyres with a hand pump. It was arranged that the small plane and its pilot should spend the night with us and start taking the remaining four passengers off one by one to Mpika at dawn, leaving our crew to undertake the risky job of getting our large aircraft off under her own steam with so short a run. Blackett's Secretary went first, then Blackett, leaving only the young South African and myself.

Attwood then decided that he would risk taking one passenger, so we tossed for it. I lost and stayed behind to watch Attwood miss the trees at the end of the clearing by a foot before I took off in the light plane. Imperial Airways Rest House at Mpika provided us with a luxurious bath and a comfortable bed, and next evening we were in Nairobi where Elspeth was waiting without anxiety, having merely been told by Imperial Airways that my plane was 'delayed'.

Nothing daunted by my adventure, Elspeth and I flew back to England a few days later by Imperial Airways, stopping for the night at Juba, Khartoum, Luxor and Alexandria. This had its advantages, as at Luxor we were given a whole morning to see the Temples. From Alexandria a flying boat took us on via Athens to Brindisi, a really enjoyable flight with lovely views of bare rocky Aegean islands set in the bluest of blue seas. Since aeroplanes were still unable to fly high enough to cross the Alps in safety, we were sent by train from Brindisi to Paris and then on by air to Croydon. Even if all went according to schedule, flying from Nairobi to London took a week.

Back in London and installed in a furnished flat in Clarges Street, I opened an office in Kingsway and worked out with the Indian Tea interests my plans for launching, jointly with Ceylon, a United Kingdom campaign on behalf of Empire teas. Meantime Colombo had accepted all my proposals for South Africa, and the campaign was being started. In London, too, I engaged a marketing man from Australia House with whose work I had been much impressed in my E.M.B. days and despatched him to Australia to prepare the ground there. In Colombo I had found great enthusiasm when I had suggested that we should have a documentary film made of the island and its life, bringing in tea. In London therefore I saw Grierson, now in charge of the Post Office Film Unit and, through him, arranged for Basil Wright to make the film. The result was the historic documentary *Song of Ceylon* which is still being shown thirty-five years later.

Finding the need for a Press Officer to cover the growing

international tea effort and to write leaflets and booklets for use in the various campaigns, I engaged Philip Jordan, then free-lancing. He was later to become Attlee's P.R.O. at 10 Downing Street. Philip was an odd and most entertaining character whose company Elspeth and I much enjoyed, but when I sent him to Ceylon to acquire the necessary background, his brand of ultra-sophistication proved something of a shock to the tea-planting community, and I never felt that his heart was in the job though he wrote and handled the press well enough.

Elspeth meantime was busy starting to write up the material she had amassed for her life of Delamere. In October I started off on my travels again, this time Elspeth with me, on a C.P.R. boat for Montreal, in company with Ernest Gourlay, the Commissioner I had chosen for Canada, and his wife Joan. On the advice of my Montreal advertising agents I found a retreat for Elspeth deep in the Laurentian mountains north of Montreal where she would be able to get on with her writing while Gourlay and I set off by train across Canada to make contact with the tea-packing firms in the various cities.

One abiding memory of this trip is of our being invited to a businessmen's Club breakfast in the Vancouver hotel where we were staying. We were assured that all Vancouver's tycoons would be there, and sharp at 8 a.m. we presented ourselves in a large private dining-room in the hotel to be warmly greeted by the President of the Club and given paper hats to wear inscribed in red letters with the words 'honoured guest'. We then had to partake, on empty stomachs, of round after round of very potent dry martinis. When we finally sat down to breakfast the eggs and bacon swam dizzily before my eyes. Breakfast was followed by speeches in which various tough-looking tycoons proclaimed their belief in ethical business practices. I was asked to say a few words about our tea mission and had the greatest difficulty in standing up to fulfil this request. At 9.30 the tycoons repaired to their offices while Gourlay and I thankfully took the lift to lie on our beds until we embarked on our train for the East. Soon afterwards, Elspeth and I left Montreal for New York. It was my first visit to the United States and I found New York the most exciting and vital city I had ever been in. The Indian Tea interests from London had been conducting a small and quite futile promotion campaign in America on behalf of Indian tea, and the object of my visit was to explore the market so as to be able to persuade them to abandon their campaign in favour of a joint effort with Ceylon and the Dutch, on a scale large enough to revitalize the American tea trade and to show the American consumer that tea was not just a drink for invalids, cissies or the English, and that pouring warm water on to a little tea bag in an open cup did not produce a beverage worth drinking. Two days before Christmas we sailed for Southampton.

1933 had certainly been a memorable year for me and I had enjoyed almost every moment of it. Heaven knows how many thousand miles I had travelled. I had seen new countries, Ceylon, India and Kenya, and made a host of new acquaintances. What gave me most satisfaction was that I had succeeded in establishing a new organization with world-wide scope in the running of which I should have a free hand. Since the Empire Marketing Board had now come to an untimely end and Tallents gone to the Post Office to organize its information and publicity, I had every reason to be thankful for my luck.

ii

The five years that followed 1933 repeated much the same pattern of work and travel. I made a point of visiting all my tea promotion campaigns every year, and Elspeth normally travelled with me. We covered what was new ground to both of us in the Netherlands East Indies, Belgium, Holland and Scandinavia. We also usually managed to fit in a short holiday in Kenya after visits to South Africa. In London an International Tea Board representing India, Ceylon and the Netherlands East Indies was soon established with myself as its Chief executive and new campaigns were started in the U.S.A., Egypt, Holland, Belgium and Sweden. Satisfactory results in the way of increased tea consumption began to follow and our sponsors—the Governments and producers of the three countries—showed their appreciation by a steady increase in the cess they levied to support our expanding work. Elspeth was also beginning to make her name as an author. *White Man's Country*, as her life of Lord Delamere was called, was published by Macmillans in 1935 and was at once recognized as the definitive history of white settlement in East Africa. Three detective novels followed, all with Kenya backgrounds and mostly written on board ship as Elspeth's preferable alternative to playing shuffleboard. In due course she wrote what was to be one of the best of her books, *Red Strangers*, the story of the coming of the white man to Kenya and the impact made on African tribal society. Macmillans were all set to publish the book, but at the last moment they wrote to Elspeth that, while references to female circumcision would no doubt be appropriate in a Macmillan travel book, they might shock readers of a Macmillan novel. They had therefore arranged for one of the senior staff to rewrite the passages concerned. The resulting circumlocutions were so ludicrous that Elspeth wisely withdrew the book from Macmillans and offered it to Chatto and Windus who were Aldous' publishers and whose senior partner we knew. Chattos had no qualms about female circumcision. Since *Red Strangers*, Chattos have published all Elspeth's books.

Certain of our travels stand out in retrospect. The journey by boat down the Nile from Uganda to Khartoum is one. Another is a safari to the Ngoro-Goro crater and the Serengetti plains in Tanganyika, where the lions were so unafraid of man that we had no need of telescopic lenses to take close-up photographs of them from our cars.

But from all our travels the place that has stayed most vividly in my memory is the island of Bali where Elspeth and I stopped for several days on our way by a small Dutch boat from Sydney to Java. Bali looked even more entrancing than we had imagined as we drove across the island to Den

Pasar in the south where the Dutch had built a most comfortable hotel. Wherever the land was hilly, narrow terraces covered the slopes, some filled with water that reflected the sky, others green with young rice. In the irrigated fields on flat land buffaloes were ploughing the swampy earth, the ploughmen wearing mushroom straw hats, and in each field a flock of white ducks rootled in the mud, never straying far from a bamboo pole flying a white rag of a flag which served as their rallying point. In dry fields, men were harvesting the rice into small neatly tied sheaves. Men and women were a warm brown in colour, the women all bare-breasted above a tightly tied long skirt. They were as attractive as legend had portrayed them, small and slight with breasts uniformly round and firm. Women pounding rice with long poles, women sitting fashioning clay pots, women walking to market with produce-laden woven baskets on their heads ; all displayed grace and beauty. Shrines and temples, thickly covered with fantastic carvings of gods, men, devils and animals were everywhere. There was music and dancing, the music from the rows of percussion instruments of the Gamelong orchestras with their odd beat ; the dancing in graceful stylized postures with hands fluttering on stiffly extended arms. It seemed to be an idyllic island of happy smiling people whose way of life and all whose artefacts were infused with beauty, and where, as we saw in the village markets, the fruits of the earth were so abundant that we reckoned that a family could live well on the equivalent of a penny a day.

My responsibility for our Tea campaign involved a long annual visit to the United States. I did not believe that New York or Boston necessarily reflected the U.S.A. as a whole. I thought therefore that in order to direct a campaign aimed at influencing a social habit on a nation-wide scale, it was desirable that I should get the feel of all the different regions, and that this could not be done from the insulation of an air-conditioned train. So in order to acquire the contacts with people and places that travel by road would give me, I used to hire an open car for journeys that, one time or another, took Elspeth and me into almost every State in the Union. Our route generally took us first to Brandon on the James River in Virginia to stay with Otway and Maisie Byrd in their lovely old colonial house, unaltered since the days of slavery except for the installation of every modern comfort. Otway lived the life of a nineteenth-century English squire with his home farm, his duck shooting on the river and his annual fishing holiday, though in Canada instead of Scotland. In Virginia, too, I once had a memorable Whitsun weekend being conducted all over the Civil War battlefields by Douglas Southall Freeman, General Lee's biographer. Luckily I was well read on the subject having long been an admirer of Lee, Stonewall Jackson and Jeb Stuart. I was much impressed by the care with which the Americans preserved their historical monuments. Every battlefield was fully signposted with the disposition of the troops on both sides, and I had nowhere in the world seen anything comparable to the town of Williamsburg, completely recreated with the aid of Rockefeller money in every detail of its eighteenth-century colonial state, even to the furniture in the houses. Perhaps, I thought, if your country's history is only a short one, you take special care to preserve it. In Freeman's company I must have displayed a romantic sympathy with the Southern cause, as he presented me with the four volumes of his life of Lee with the inscription, 'I saw in your eyes the light that for generations has always shone when a Huxley gazed on the struggle of right against wrong, of the weak against the strong'.

South from Virginia came States where tea was then almost unknown except as a seasonal summer drink in the form of thirst-quenching iced tea. On the way to New Orleans we bathed in the Gulf of Mexico in a mud-coloured sea, the temperature of warm soup, and waded out for what seemed to be miles with the water only up to our waists. Crossing Texas we realized that State's huge expanse when, on leaving San Antonio, we came on a signpost reading 'El Paso, 708 miles'. Further north and west there was the fantastic scenery of Utah's Zion National Park, the steep sides of the mountains striped in layers of bright colours like a Neapolitan ice-cream, and, of course, the Grand Canyon, familiar from pictures and descriptions, but none the less breath-taking in the impact of its sheer size and depth.

iii

By means of my American travels I became familiar with the American way of life and began to understand the American outlook. I soon realized that the use of a common language could be an impediment rather than a help to mutual understanding. Because of it, English people tended to expect Americans to behave like Englishmen and to look at the world through English eyes, and they felt resentment when Americans did not do so. Englishmen also tended to forget how much of the population of the United States was of non-British stock, and that such people had no common historical ties with us, or, like the Irish, had good reason to dislike us. One needed, too, to visit some mid-western town like Wichita, Kansas, well over 1,000 miles from either the Atlantic or Pacific coasts, to understand how remote Europe and its problems must seem to its inhabitants, since neither air travel nor the rocket were yet shortening distances. In the commercial world in which I moved I certainly had some experiences which seemed very strange to my English eyes.

After my first exploratory visit I had told my sponsors that a promotion campaign with an annual expenditure of the order of a million dollars would be needed to make a worthwhile nation-wide impact on the American consumer and tea trade. Such an advertising appropriation was a large one even for America in those days of the depression. I therefore welcomed the proposal that before any final commitment was entered into, representatives of the Indian and Dutch tea interests should join me in visiting America to make a joint report.

My colleagues were Milligan, lately retired from the

A swarm of locusts on the Kenya-Uganda border,
photographed by G.H., 1938
Lions round a kill on the Serengeti Plains, Tanganyika,
photographed by Elspeth, 1938

NORTH YORK MOORS NATIONAL PARK · NORTHUMBERLAND NATIONAL PARK

NATIONAL PARKS

CAREW CASTLE, seen here in a water-colour by Paul Sandby (1725-1809), stands at the head of a tidal creek of Milford Haven in the Pembrokeshire Coast National Park. This lovely setting remains unspoiled to this day. The castle was probably founded by the Norman, Gerald de Windsor, Constable of Pembroke, but the present building is mostly late thirteenth century built by Sir Nicholas de Carew. The north front with its mullioned windows was reconstructed in Elizabethan times. The ten National Parks of England and Wales have been established to keep unspoiled such beautiful scenes so that we and our heirs may continue to enjoy this heritage, whatever changes in our way of life the future may bring.

OUR HERITAGE

When visiting the National Parks take care to observe the Country Code

Guard against all risk of fire · Fasten all gates · Keep dogs under proper control · Keep to the paths across farm land

Avoid damaging fences, hedges and walls · Leave no litter · Safeguard water supplies

Protect wild life, wild plants, and trees · Go carefully on country roads · Respect the life of the countryside

PEMBROKESHIRE COAST NATIONAL PARK · BRECON BEACONS NATIONAL PARK

A National Parks Commission poster; one of 'Our Heritage' series

Prepared for the National Parks Commission by the
Central Office of Information

Indian Civil Service, a stout lazy man more interested in his belly than in the problems of tea promotion about which he knew nothing, and Lageman, who had been a director of a plantation company in Java. The latter was an able, very correct and painstaking individual, but deeply imbued with the suspicion, common to many Dutchmen, that he was being got at. We crossed the Atlantic separately to meet in New York.

Shortly before Elspeth and I left London, in advance of my colleagues, Philip Jordan had introduced us at the Café Royal to an American Public Relations friend who displayed a great interest in our mission. He must have cabled to contacts in New York, since as soon as the Customs officials had boarded our liner on its way up the Hudson, a bell-boy knocked at our cabin door bearing a message asking me to see the Customs officers in the dining saloon. Being in the middle of packing I was not pleased by the summons and wondered what it could be about. My name was announced as I entered the saloon and I was somewhat taken aback when a Customs officer shook me warmly by the hand saying that he was happy to accord me the freedom of the port of New York by courtesy of the N. D. Ayer Advertising Company. Though Elspeth and I had nothing dutiable to declare, it was certainly convenient to march through the Customs Shed and reach our hotel while other passengers' luggage was still being examined.

Hardly had we unpacked in our hotel room before our telephone rang. The caller gave his name as George Palmer Putnam. He was, he said, a member of the publishing family and the husband of Amelia Earheart, who had become world famous through her solo flying exploits. Hearing of our arrival, he wanted to indulge his liking for the company of English visitors, and would we spend the next day—Sunday—at his house at Rye and meet Amelia Earheart? A friend of his would pick us up at our hotel in the morning. Having made no other plans, we accepted the invitation, though the whole business sounded rather fishy.

Next morning a very personable young man duly called

for us. During the drive to Rye, he mentioned that he was in advertising with a firm called William Esty. Coupling this piece of information with the greeting from the N. D. Ayer Company I realized that news of the prospective tea campaign must have reached Madison Avenue and that I was the rich prize which New York admen were anxious to secure. Somehow or other, Putnam must, I thought, be involved in the racket. However, we enjoyed a very pleasant Sunday at Rye. Putnam proved a perfect host and Amelia Earheart, with her short fair hair and boyish look, a most interesting person to meet. In an hour or two we were all on christian name terms in the American manner, and it was not until shortly before we left that George Putnam broached his interest in my mission. Had I yet appointed an advertising agency, he asked? When I told him that I was waiting to do so until my two colleagues arrived, he urged that before we came to any final decision I should make a point of visiting the William Esty agency. This I gladly undertook to do. In the next few days I had letters and telephone calls from a number of agencies and called on several of them, including the N. D. Ayer firm, who had the Ford Motor account. In none of them did I find the kind of approach to my tea problem that I felt would be the right one until I visited the Esty agency and talked to Bill Esty, its remarkable head. Esty had been one of the top executives in the huge J. Walter Thompson agency and had been responsible for the Lux soap advertising for the Lever combine in which he had been very successful by getting film stars to endorse the merits of the soap. In the belief that if he set up his own agency he would get the Lever account, he and his colleagues in the Lux team had broken away from J. Walter Thompson's only to find that Lever's preferred to stick to the latter. Esty had then vainly tried to secure other accounts and was down to his last few dollars when he heard that 'Camel' cigarettes were thinking of changing their agency as they had been losing ground to 'Lucky Strikes' in the fiercely competitive cigarette field where sales depended so much on the appeal of the advertising. 'Luckies' advertise-

ments had been successfully exploiting somewhat bogus
scientific claims for the properties of their cigarettes to the
intense annoyance of the Reynolds Corporation who owned
'Camels'. So Esty submitted to Reynolds an advertising
scheme which blew 'Luckies' claims sky high. Based on
illustrations explaining how conjuring tricks were performed—a topic which Esty knew would attract the attention of newspaper and magazine readers—the theme was
'its fun to be fooled', thus debunking the 'Lucky' advertising, and going on to say that what really mattered was that
'Camels' put the best tobacco into their cigarettes. The
Reynolds firm were so delighted with this that they gave
Esty their account, one of the largest in the United States.
As 'Camels' were soon outselling 'Luckies', the Esty
agency was very profitably established and had since
secured a few smaller accounts. I found myself very taken
with Bill Esty's completely objective and, indeed, cynical
approach to advertising. Here were none of the fine phrases
of service to the community and so forth, but an understanding of what really motivated people in the mass and of
how to exploit this understanding. Here, too, was a tough,
purely American approach such as I wanted to underly our
tea promotion in order to get right away from the prevalent
notion that tea was just an English beverage. It was typical
of Esty's outlook that he should have installed in the copy-
writer's room a large reproduction of a modern painting
of a popular Coney Island beach, packed with hideous
humanity enjoying a Sunday outing. 'Remember this is the
audience you are addressing'—was the injunction inscribed
in large letters below the picture. And Esty knew his advertising must appeal to such desires as keeping up with the
Joneses, satisfying some material want or following the example of success symbols such as All-American footballers
for men and film stars for women. I was also very much impressed by Esty's team, his art director, his head copy-
writer and his space buyer, and since Esty's had few other
accounts, we should be sure of his full personal attention.
Whatever George Putnam's motives may have been, and I

imagined that he would collect a commission from the Esty Agency, his advice, I thought, had been good.

When Milligan and Lageman arrived I found that the former had met a United States Senator on board the ship who had strongly recommended an advertising agency in which he had a financial interest. Milligan thought that, coming from such a source, the Senator's recommendation should be followed. Lageman, however, had become intensely suspicious of any form of approach. How then to get my colleagues to agree with me to appoint the Esty Agency? Going to Putnam I put my cards on the table, telling him that though I wanted the Esty agency, it was up to him to convince my two colleagues. A day or two later he telephoned that he had the answer. Would we all three go to tea on Sunday with his old friend, Mrs. Helen Ogden Reid, the publisher of the *New York Herald Tribune* newspaper, in her Park Avenue mansion?

My colleagues, who in the meantime had met through me George Putnam and Amelia Earheart, were flattered by the invitation and were duly impressed by the English butler who opened the door when we arrived and by the charm and dignity of Mrs. Ogden Reid. In the course of a very elegant and English tea, Putnam told Mrs. Reid about our mission. Since, he said, she must be well acquainted with the work of all the leading advertising agencies in her capacity as the *Herald Tribune*'s publisher, would she give us her independent advice on the Agency we should select? Mrs. Reid at first demurred on the grounds that it would be invidious for her to show a preference, but when pressed by Putnam said that she thought we should certainly consider the Esty Agency which she felt was very well qualified to undertake our work. How Putnam had arranged this performance I never asked, but it certainly worked. Milligan felt that here was a recommendation more valuable than that of his Senator, and even Lageman felt satisfied that Mrs. Reid's advice must be disinterested. The Esty Agency was therefore recommended as the advertising agency for the joint tea campaign in the report which we sent back to our sponsors, the report fully endorsing my views as to the need to join our forces in promoting tea as such, irrespective of its origin, backed by a million dollar a year expenditure.

The Esty appointment was one which I never regretted. Bill Esty's advertising flair was as good as I thought it would be, and in the course of the next ten years American consumption of Indian, Ceylon and Netherlands East Indies teas was doubled. It was through Esty, too, that I gained two notable recruits to assist in our campaign. One was Elmo Roper for our market research. His organization was the most reliable and had the highest standing among the American market and public opinion researchers—or 'pollsters' as they are now called—and the results of his research into American attitudes to tea were of invaluable assistance in helping to direct our campaign. Equally valuable was the other recruit in the person of Earl Newsom whose newly formed firm took charge of our Public Relations work. I was, I believe, his first client, though his work was so outstanding that later he numbered both Ford and Rockefeller among the important organizations who employed him. Both Elmo and Earl soon became and still are my very good personal friends, but it was with Bill Esty and his wife that Elspeth and I established our closest relations.

From those pre-war years I especially remember one other business experience that, to my English eyes, seemed the strangest of all. The American tea campaign had been running for a year or so, and Elspeth and I, back in New York, had just finished breakfast in our hotel room when the desk telephone rang to say that a Colonel somebody or other from Washington wanted urgently to see me. His name was unknown to me and I had no idea what he wanted but felt that I should find out by inviting him up. There entered a good-looking middle-aged man who informed me that he had come from the White House at the request of Mrs. Roosevelt whose personal representative he was. Mrs. Roosevelt, he said, would like to sponsor our tea campaign on the radio, and his car was waiting to drive Elspeth and myself to the White House to discuss this with her. I knew of course that the President's wife had been broadcasting on behalf of various products, including Beauty-Rest beds, her fees being given to one or other of her favourite charities, but I had no idea that such business arrangements were conducted on this kind of personal basis, which, as an Englishman, I found highly embarrassing. I therefore stalled by telling the Colonel that on all advertising matters I made a rule of being guided by my advertising agents whom I would consult on the proposition, or whom he should himself approach. The Colonel seemed very reluctant to accept this answer, repeating that it was a personal matter between Mrs. Roosevelt and myself and finally offering on her behalf that if I would accept the proposal Mrs. Roosevelt would give a series of tea parties at the White House to which members of the tea trade would be invited and some of which the President would attend in person. Feeling increasingly embarrassed I stuck to my guns and finally got rid of the Colonel and telephoned Esty. He seemed greatly relieved to hear that I had not fallen for the proposal, saying that as a commercial asset the First Lady's name stank and that her sponsorship of our campaign would do more harm than good. Esty, a fanatical republican in politics, loathed the Roosevelts and on this occasion I now think that his prejudices outweighed his better judgement and I regret that I never paid the visit to the White House.

Although Bill Esty shared his political views with most other American businessmen, no one could in other respects have been less typical of the breed. By nature reserved and a bad mixer, he had the strongest dislike for the hail-fellow heartiness of his business associates in advertising, and avoided all possible contact with them outside his office. I believe, indeed, that he was only happy to establish a personal relationship with Elspeth and myself because we were transient visitors from abroad and could not make any permanent intrusion into his private world. Whatever the reason we were given his full personal friendship. He was now just on forty, having been old enough to serve in France in the war where he had been badly gassed. His first wife had recently died leaving him with a boy and a girl of eleven and nine and he had married Alice as his second wife. Of Swedish descent she not only had great beauty, but was also musically talented with a lovely contralto voice. She was, too, very sweet-natured and highly competent. In New York the Esty's had an apartment overlooking the East River but it was their home in New Canaan, Connecticut, that formed the centre of their family life and it was there that Elspeth and I spent most weekends when we were in New York. Bill was a crime expert with an encyclopaedic knowledge of American and British murder trials and his bookshelves were filled with books on the subject together with detective novels. He was greatly pleased when Elspeth dedicated the American edition of her *Murder on Safari* to him and Alice. Coming from an academic background, Bill was also a mine of odd historical and geographical information, and meals were always enlivened by 'quizzes' for the benefit of the children to whom he was devoted. He took a special pleasure in anything that had a cynical twist and had amassed a fine collection of blue and white English eighteenth-century household pottery which the enterprising Staffordshire potters had decorated with portraits of Washington, Jefferson and other American Revolutionary heroes and inscribed with American patriotic slogans, in order to sell them to America at the time of the American War of Independence. Bill thought that this was a very happy example of British commercial skill.

iv

Although we were spending much more of each year on our travels abroad than in England, Elspeth and I soon got tired of living in furnished rooms when we were in London, so we leased a pleasant, airy, unfurnished flat on the top floor of a new block in Kensington, where we were able to entertain our friends. Our English weekends were always spent in the country. Occasionally we would again go tramping over the South Downs, but usually we went to my father's on Boars Hill or to Balcombe Place in Sussex. My father had now given up his part-time consulting work in London to the great grief of his devoted patients, and his farm had become his chief interest. Until her very happy marriage in 1935 to Geoffrey Cooke who worked in the Bank of England, my younger sister Anne lived with her father, and all his children and grandchildren continued to pay him frequent visits. He made many friends, too, among his interesting neighbours on Boars Hill such as Arthur Evans, the famous archaeologist and Reginald Conpland, the historian. No one, indeed, who met him could fail to be drawn by the simple sincerity of his character, wholly devoid of any pretence and deeply understanding of the human condition and tolerant of its failings. He had taken to Elspeth at once and her writing and our travels were a great interest to him. As with most old people he liked punctuality, order and regularity. I can remember the ingenious way by which he overcame the nuisance of Anne's dog's dilatoriness in returning to the house when let out last thing at night. Attaching a fishing line on a reel to the dog's collar, he reeled the dog in like a fish.

Balcombe, our other frequent weekend resort, was the home of Lady Denman, one of my mother-in-law's oldest and closest friends. 'Trudie' Denman was one of the really great women of our times. Her father, Weetman Pearson, the first Lord Cowdray, had turned the small family business of S. Pearson & Sons which he inherited into one of the world's greatest contracting firms, building docks, harbours, dams and railways all over the globe. More important than the great wealth with which he had endowed his only daughter, Trudie had inherited much of the character and qualities that had enabled Weetman Pearson to create his empire—his integrity, judgement, drive and perseverance and his liberal outlook. Married off at nineteen by her socially ambitious mother to thirty-three-year-old Lord Denman, then a rising hope of the Liberal Party of which the Pearsons were staunch adherents, Trudie had spent nearly four unhappy years in Australia where Denman was Governor-General from 1911 to 1914, in the growing realization of how unsuited to each other she and her husband were, though their marriage was never broken up.

One of her ruling traits was a passionate sense of justice, especially on behalf of women. In Australia she had seen something of the hard, dull and often lonely lives of the women in the 'outback', and on her return home she took up the cause of English and Welsh country women, becoming in 1915 the first Chairman of the newly formed Women's Institute movement. In 1916 only twenty-four Institutes had been formed, but by 1936 after twenty years of Trudie's dynamic leadership their number had grown to over 5,500 with more than 350,000 members. Nor was it only in bringing fresh interests and opportunities into the lives of country women that Trudie inspired the movement. She also made the Women's Institutes exercise a very considerable influence on national and rural policies.

The same determination to better the lot of her fellow women made Trudie in 1930 take up the second great interest in her life, when she became the first Chairman of the National Birth Control Council at a time when family planning was very far from being the respectable and openly discussed subject it has since become. The 3,000-acre Balcombe Estate had been a present to Trudie from her father in 1905. The house, Balcombe Place, solidly built in stone in Victorian-Elizabethan style, had no external distinction but was immensely and unpretentiously comfortable. Trudie's sense of humour, her love of simple things, her indifference to wealth or social pretensions and her interest in people, all combined to make weekends at Balcombe a delightful experience. The atmosphere was always gay, the small circle of fellow guests was composed of thoroughly agreeable friends, and the talk stimulating and amusing. Trudie was a devotee of golf and tennis, so these formed part of our weekend occupations as did her other pastime of collecting wood and making bonfires.

In spite of having such pleasant weekends at Boars Hill

or Balcombe, always available to us when we were in England, Elspeth and I had begun to hanker for a permanent country house of our own. We wanted it to be within easy motoring reach of Oxford and my father, and after much searching we were lucky enough to find in 1938 an old farmhouse with fifty acres of land at the edge of the then completely unspoilt village of Oaksey in pleasant, open though flat, country half-way between Cirencester and Malmesbury and just over the Wiltshire border from Gloucestershire. Oaksey, besides being near enough by road to my father, had the great advantage of being within four miles of Kemble Station whence non-stop trains ran to London in an hour and a half. Woodfolds, as our house was called, had been built about 1670 in the Cotswold grey stone with the Cotswold stone-tiled roof that gave such charm to the simplest of farmhouses. It had been left untouched since it was built and had neither water, drainage or lighting, but Thomas Rayson, our architect friend from Oxford who had refused for various reasons to allow us to buy a number of other houses we had looked at, found it structurally sound and at once saw its possibilities. The price at which we bought it at auction was such a low one, even for those days, that we could afford to give Rayson a free hand in making additions and alterations and in installing all modern conveniences. It was, however, not until shortly before the outbreak of war in 1939 that Elspeth and I were able to move in. Ever since, Woodfolds has been our most happy and comfortable home.

CHAPTER VIII

i

A<small>T</small> the time of the Munich crisis I was flying back from South Africa to Kenya to join Elspeth before we both returned to London. At Njoro I found two letters awaiting me. One was from Stephen Tallents to say that he had been asked by the Government to draw up plans for setting up a Ministry of Information in case of war. He wanted to enlist his old E.M.B. publicity team and would I get in touch with him as soon as I got home. The other letter was from Sir John Reith, who had recently left the B.B.C. to become head of Imperial Airways. He asked me whether I was willing to be considered for the appointment of Imperial Airways' 'public relations officer with responsibility equivalent to that of Sir Stephen Tallents at the B.B.C.' I had no wish to desert Tea and I also knew of the frustrations that Tallents had suffered under Reith at the B.B.C. when he had gone there from the Post Office. I thought, however, that in process of refusing Reith's offer I might have a good opportunity to air certain public relations' principles which I had imbibed from Earl Newsom and from my own experience.

It was a subject in which I had become increasingly interested. How did I define 'Public Relations' and why did I think that the subject was important? My definition of 'Public Relations' was what the name implied, the relations of an organization, whether a business, or a Government Department or, as in the case of tea, a whole industry, with all the 'publics' with which it came in contact, employees, shareholders, local communities, customers, as well as the public at large. Such relations had, of course, always existed as part of man's relationship to man. But some seventy years earlier a Frenchman named Le Bon had written a book in which he had stated that 'the destinies of nations are elaborated in the heart of the masses and no longer in the councils of princes', and that 'the divine right of the masses is about to replace the divine right of Kings'. Le Bon had called his book *The Era of Crowds*. He might equally have called it the era of public opinion, and this passing of sovereignty from individuals and small groups of people to the masses was the reason for the conscious emergence of 'Public Relations' and their practice. Any institution which hoped to prosper in the new social and economic climate had now to gain the confidence of people ; and it was a task which had grown increasingly important with power and responsibility tending to become more and more concentrated in large units, with huge industrial organizations replacing small individual business enterprises, and with Governments continually enlarging their functions and impinging ever more widely on the daily lives of the governed. The larger the unit the more remote from people it became, the managerial responsibility in the human field the more complex, and the consequences of failure to discharge this responsibility the more serious.

It had been in the U.S.A. in 1903 that 'Public Relations' had begun to attain recognition as a subject worth studying, when a young New York journalist named Ivy Lee had set himself up as a publicity man for business. It was a time when big business had become dominant over the life of the nation, and being committed to the proposition that the less the public knew of its operations the better, had so alienated public opinion that muck-raking and trust-busting were the order of the day. Big business had then begun to discover that a high-handed disregard for public opinion could be badly damaging. No industry has been more contemptuous of public opinion than the anthracite coal owners, and public opinion led by the Press had moved overwhelmingly on the side of the workers who had in consequence been able to achieve a real victory. In 1906 the industry called in Ivy Lee to its aid. He proceeded to change the course of corporate relations by demonstrating the usefulness of full information, accurately and attractively given to all the 'publics' concerned through all the media of mass communication.

He considered that business needed a new kind of lawyer, not merely one who defended his clients in court, but one who counselled his client how to act so as to avoid trouble with the public as well as with the law. His summing-up of his work for the Pennsylvania Railway, whose reputation with the public had also been outstandingly bad and who also retained Lee in 1906, was that he had taught the management to gain the goodwill of the public by deserving it, since he maintained that an elementary requisite of any sound publicity must be the giving of the best possible service. A little later he was persuaded to advise the Rockefeller family on their publicity problems. They were among the most maligned of America's millionaires, their reputation being that of close-fisted, ruthless exploiters of their fellow men. They were also among the most reticent in replying publicly to any criticism. Lee gave them a public hearing and made John D. Rockefeller understood and respected as a man who gave hundreds of millions of dollars to charities, instead of being regarded as a sinister corporate machine.

Lee was also the original public relations counsellor for some of the world's largest and wealthiest corporations such as Standard Oil, Bethlehem Steel, the Chrysler corporation, American Tobacco and others, advising his clients on the actions he thought they should take in order to achieve public goodwill. For his day the nature of his advice was often radical. He urged American Tobacco, for instance, to start a profit-sharing plan. He advised the Pennsylvania Railway to beautify its stations, to install more safety equipment and to pay top wages. He counselled the banks to divorce savings deposit banking from speculative investment banking. He told the Movie industry to stop inflated advertising. Above all he advised all his clients to establish adequate channels of communication on a two-way basis between management and its various 'publics' so that understanding could be achieved. Ivy Lee died in 1934, but not before he left the legacy to the new profession of public relations that in a free and democratic society no person, product or policy could succeed without public acceptance, and that public acceptance could not be dictated but must be earned.

In spite of the spread of Ivy Lee's philosophy I had found that even in America and far more in Britain the subject of Public Relations was surrounded by ignorance and prejudice and its practitioners often thought of as charlatans, a reputation which indeed some of them brought on themselves. Many people believed that Public Relations was just another and more respectable-sounding name for publicity and that the chief function of public relations practitioners was to create some entirely contrived situation, event or story, usually about some show-business personality, which the Press would then headline.

At the other end of the scale was my brother-in-law, Sir Edward Harding, the permanent head of the Dominions Office, who informed me in all seriousness that his information officer was so good at his job of keeping the Press away from the Department and its work that there had not been a mention of it in the Press for the last twelve months. In between there was the very commonly held belief in business circles that public relations practice consisted in devising some ingenious stunt to beguile newspaper editors into printing, free of charge, news about a product that should have properly gone into the editorial waste-paper basket or have been paid for in the advertising columns. This attitude was encouraged by some newspaper advertisement managers who, in the competition to attract advertisers, would offer free editorial publicity as an added inducement to taking advertising space.

As I saw it, Public Relations were an integral function of management itself, and an understanding of the subject formed an important element in managerial thinking and policy formation. It followed that the responsibility for public relations should either be placed at top management level or that the officer concerned should have a status that gave him direct access to the managerial heads in order that he could advise them authoritatively on all the factors likely to affect a situation before and not after policy was decided and action taken. I believed, indeed, that for public relations to be forced on to the defensive was to lose the battle. To be successful they must be dynamic and hold the initiative. American practice was already recognizing this and was placing a special Public Relations responsibility on a member of the Board of Directors. But in Britain successful Public Relations seemed to depend on the degree of understanding the head of an organization possessed of the subject. For instance my association with Frank Pick had shown me how in his position of Managing Director of London's Tubes and Buses, the public relations activities that he personally inspired had helped to win public goodwill. Another good instance, I felt, of top public relations thinking, had been in the Post Office where Tallents, as its Information head, had found in Kingsley Wood, a sympathetic and understanding Postmaster-General. With his backing Tallents had been successful in getting the Post Office a greatly improved and up-to-date image, his efforts including attention to such details as the quality of the ink and pens for use by the public in post offices.

Public Relations functions, I believed, fell under four main heads. To understand the changing points of view of the various groups of people with whom an organization was involved; to impart clearly that understanding to managements; competently to estimate reactions to an organization's actions and to be on the alert to suggest desirable ones; to do a really effective job in the whole field and range of human communications. It was under this last head that I thought the success or failure of Public Relations basically lay. Communications were the cement that held society together. Rumour was the disease that spread its infection when communication broke down, rumour being negative communication that could only be cured by positive communication. I was and still am convinced that most trouble in human relationships is caused by a failure in communication and that the study and practice of communication techniques, including semantics, should be the special responsibility of Public Relations, the scope ranging from guiding and inspiring the direct contact of individuals, which would always form the most important of all channels, through the whole field of the spoken word, the written word and visual presentation. Like charity, Public Relations, in my view, began at home in the sphere of personnel management and I believed that it was in the failure of managements to establish effective communications with employees that the root cause of most industrial trouble lay.

There were other general principles that needed to be understood. The commonly held fallacy, for instance, that all that was needed was to 'educate' the public in the facts. Unfortunately people would not just stand still to be 'educated'. The majority had neither the time nor the inclination to listen. Moreover, all evidence seemed to show that most people's opinions were emotional attitudes which they shared with groups of people with whom they wanted consciously or subconsciously to be identified. Ideas and opinions could, I thought, only be sold firstly if they were seen clearly to affect personal interests, hopes or fears. Otherwise it was like trying to sell ice-cream to Eskimoes.

Secondly, I believed that people were not likely to buy ideas divorced from action. Very few were interested in abstract notions, and actions would always speak louder than words. Thirdly, it seemed that people tended to buy ideas and opinions only from those they trusted. Individuals and organizations had first to gain public confidence before they could hope to put over their viewpoints.

Another principle was that Public Relations should resist getting too much involved in public arguments. The trouble about arguments, especially arguments in public, is that they often become contests in which people with no very strong prior opinions on a subject find themselves hotly defending their point of view and acquiring a vested interest in a position so that it becomes a matter of 'face' to maintain it.

There is, too, a tendency for public relations practitioners to make the organization they work for look like a gigantic

G.H., Cleggie and Charles at Woodfolds, 1960

Woodfolds from the garden

G.H. in 1967 age 73

stuffed shirt. When thinking about our own organization we are all apt to lose our sense of proportion and become awed in our own presence. Public confidence, I felt, was much more likely to be won by a natural, friendly, unpretentious and colloquial approach, provided that in trying to play down to an audience one avoided revealing a secret belief in its inferiority. Only very recently the Post Office has given a striking example of how not to conduct public relations by the manner in which it sought to gain public goodwill to the introduction of its two-tier postal service. Its approach to the public aimed at being colloquial but was only patronizing ; humbug was employed to try to conceal the patent fact that letters would cost more ; and the action that followed, initially at least, belied the improved service that the public was promised.

I was, of course, well aware that no organization could expect to exist and move and achieve its ends without courting some trouble for itself. But Public Relations consciousness should learn to distinguish those unfavourable attitudes which would be vital from those which would be inevitable but not vital. Above all, I believed that the first lesson in public relations practice was to learn when to hold off. Shouting too loudly only made people deaf. Sitting tight, taking no action, was, I felt, often the best answer to a public relations problem. But such 'inaction' must be a positive 'action' deliberately undertaken and not just the result of inertia.

It was with a summary of these views that I regaled a rather startled Reith and Clive Pearson, a member of his Imperial Airways Board, at lunch at Brooks' Club when I got back to London. As a frequent passenger on Imperial Airways I had formed some very definite views on the managerial policies, attitudes and methods which would best encourage the travelling public to take to flying and which would be most effective in disabusing the quite prevalent idea embodied in the catch-phrase, 'if you've time to spare, go by air'.

I knew that it was only from on top that my views would

have a chance of gaining acceptance, so I told Reith that I would only consider the appointment he was offering if, as Public Relations Chief, I had a seat on the Board or, at least, was given the right to have a full voice in any policy-making. I was well aware that such an attitude was far from what Reith would be looking for in his public relations officer, but I had been given the opportunity of airing my views and was not in the least surprised at being spared the choice of having to leave Tea, nor by Reith's subsequent appointment of the kind of tame cat that he had apparently hoped to find in me.

ii

As soon as I had got back to London I had written to Tallents in the expectation of working with him on the plans for a war-time Ministry of Information, in response to the invitation he had sent me when I was in Africa.

It was with dismay that I now learned that the first draft plans which he had submitted had been contemptuously rejected, and that the assignment had been given to the Public Trustee, no doubt a worthy civil servant, but without the slightest experience of the subject. Tallents' unorthodoxy and his success in getting away with unbureaucratic conduct had done him no good in bureaucratic circles. His plans had envisaged the recruitment of a small but experienced skeleton staff, each of whose functions would be capable of expansion in the event of war in such direction as circumstances might dictate. How much folly, waste and confusion would have been avoided if the Ministry had started its work along the modest and sensible lines that Tallents had recommended. But this was not to be.

Cecil King in his autobiography has told how he offered his very considerable experience for the formation of a Ministry of Information, only to discover the 'immutable principle' that 'no one at the Ministry of Information must know anything about propaganda, popular opinion, mass communications or anything of the kind!' Cecil King's indictment was only too true as I was to find, and I am only surprised that I should have been invited to take part in the planning.

One day early in 1939 I had a letter from Sir Campbell Stuart, a Director of *The Times*, asking if I would go and see him. He was a cousin of my Canadian Aunt Bessie, the wife of my mother's youngest brother, Harry Stobart, but I had not previously met him. Campbell Stuart seemed to be living in a world surrounded by potential spies, as during our talk he surprised me by suddenly jumping up to open the door of his office to make sure that no one was eaves-dropping. Pledging me to secrecy he told me that the Government had set up a small committee to draw up the detailed plans for a war-time Ministry of Information and that I was invited to join this Committee. When I began to attend regular meetings of the Committee at a house in Belgravia, I was surprised to find that none of my fellow planners seemed to have any experience or qualifications for our task, though determined to ensure that a full-fledged Ministry of Information, completely staffed in every depart-ment down to the last typist, should be able to spring into instant action the hour war was declared.

Unfortunately none of us knew what shape a war might take or to meet what needs the Ministry's efforts should be directed. As Cecil King has written, 'it was a lunatic set-up'. To give an instance of my Committee's deliberations; at one meeting in the spring the subject of posters was raised, to be printed ready for display the day war broke out. When asked for my opinion, I replied that posters were not de-signed *in vacuo*, but were a medium to carry some brief specific message, and that until we were sure what message was needed we should refrain from committing ourselves. This was very coldly received and I could see that I had destroyed my reputation as a poster expert.

Sure enough, the moment war was declared, a complete Ministry occupying the Senate House of London University started to function. It was, however, only the 'phoney' war that was waged for the first six months, when exhortatory messages to the public were quite futile and almost the whole Ministry a waste of time and money. Naturally the Press were quick to hold up to ridicule the whole set-up with its huge staff swarming round like aimless ants. I was fortunate in that my reputation had by then sunk so low that I was given no executive post and was only asked to become a member of a so-called 'Brains Trust' in the Ministry's Home Division. My fellow members of this 'Brains Trust' were Richard Crossman, Gordon Selfridge junior and Lady Grigg. I never discovered, nor I think did my colleagues, what our exact functions were supposed to be. I could only imagine that we were there to sit hatching out bright ideas. If so we were a failure and I very soon got so exasperated at the utter futility of my position that I sent in my resignation.

My Tea Board had generously agreed to free me to do any war work while continuing to pay my full salary, provided that I would keep a watching brief over Tea promotion. We had decided to continue, for the time being at least, all our campaigns except that in the United Kingdom. There we felt that, with the probability of tea being rationed, we should stop all our consumer advertising. On the other hand I was anxious that we should not indefinitely neglect tea's most important market, especially since advertising for other beverages such as cocoa was being increased. I thought, therefore, that public relations might be employed to keep tea's virtues prominently before the public through identifying them with the war effort. Many of our United Kingdom staff were, of course, joining the Forces, but Barnes, my Bureau's energetic head would be available, together with Hereward Phillips, its able Public Relations Officer. With them I looked for opportunities whereby tea could give war services that would merit and attract public attention and approval.

One thing that struck us was that large numbers of small Home Defence Units, such as anti-aircraft, searchlight and balloon-barrage posts, were being scattered all over the country in lonely and isolated spots far from shops or cafés and out of reach of static canteens. What we felt was needed was to bring canteen services to such posts by means of mobile vans, the tea being brewed at a depot and carried on the vans in a new form of insulated urn which our Bureau had recently developed. But the idea of mobile canteens was completely novel and no one had any experience of how to build and run them. In order to gain experience and demonstrate their utility we agreed that we should ourselves build and run a few prototypes. We also felt that we ought to find the right body to sponsor the 'Tea Cars', as we decided to call them, if, as we hoped, we could prove that they filled a real need. The most suitable sponsor seemed to be the Y.M.C.A., as the largest of the voluntary organizations that would be giving canteen services to the Forces. Sir Alfred Pickford, the Chairman of my International Tea Board, and I, therefore approached the Secretary of the Y.M.C.A.'s National Council, offering to provide and run four Tea Cars under the Y.M.C.A.'s name and auspices. Our approach was sympathetically received, and before September was out Pickford and I were able to make a formal presentation to the Y.M.C.A. of the first Y.M.C.A. Tea Car, which started working from the Y.M.C.A. centre at Plaistow in the East End of London. Within two days the officers commanding the Anti-Aircraft and Balloon-Barrage sites in the area had given the scheme their official blessing, and their men were welcoming the Tea Car as a godsend. We at once purchased and equipped three more cars. Besides tea they carried writing paper, books, cigarettes, sweets and snacks. At the end of a month the success of the Cars was fully established and, with the tea selling at 1d. per cup, we had shown that they could be operated at a small profit. The Y.M.C.A. were so delighted at the excellent advertisement for their war service that the Cars were giving that they decided to adopt them as an integral part of their war effort and to include them in their appeals for funds. They also invited Pickford and myself to become members of their War Emergency Committee.

Meantime, however, our Y.M.C.A. Tea Car project had

been rapidly gathering impetus. By the end of 1939 forty Tea Cars were in service and many more in production, all except the first four built and equipped from Y.M.C.A. funds and manned by Y.M.C.A. voluntary workers. In February the first convoy of specially built and equipped Y.M.C.A. Tea Cars joined the British Expeditionary Force in France after having been inspected by the King and Queen in the forecourt of Buckingham Palace. I was present at the inspection and was very much impressed by the interest the King and Queen took and by the thoroughness of their inspection. The Tea Cars proved to be as popular with the troops in France as they were at home and their work attracted even wider publicity for the Y.M.C.A. and for Tea.

It was, however, in the bombing Blitz on Britain that the Tea Cars most dramatically proved their worth, their unpaid women drivers working day and night in the big cities and risking life and limb, while the bombs were still falling, to bring not only hot tea and food but also heartening comfort and cheer to the cold and homeless victims amidst the wreck of their homes, and to the fire-fighters and Air Raid Wardens digging in the rubble for survivors. By this time the Y.M.C.A. had some 500 Tea Cars in service, and other organizations such as the Church and Salvation Armies and the Women's Voluntary Services had also begun to build and run similar mobile canteens. Fourteen Y.M.C.A. Tea Cars were destroyed by bombs in the Blitz and twenty-four badly damaged, but the work of the Tea Cars was so much appreciated that the Lord Mayor of London's National Air Raid Distress Fund made a special donation of £10,000 to the Y.M.C.A. 'in recognition of the losses sustained in course of the widespread service of the Y.M.C.A. mobile canteens to the civil population throughout the country'. By the end of August 1941 the Y.M.C.A. had been enabled to put over a thousand Tea Cars into service, at a capital cost of several hundred thousand pounds—all as a result of our initial contribution of £3,000 for the four prototypes.

In London during the Blitz I usually took a room in the

Cumberland Hotel where I felt no need to disturb my night's rest by going down to a shelter when the sirens sounded. Most Friday evenings I was able to get down to Woodfolds for the weekend. On its formation I had joined the Oaksey platoon of the Local Defence Volunteers—the precursors of the Home Guard—armed initially with pikes and our own sporting shot guns. Most of us were World War I veterans and through weekend nights with them I got to know and appreciate the sterling qualities of my village neighbours, almost all agricultural workers.

Meantime, Elspeth had become one of Wiltshire's organizers of the Women's Land Army, whose national head was Trudie Denman. At Woodfolds we had our own hens and ducks to supplement our food rations, and our American friends kept on sending such a generous supply of food parcels throughout the war that we were always able to help out our less-fortunate neighbours. But our most memorable instance of American generosity came from Bill Esty. Shortly after the fall of France, when all America was expecting Hitler successfully to invade England, I got a note from Bill. It read as follows : 'Gervas, please remember that I have ready to forward anywhere you say, any time you say, up to ten thousand dollars in any currency you would want. Alice knows nothing of this ; it's just between you and me, dear Gervas.'

The second sphere in which we set out to help Tea make a special contribution to the war effort was in the factories. Our work here lacked the dramatic quality of the Tea Cars and was much less publicized, but it was of real assistance to war-time production on the home front, as well as to the future of tea consumption in the United Kingdom.

The shock of the fall of France and the loss of all our Expeditionary Force's weapons made the whole nation conscious that only a colossal and unprecedented production effort could re-equip the Army and strengthen the Air Force in time to avert disaster. In response to the call the factories were now working night and day, often under the handicap of the bombing of our industrial centres. Realizing that good food and refreshment for the workers was a necessity if production was going to be increased, the Government passed a Bill making it obligatory for all factories employing more than 250 people on war production to provide a canteen for their workers. Official appeals were also made to make the fullest use of existing factory canteens. The needs of the day swept away former apathy on the part of managements towards the idea of rest breaks with refreshments. Their difficulty now was that they had neither the knowledge nor the time to devote to planning efficient canteen and refreshment services, and experienced caterers or catering advisers were very scarce. It seemed to Barnes and myself that here lay an opportunity for our Tea Bureau to help fill the gap by providing industry with a free catering advisory service and that Tea could thus make a further contribution to the national war effort. In the late autumn of 1940 I therefore formed a special branch of our Bureau called National Catering Services. Barnes recruited to its staff a number of men and women with practical catering experience, headed by Clifford Gardiner from a leading firm of catering equipment manufacturers. It had been Gardiner who had developed the insulated urn which had formed the basis of all our mobile tea services. Although our role in the factory sphere was to be an advisory one, I decided that in order that our advisory services should be firmly based on first-hand experience of war-time in-factory catering problems and costings, we should ourselves undertake all the catering operations in a few typical large factories. At the beginning of 1941 we therefore made ourselves responsible for the complete canteen and refreshment services in a new factory in the Midlands employing 7,000 people engaged on the building of fighter aircraft and working day and night shifts seven days a week. The management had been in difficulties over their canteen arrangements, and production was being adversely affected, the new canteen being only partially equipped and its staff untrained. No more arduous task could then have faced our National Catering Services for their initial assignment in supplying good hot meals in the canteen at midday and midnight for the shift workers, special meals in directors', executive and clerical dining-rooms and quick tea-trolley services to the workers at their benches during all mid-shift breaks. But our staff gained invaluable experience and data, amongst the latter being the fact that large-scale selling of tea at a penny a cup yielded a very substantial profit which could be used to improve and cheapen the main meals in the canteen.

On the purely advisory side our National Catering Services' first assignment was with the fifty Royal Ordnance factories, employing over 500,000 workers. They were in trouble over their tea and snack services, for which we devised a time-saving and efficient trolley service. Other requests for our free advisory services quickly followed, and before long we felt we had enough experience to produce a concise and practical text-book which we called *Canteens at Work*. Published by the Oxford University Press, the book was accorded a very warm welcome by the Ministry of Supply, the Trades Union Congress and the Federation of British Industries, and led to many more requests for our advisory services. By the end of the war our Catering Services branch, equipped with its own drawing office for plans, had been employed by more than 3,000 large factories covering a very wide range of industries, each with its own catering problems, while we ourselves were operating the complete canteen and tea services in five diverse factories. What war-time experience had conclusively proved to managements was that quick and efficient mid-shift tea services did, as we had claimed, improve production, reduce absenteeism through illness and make for better labour relations. Mid-shift factory tea services were now firmly established for the post-war era.

CHAPTER IX

i

The entry of the United States into the war brought to all of us in Britain the happy certainty that, however gloomy the present outlook, final victory must eventually be ours. So far as my own destinies were concerned, Pearl Harbour was, to my great surprise, to take me back into the Ministry of Information and to give me the most interesting work I had ever undertaken.

In the middle of July 1942, I got a letter from Cyril Radcliffe, later Lord Radcliffe, the Director-General of the Ministry, asking if I would go and see him. I had had no contact with the Ministry since I had left it nearly three years earlier. I knew that it had proved the graveyard of successive Ministers and Director-Generals, amongst the latter my old friend Frank Pick, but I had also heard that, with the appointment of Brendan Bracken as Minister and Radcliffe as Director-General, a transformation had been effected and that the Ministry was now an efficient, smooth-running body.

I had met Radcliffe once or twice before the war at the house of mutual friends and had been very much impressed by what I had seen of him. It had been clear that he had a brilliantly sharp brain which had given him a high reputation as a lawyer, and I had also found him a man of wit and considerable charm as well as of formidable force of character.

When I called at the Ministry, he told me that America was beginning to send over for training in England increasing numbers of their armed forces and that the responsibility for good relations between our civilian population and the arriving Americans had been given to the Lord President of the Council, Sir John Anderson, who had appointed a small committee under Sir Edward Grigg (later

Lord Altrincham) to take charge of this assignment. Its first act had been to issue a widely publicized appeal for the names of would-be hosts who wished to offer hospitality to the visitors. The response had been so overwhelming as completely to swamp the resources of Grigg's office, but the members of the American forces seemed very reluctant to ask for invitations and the would-be hosts were now indignantly demanding why no acknowledgment or response was forthcoming to their offers of hospitality.

The whole business had got into such a muddle that Bracken and his Ministry of Information were now being asked to take over the responsibility. It was evident that Radcliffe knew about my past experience and that I was familiar with American thought and ways, and he asked me if I would be interested in rejoining the Ministry to take on the assignment working directly under him and Bracken. It was a challenge that I felt I could not possibly refuse, but I stipulated that I would only come in a voluntary capacity and must be free to devote some time to my Tea and Y.M.C.A. obligations.

A week later I had rejoined the Ministry and had my first meeting with Brendan Bracken. His appearance was, indeed, a remarkable one, with a round boyish face under a wild thatch of improbable and very light hair. What at once greatly attracted me was the friendly warmth of his personality and his informality. My admiration and affection for him only increased as time went on and I had never met a chief for whom it was more fun to work. It proved, too, to be rewarding to be under someone who was so close to the Prime Minister that his views on any subject had a good chance of immediate acceptance. Much as I admired Amery it had always been a disadvantage that he often failed to carry his Cabinet colleagues with him.

No two men could have been more dissimilar than Bracken and Radcliffe, but each complemented the other's qualities and between them they had certainly succeeded in turning the Ministry into a very different place from the one I had left in despair. Even their combination could not prevent the petty jealousies, backbiting and jockeying for position that went on amongst some of the staff in so large an organization, but I was very fortunate in that, thanks to my Tea Board's generosity in continuing to pay my full salary, I was outside any competition for place or pay.

The transfer of the responsibility for our civilian population's relations with the American forces was very much welcomed inside the Ministry and I had gathered that the American Division expected that they would be placed in charge. In the plans, however, that I formed and that I now outlined to Bracken and Radcliffe, I had other views. I told them that I believed that it was folly for any central authority to try to arrange hospitality for our American visitors in their thousands and that I was not in the least surprised at the failure of the attempt, since few self-respecting American soldiers would be likely to accept 'blind dates' with people, who in popular American belief, would turn out to be 'snooty Limeys'. I felt therefore that the whole procedure should be scrapped.

My conviction was that personal contacts must form the first channel through which to establish relations that would lead to friendship and hospitality. But personal contacts could only be made at ground level in the localities where the American troops were stationed. As at a dance, local 'Paul Jones'' were needed to break down initial barriers. Fortunately the Ministry had its own Information Officers and staffs in the Regions into which war-time Britain had been divided. They should, I thought, furnish the basis for local contacts, to further which they should enlist the help of the local branches of the voluntary societies such as the Y.M.C.A., the Women's Voluntary Services, the Church and Salvation Armies, the English Speaking Union, the Women's Institutes, many of whom were active in providing amenities for our own Forces. Our own role at the Ministry's Headquarters should be confined to keeping in close touch with our Regional Information officers and to winning the support of the headquarters of the Voluntary Societies so that they should get their local branches to work in with our

Regional Information officers in taking every opportunity of making contact with the Americans. Bracken should, I recommended, himself preside at an immediate meeting of all our Regional Information officers, who would subsequently meet with me regularly, while I undertook to sound out the headquarters of the Voluntary Societies with the object of their heads attending an early meeting with Bracken and thereafter meeting him at a monthly Conference when they could discuss with us any difficulties or problems that had arisen. Since the Regional Information Officers came under the Ministry's Home Division I proposed that I should be attached to it. No new department or organization would need to be set up and all that I would want would be an office room and a secretary. From my talks with Radcliffe I had gathered that he had been thinking much along these lines and he and Bracken fully endorsed my recommendations. I felt sorry to disappoint the Ministry's American Division whose staff seemed both efficient and likeable, the more since I had not found the head of the Home Division a particularly sympathetic character. Fortunately his number two, Henry Maxwell, was a most delightful and amusing man with whom it would be a real pleasure to collaborate.

In the event our plans seemed to work out very well. Our Regional Information Officers were enthusiastic, and I got the promise of their fullest support from the heads of all the Voluntary Societies. Lady Reading, the formidable chief of the Women's Voluntary Services, with whom I dined in her house in Grosvenor Square, going so far as to assign one of her best lieutenants, Elsa Dunbar, to take special charge of the W.V.S.'s activities in this sphere.

Before long, local reception and hospitality committees were being formed to arrange get-togethers of all kinds with the Americans when they arrived, and, from the American side, we were getting very pleasing reports of the welcome their Forces were being accorded.

Bracken made a special point of presiding at our monthly meeting with the heads of the Voluntary Societies and had them eating out of his hand. I remember one typical instance of his flair with people, when he opened the meeting by asking us all to stand in silence in memory of a great leader who had 'passed on'. I myself was unaware that the head of the Church Army had just died and I subsequently ascertained that neither of Bracken's private secretaries had briefed him, but it had not escaped his eye, and his gesture was much appreciated by his audience. I found it very enjoyable as well as interesting to get out into the country, visiting our Information Officers in the Regions, meeting commanders of American units and seeing the efforts of the Voluntary Societies in the field. With Bracken at luncheons which he gave at the Ministry I met General Eisenhower and Winant, the American Ambassador. Both were easy to get on with and helpful, and Eisenhower could always be relied on to meet us half way in his determination to be more than fair to the British over anything concerning his forces.

By the time of the big build-up of the American Forces for the Normandy landings, I had become heavily engaged in another side of the Ministry, so we evolved a more elaborate procedure for dealing with civilian relations with the much larger numbers of American troops who were now based in England. This was to set up a small Anglo-American Committee with myself as Chairman and Sir Godfrey Haggard, an ex-consul-general in America, as its whole-time executive. Nominally Bracken was the Committee's Chairman with Winant, the American Ambassador, and the heads of our and the American Forces as its members, but in practice I represented Bracken, Herbert Agar represented Winant, and appropriate subordinates the British and American Forces. As its joint secretaries the committee had Henry Maxwell and the able and delightful Janet Murrow, the wife of the famous American broadcaster, Ed Murrow. The idea was that the Committee would be in a position to deal promptly with any difficulties or complaints that might arise, since the appropriate member could go straight to the fountain head of the responsible department concerned. In practice the Committee worked well in an atmosphere of complete accord and goodwill. After the war was over I persuaded my friend Elmer Roper to conduct a survey of a cross-section of American ex-servicemen in order to ascertain what their feelings were towards the inhabitants of the various European countries where they had been stationed. The survey showed that we in Britain were decisively well on top in popularity, with the Germans second, the Italians third and the French right at the bottom.

The other assignment with which I had become deeply involved at the Ministry was with its Empire Division, when Bracken and Radcliffe asked me one day in 1943 if I would take over its Directorship. I was not at all keen to get involved in the Ministry's executive machine but found it impossible to refuse Radcliffe's request. The Division, he told me, was frankly in a mess and I found that this was only too true. Its Director whom I replaced was an ineffective type whose main concern was with minutes and files. Of its three sections, the Dominions' one was in good shape under a sensible academic head, and Bracken had been inspired to send John Betjeman to Dublin as the Ministry's very popular representative there. But the Indian section seemed to have no function at all, since nothing could be done without the agreement of the India Office and the Government of India who effectively barred any activities on the part of the Ministry. So far as the Colonial section was concerned, it seemed, under its ambitious head, to be in a permanent state of warfare with the Colonial Office's own Information department which, in turn, was frustrated by the hostility of the office's senior civil servants to any form of publicity. I did find, however, attached to the Ministry's Empire Division, an invaluable ally in Professor Vincent Harlow, the writer and historian. Luckily, too, there were no difficulties with the correspondents of Empire newspapers in London whom it was the Ministry's job to assist, since Bracken himself was always prepared to meet and talk to them. I overcame the impasse between my Colonial section and the Colonial office by the simple expedient of arranging with Lloyd, the Colonial Office's very sympathetic permanent head, for a weekly meeting at the Colonial Office to decide what needed attention and who should attend to it. But I also found an almost complete impasse between the Colonial Office and the B.B.C., the Colonial Office complaining that the B.B.C. refused to broadcast any material it supplied, while the B.B.C. complained—and I thought with some justice—that what the Colonial Office supplied was quite unsuited for effective broadcasting.

Discussing the situation with Bracken I suggested that the only remedy was to attach someone to the Colonial Office who would be acceptable to both sides and who understood both what should be broadcast to and about the Colonies and also the kind of material that B.B.C. producers —who were the determining factor—would like to use. Bracken agreed with me but asked me where such a person was to be found. I replied that I only knew of one person and that was Elspeth, who had been working in the Press Department of the B.B.C. for nearly a year. Her services were promptly enlisted and she joined the Colonial Office where she formed a most successful bridge between the Office and the B.B.C., only resigning towards the end of 1943 for the happy reason that she was expecting a child in February.

ii

Once we were both settled in England for the duration of the war, with our travels for the time being at an end, Elspeth and I had decided that it was time to try to start a family. We had, however, no success until we consulted the aptly named gynaecologist, Dr. Beckett Ovary, who performed a minor operation on Elspeth. For her confinement she came up to a nursing home in London and in due course produced a fine, healthy red-haired son. Some sporadic air-raids had begun again on London at the time, and amid the sound of explosions, I waited anxiously for news from the nursing home at the flat in Earl's Court which I was sharing with my brother Michael. It was a relief a few days later to drive Elspeth and Charles Grant, as we decided to name the boy, back to the peace of Woodfolds on a lovely sunny February day, accompanied by a very efficient and likeable nurse.

I returned to my work at the Ministry, happier, I think, than at any other time in my life. Highly unpleasant as I found the 'doodle-bugs' in London later that year, followed by the V2 rockets, I was free from worry about Elspeth and Charles who continued to flourish at Woodfolds. It was there that we heard the news of V.E. Day. I gave thanks to the good fortune that had not only brought me safely through two world wars, but which in the second one had given me such personal happiness and the chance to do interesting and worthwhile work.

Good fortune had also attended my brothers and sisters. My brother Michael who had left the Foreign Office in the thirties to found and edit *The Geographical Magazine*, had returned to the Foreign Office and had spent some of the war years in the United States. Kit, my soldier brother, who had been through Staff College shortly before the war, had gone to France in 1939 on the staff of a Corps and had escaped unhurt from Dunkirk. He had then held various staff jobs in England, becoming an instructor at the Staff College, and had ended the war in command of a Brigade in Normandy and the crossing of the Rhine. Marjorie, my elder sister, had been with her husband in South Africa where he had been appointed High Commissioner and where thirty years later I was to find her still remembered with warm affection. My younger sister Anne's husband, Geoffrey Cooke, kindest of men and best of husbands, had been with the Home Forces, and she had rejoined my father on Boars Hill with her two small children. My father was to celebrate his eightieth birthday at the beginning of 1945, but he was feeling his advancing years and in 1943 had sold his farm and house on Boars Hill when he was offered and bought two small houses at Shackleford in Surrey which had belonged to his old friend Sir Edgar Horne, the Chairman of the Prudential. My father installed himself in one, a very charming enlarged and modernized old cottage whose garden was bounded by serpentine red-rick walls, while Anne and her children moved into the studio cottage next door. My father's health was, however, now fast deteriorating and he had to undergo two serious operations. I well remember him saying to me when I visited him in a Guildford nursing home after the second operation, 'Why couldn't they let me go peacefully when I was under the anaesthetic instead of keeping me alive for a few months of pain and discomfort.' Although he would never say so, I am sure that with his compassionate understanding he must in the course of his practice have refused to prolong the misery of patients in hopeless cases.

I was able to visit him regularly from London to spend a night with him, and we seemed to be closer to each other than ever before. He died early in 1946 just after I had sailed on my first post-war visit to America. Few men can have been more widely loved, and certainly no children ever had a kinder, more generous and more tolerant father. I was only happy to know that I had been able to give him some pleasure in his last years.

CHAPTER X

i

I WAS 51 when the war ended, and it was not until the end of 1967 when I was close on 74, that I retired from my various activities that filled the twenty-two years between. They were to be the happiest as well as the most varied and interesting years in my life.

Resigning from the Ministry of Information immediately after the 1945 General Election, my · first preoccupation was with Tea. It was still rationed in Britain but it was clearly important for Tea's future consumption in its biggest market that it should not lose the immense goodwill which it had won during the war amongst civilians and the armed forces alike. When Elspeth and I were reconstructing Woodfolds in 1938 we had paid a number of useful visits to the Building Centre in London where the Building Industry had displayed its latest models in the way of windows, doors, lighting and so on. The thought had then occurred to me that the world Tea Industry might advantageously have its London centre where it could be on view to the public in all the aspects of its history, production, marketing and consumption, as well as in the display of all the newest designs in Tea things. This idea I was now able to put into execution.

The all-important central site for the Centre was found in an old building in Regent Street a few yards below Piccadilly Circus. After reconstruction I got Mischa Black to undertake the original decoration in order to give Tea the most modern setting for its display to the world. Since then the Centre's attractions have been renewed from time to time under Denys Forrest who became the Centre's first Information Officer and subsequently took charge of our U.K. campaign. From the day of its opening the Centre drew large numbers of visitors, and proved so successful a promotion weapon that, in the next decade, we opened similar though smaller centres in Glasgow, Manchester, Birmingham and Exeter. In Australia, Tea Centres in Sydney and Melbourne proved equally popular.

Meantime, I was busy reviving all our overseas campaigns and adding a new one in West Africa. I had relieved myself of some of the burden of incessant travel by recruiting an assistant in the person of Antony Tasker, the stepson of Harold Raymond, the head of Chatto's, Elspeth's publishers. At the beginning of 1948, I took him with me when I visited Ceylon and India to report to my Board's parent bodies on our war work and on our plans for the future.

Apart from this journey to Ceylon, India and Egypt, I confined my own early post-war travels to an annual visit to the U.S.A. and Canada, leaving the regular inspection of our other oversea campaign to Tasker. Alas, home ties and post-war costs prevented Elspeth from sharing my American visits, but Bill and Alice Esty became even closer friends than before, and when I was in New York, most of my weekends were spent with them in New Canaan.

One great pleasure of my annual visit to America was the opportunity it gave me of seeing Aldous and his devoted wife Maria whom I had always greatly liked and admired. Fortunately it was necessary for my work that I should call on the tea trade on the Pacific coast, and Maria would meet my train at Los Angeles station and drive me out of the city to their suburban home for a wholly delightful night or two's stay. However long it had been since we had last met there seemed to have been no break at all in our relationship. Aldous' beautiful speaking voice, his choice of words and the fantastic range of his interests, which even embraced one's own small doings, always held a unique fascination for me as 'we tired the sun with talking and sent him down the sky'.

Once or twice I also met Aldous and Maria in New York, and on one such occasion delighted the Estys, Newsoms and Ropers by giving a dinner party for them to meet Aldous. The dinner was a great success. Aldous displayed a fascinated and wholly objective interest in the arts and techniques of advertising, public relations and market research. Stimulated by his charm and the intelligence of his questions, Earl and Elmo expounded their philosophies, while Bill came right out of his normal shell and was perhaps the most interesting of the three in his disclosures of how and why advertising could be made to influence the habits of the masses.

Since the sale of tea to America was a dollar earner for the sterling area, I had been able to get enough dollars from the Bank of England to continue to finance the public relations and marketing sides of the campaign but there had been no funds available for national consumer advertising. By good fortune I was in America in the late summer of 1949 when I read the headline news of the devaluation of the £. This, of course, meant that the American tea trade would be able to buy their tea from India and Ceylon more cheaply. I immediately went to see Robert Smallwood, the head of Lipton's, the largest American tea packers, and Chairman of the U.S. Tea Association. I put it to him that if the packers passed on to the consumer the reduction in prices made possible by sterling devaluation, it was unlikely that a single extra pound of tea would be consumed, since price had never been a factor in American tea consumption. Instead therefore of cutting the price of tea I urged that the American tea trade should combine in using the price bonus to form a fund to be employed jointly with my Board's funds in consumer advertising for the promotion of the tea habit, whereby all would benefit. If the tea trade would do this I felt sure that my Board would be able to get more dollars to match the trade contribution and thus restore the campaign to its full pre-war level. Smallwood at once agreed and before I left for England preparations for a joint Tea Council were under way. It was the first occasion on which tea packers had joined forces with the producers for general promotion work and it was to be the precursor of similar joint efforts in other markets.

All seemed to be going very well with the fortunes of the International Tea Board in London. Government members had been appointed to the Board by India, Ceylon and Indonesia in 1948, and in that same year I had recruited young Indian and Ceylon nationals as assistant organizing directors at headquarters. Then, towards the end of 1952, a bolt fell from the blue, when our embarrassed Indian Government member informed us that he had been ordered by the New Minister of Commerce in Delhi to say that India was withdrawing from her partnership in the Board. No reason was ever given for this sudden and surprising decision by a new Minister who was almost entirely ignorant of the Board's work, but there had been friction between the Indian and Ceylon Governments over the rights in Ceylon of the South Indian Tamils who formed most of the labour force on the Ceylon tea estates.

Strong representations made to Delhi by the Indian High Commission in London and the Indian Tea Association, representing the producers, failed to alter the Minister's decision, and India's secession was quickly followed by that of Indonesia, though the latter's contribution to the Board's funds, had, since the war, only been on a token scale. There remained, however, Ceylon, and it was to consult with her Minister of Commerce and Tea Board that I flew out to Colombo in one of the first of the jet Comets that were inaugurating a new era in air travel. In Colombo I found that all interests were determined to maintain Ceylon's promotion efforts irrespective of the defection of her partners. This we felt we could turn to Ceylon's advantage by retaining the name and goodwill of the International Board which would, in effect, become Ceylon's oversea promotion agency. In Colombo I was also able to settle my own future position to my entire satisfaction. In view of the lessened executive responsibility, my Ceylonese assistant would be the International Board's Organizing Director, while I became its fee-paid Vice-Chairman, the Board now consisting solely of Ceylon Government and producer representatives. Since my responsibility would henceforth be mainly advisory, I should have much more time for interests other than tea.

I had thought it probable that before long, when they

saw how successful Ceylon's promotion work was proving, primarily on behalf of her own teas, under the International Board's name, the Indian tea interests, both European and Indian owned, would succeed in persuading their Government to rejoin the International Board in joint promotion which was so manifestly to their advantage, but in spite of their strong and publicly expressed opinions, they failed to do so. They did, however, persuade their Government to continue to contribute to joint producer and tea trade campaigns in the U.S.A., Canada and West Germany, conducted by local Tea Councils.

My last fifteen years of tea promotion were thus spent in the service of Ceylon, my original employers. As I had, however, anticipated, increased world tea production in India, Ceylon and East Africa began once again to overtake world consumption in the absence of the united efforts of the producers to expand it. By the middle 'sixties the producers and their Governments were realizing the growing seriousness of the situation as the world tea price continued to fall. The tea industry was, in fact, going back to where it had been in the early 1930s when I came in.

But this time the respective independent Governments of the tea-producing countries refused to consider any international regulation scheme for production or export, which, as in the 'thirties, would have proved the only short-term remedy. They did agree, however, with the United Nations Food and Agricultural Organization that increased promotion efforts to expand world consumption were urgently needed for long-term recovery, though at the time of writing no agreed scheme has emerged.

In the United Kingdom, however, the tea packers themselves, alarmed at a perceptible though slight fall in both per head and total consumption in tea's largest market, had approached the Indian and Ceylon Tea Associations in London with a view to joint expenditure on a large-scale promotion campaign for tea, irrespective of its origin, in order to try to check the decline and then increase per head consumption. Such an approach from the U.K. packers was an entirely new development, as hitherto all their advertising appropriations had been spent on promoting the sale of their own brands *vis-à-vis* those of their competitors. The Indian and Ceylon Governments agreed with their producers to furnish their share of the funds and a Tea Council representing all the partners was formed, on my old U.S.A. pattern, for the control of the campaign. All the members of the Council were anxious to make full use of my experience, and I was very happy to accept the Chairmanship of the Council's Technical Committee. Our advertising was primarily addressed to the younger generation and to the catering field where our research showed tea to be losing most ground, and aided by our Advertising Agency's admirable slogan, 'Join the Tea Set', the campaign got off to a very good start. In less than two years statistics indicated that we were succeeding in checking the decline in U.K. consumption.

With the campaign fully launched I felt by the end of 1967 that it was time for me to draw out since I was close on 74 and had completed thirty-five years of tea promotion. In sending in my resignation to Ceylon I had nothing but gratitude for all the trust and goodwill which had always been given me by all branches of the tea trade the world over, and, of course, especially by the producers and Government of Ceylon. My association with tea ended with a series of luncheons, speeches of thanks and presentations which, pleasant as they were, I felt to be largely undeserved. What I valued most, perhaps, was a very lovely large silver tray, hand-made in Ceylon by Kandyan craftsmen, its rim decorated with all Ceylon's animals, and presented to me by the Ceylon Board in appreciation of my thirty-five years' service.

ii

Shortly after I had left the Ministry of Information, Sir Thomas Lloyd, the permanent head of the Colonial Office with whom I had established such a satisfactory relationship during the war, asked me to lunch with him. He told me that Creech-Jones, the new Secretary of State, wanted the Colonial Office to be more widely publicized and was pressing him to appoint a high-powered Public Relations Officer from Fleet Street to the office for the purpose. What, asked Lloyd, did I think of this? My emphatic reply was that I believed that such an appointment would have precisely the opposite effect to what Creech-Jones intended. From my experience, the main impediment to better Colonial Office public relations lay in the attitude of the Office's heads of departments who disliked the idea of any form of publicity and saw no need for anything of the kind. To appoint a highly paid outsider from Fleet Street would, I thought, merely confirm their suspicion that all public relations were some kind of racket and would make them less inclined than ever to co-operate. Lloyd agreed with me, but asked what he should do. The advice I gave was that he should try to find someone of good reputation from within the official hierarchy who might have a flair for information work, whom the senior officials would respect and with whom they might be willing to co-operate. Not long after Lloyd told me that he thought he had found the very man in Kenneth Blackburne, who had already had an outstanding record in the Colonial Service having been the youngest Colonial Secretary ever to be appointed, and who clearly had a high career in front of him. If he were appointed Information Officer, the senior officials would have to revise their opinions as to the importance of the post. Meeting Blackburne over lunch with Lloyd I at once realized how good Lloyd's choice had been, though the former was hesitant about accepting the post on the grounds of his lack of technical experience of Information work. I therefore offered to act as his adviser and to have regular meetings with him for discussing methods of work and such technical problems as might arise. Both Blackburne and Lloyd welcomed my offer and Lloyd arranged for me to be put in the Colonial Office list under the imposing title of 'Honorary Adviser on Public Relations to the Secretary of State for the Colonies'.

All worked out as we had hoped. With Kenneth Blackburne's appointment the officials' whole attitude to Information work changed as he won their respect and confidence.
My own contribution was, in fact, negligible as Kenneth
very quickly grasped all the principles and methods making
for a good information service, and our regular meetings,
agreeable as they were, afforded little more than confirmation of his views and activities. Anyway, I had found a new
valued friend and by the time Kenneth moved on to higher
things—he ended his career as Governor of Jamaica—the
Colonial Office Information services had been established
as among the best in Whitehall.

My Colonial Office advisory post must have been one of
the reasons for my being asked in the autumn of 1952 to
become a member of an Independent Committee of Inquiry
into the Government's oversea Information Services. The
Committee was a small one of only seven members. Our
Chairman was the Earl of Drogheda, an elderly man of
great charm who had long experience of committee work
in the House of Lords. Two of our members came from big
industry in the persons of directors of Shell and Unilever
respectively. Then there was Victor Feather, the Assistant
Secretary of the T.U.C., Donald McLachlan, the Assistant
Editor of the *Economist*, and Mrs. Mary Stocks. Victor
Feather was a mine of stalwart good sense with his north
country background of the best type of craft Trades
Unionism. His feet were always firmly planted on the
ground and he was never dogmatic. Donald McLachlan
brought a very able mind and much newspaper experience
to our work, and Mary Stocks' quick mind, wit and wide
experience of Government Commission work was a great
asset. We were also very lucky in our Secretary, Robert
Marett from the Foreign Office who, though never obtru-
sive, always helped to keep us firmly on our course. In the
nine months which it took us to fulfil our formidable assignment we had sixty-seven meetings in the course of which we
took evidence from all the Departments concerned, the
Foreign Office, the Commonwealth Relations Office, the

Colonial Office, the Board of Trade, the Central Office of Information, the British Council and the B.B.C., besides each of us visiting an oversea country to see the work in the field, my own visit being to Ceylon.

Our general conclusions were that the oversea Information Services played a valuable role in support of our Foreign, Commonwealth and Colonial policies and of our trade, and must be regarded as part of the normal apparatus of diplomacy of a Great Power, though propaganda was no substitute for policy, and its effect on the course of events was usually only marginal, even if in certain circumstances it might be decisive in tipping the balance between diplomatic success or failure. We found that repeated and hastily applied last-moment cuts in the Government's expenditure on the oversea Information Services had led to much waste and inefficiency. So while we recommended that more money should be provided, it must be in accordance with a long-term plan.

After our unanimous report had been submitted there came complete silence. We knew, of course, that our report with its endorsement of the value of the Information Services and its recommendation for increased expenditure on them would be unpopular with the Treasury and generally in Whitehall, and it began to look as if our report had been quietly pigeon-holed; although a summary of it in the form of a White Paper was presented to Parliament in the spring of 1954. It was not, however, until a year later when Dr. Charles Hill, the Postmaster-General, took over the co-ordination of Government Information work, that action on our recommendations began to take place. As one of my ex-Drogheda colleagues remarked to me, 'it's a Hill wind that blows nobody any good !'

Towards the end of 1953 I was as surprised as I was gratified to get a letter asking if I would be willing to accept a Companionship of the Order of St. Michael and St. George (in brief a C.M.G.) in the 1954 New Year Honours. Little as I might feel I'd earned it and although neither Elspeth nor I had ever harkened for or set much store by such distinctions, my vanity was far too great to think of anything but pleased acceptance, and by keeping the letter to myself I was able to give Elspeth a considerable surprise when she read the Honours List in *The Times* on New Year's Day. Eight years later she herself was awarded the C.B.E. which I felt was a very proper tribute to her reputation and Services.

One assignment given me by the Colonial Office in 1958 afforded a most interesting and enjoyable experience. This was to visit Uganda as Chairman of an independent Committee of Inquiry into its Information Department and Services. I was fortunate in the British members of the Committee—Philip Noakes of the Colonial Office and Eliot Watrous of the B.B.C.—who accompanied me, and in the five local Ugandan members, one British, one Indian and three African, while the Governor, Sir Frederick Crawford, had chosen a most able and knowledgeable civil servant— Henry Morris—as the Committee's secretary.

I felt that at the outset the Committee must agree on a definition of the basic functions of a Colony's Government information services. In Uganda a Department of Information had been set up six years earlier but we found it in an unhappy state with its morale very low. Sir Andrew Cohen, the late Governor, had, I considered, got his priorities all wrong when he had laid down that the Department's principal task was to publicize Uganda abroad. I therefore got the Committee to agree that the primary tasks of an Information Department, as an integral part of the country's administration, were to interpret the Government's policies and actions to the public, to assist the Government in keeping in close touch with the public's reactions, to help in creating a well-informed public opinion, and to encourage the people to take an increasing interest in the economic, cultural and political development of their country. Publicizing Uganda abroad I relegated to only a secondary function.

The most enjoyable part of my Committee's activities was its tours all over the country, visiting many areas of great scenic beauty, including the Queen Elizabeth and Murchison Falls National Parks with their wealth of wild life. Back in Kampala where my Committee held its sessions, I had an interesting evening, meeting senior Ministers and members of the Lukiko, the Buganda parliament. Talking to them, I might have been at a gathering of ultra-Tory members of the Carlton Club in Pall Mall, as they urged me not to be led astray by talk of democratic changes, which, they assured me, were not wanted by King Freddie or the great majority of the Baganda.

Henry Morris, Noakes and I made ourselves responsible for drafting the Committee's report which we accomplished in three days and evenings of continuous sessions, with Watrous and our Indian member drafting the recommendations on broadcasting. The Committee's report, which covered in some detail all aspects and media of Information, recommended that the information services should no longer be left to the interplay of departmental interests, but that the Information Department should be so staffed and financed as to be able to assume direct or agency responsibility for the production and distribution of all information material. In regard to broadcasting, in which sphere the existing Information Department was giving a very poor service in English and seven vernacular languages, our recommendation was that, pending the establishment of an independent Corporation on the lines of the B.B.C., the Government broadcasting service should be under a separate Department with a qualified director seconded from the B.B.C. and supplied with adequate funds and a trained staff, the increased cost being partly met by the acceptance of 'spot' commercial advertisements.

Our report was very well received both by the Government of Uganda and by the Colonial Office, and I got warm letters of appreciation from the Governor and from the Colonial Office.

It must have been due to my membership of the Drogheda Committee that in 1954 I was invited to join the
Executive Committee of the British Council, whose activities the Drogheda Committee had closely examined and
commended, although we had felt that the Council's immediate post-war expansion had greatly overstrained its staff
and financial resources which had been further weakened by
subsequent Treasury cuts imposed without regard for the
Council's essentially long-term role. The Council had also
become a regular target for ill-informed and malicious
attacks by the Beaverbrook press which held it up to ridicule
by picking out isolated instances of activities in the Arts'
field and entirely ignoring its valuable long-term contribution to our political and commercial interests by its overseas centres and libraries, and by its care for overseas
students visiting Britain on Council scholarships, bursaries
and tours. I was no stranger to the concepts that lay behind
the Council, since well before its establishment in 1934 in
order to counter German and Italian propaganda in the
Middle East, Stephen Tallents, shocked by finding Britain
so ill-represented at the Barcelona Exhibition in 1929, had
written an essay called 'The Projection of England' which
had been first published in booklet form in 1932.

I had frequently discussed the subject with him at the
time of its writing, and in the essay he had pleaded for the
carrying out of just those wide functions which the Council
subsequently fulfilled.

When I joined the Council's Executive Committee Paul
Sinker, a man of outstanding ability and drive with an
academic and Treasury background, had recently become
the Council's Director-General. His administration was
already greatly increasing the Council's standing and efficiency, and a year or two later its prestige was further enhanced when it was fortunate enough to secure the services
as its Chairman of Lord Bridges, the former secretary to the
Cabinet and Head of the Treasury. Under Bridges and

Sinker, the Council's staff at headquarters administered its affairs so efficiently that the Executive Committee rarely did little more than rubber-stamp what the officials had already decided. One occasion, however, I well remember, when certain members demanded that the Council should with-draw completely from South Africa, alleging that its pres-ence there was compromising with evil and damaging the Council's reputation in the rest of the world. These same members, nevertheless, were the most clamant in pressing for closer cultural contacts with the Soviet Union whose domestic policies might have seemed even more objection-able than those of the South African Government.

Being one of the few members familiar with South Africa, I took an active part in the heated debate that took place. I argued that withdrawal by the Council would be the height of folly and would only hurt the Bantu and progressive white South Africans, while entrenching the conservative Afri-kaners more firmly than ever in their laager of indifference to world opinion and of their genuine belief in the rightness of their apartheid policy. I was as convinced then, as I am now, that the one helpful line to adopt in regard to South Africa was to enlarge and not restrict every possible contact with the outside world both commercially and culturally, and thus to try to draw the Afrikaner out of the laager which past history had made him build not without justification. Instead of withdrawing from South Africa I urged that the Council should expand its work there. I upheld my con-victions in the face of acrimonious hostility on the part of a few of my fellow members, one, a well-known and much publicized personality, rebuking me for using the term 'Bantu' to denote black South Africans, saying that it was a 'dirty word'. I had, however, the satisfaction of seeing the demand for the Council's withdrawal defeated under Bridges' wise and conciliatory guidance.

After serving for over ten years on the Executive Com-mittee I felt that there must be many others who could more usefully fill my place, and gave in my resignation, although I remain a strong believer in the Council's work.

My membership of the National Parks Commission afforded a complete contrast to that of the British Council's Executive Committee. The Commission's thirteen members not only discussed and formulated all policy matters when they met at the Commission's offices in Regent's Park for two whole days a month, but also individually shared the more important sides of its executive functions, carrying out site inspections of proposed developments, giving evidence at public inquiries and so on, and in the course of such work, getting to know the county planning authorities as well as becoming familiar with much of the loveliest and wildest scenery in England and Wales. The Commission's very small paid staff, efficient, hard-working and helpful, were content to carry out the routine work and to assist the Commissioners with advice and briefs.

It had been in pursuance of a Bill passed by Parliament at the end of 1949 that the Commission had been set up to exercise general supervision of the Parks, though local Committees were to be the planning authority for each Park planning control and not acquisition of land being their basis.

By the time I joined it in 1955 eight areas comprising the finest large stretches of unspoiled countryside in England and Wales had already been designated by the Commission as National Parks—the Peak, the Lakes, Snowdonia, Dartmoor, Exmoor, the Pembrokeshire Coast, the North York Moors and the Yorkshire Dales—while the remaining two of the ten finally chosen—Northumberland and the Brecon Beacons—were in process of designation. In all, these ten National Parks covered just over 5,000 square miles or 9% of the total area of England and Wales. The Commission was also just starting on the selection and designation as 'Areas of Outstanding Natural Beauty' of smaller pieces of country, in need of special protection by planning control, though not requiring such strict administrative arrangements as for the Parks, nor provision for their enjoyment by the public. In addition, the Commission had begun on the long and very involved work of negotiating public rights of way for long-distance footpaths and bridleways.

I owed my membership of the Commission to Stephen Tallents. Feeling that the Commission had done very little to discharge the duty laid upon it for the promotion of enjoyment of the Parks by the public, its Secretary, Harold Abrahams, lacking the funds to engage a professional publicity officer on his staff, had asked Tallents whether he knew of anyone with the requisite experience who would be willing to give his voluntary services as a Commissioner to take special responsibility for the Commission's Information functions as well as fulfilling the ordinary duties of a Commissioner. Tallents' reply had been that I should be approached. It was an invitation that I had no hesitation in accepting, since after talking to Abrahams, I felt that membership of the Commission would prove to be a most interesting and rewarding experience in the course of which I should be able to make a contribution to a cause which greatly appealed to me.

My fellow Commissioners turned out to be without exception most sympathetic people. To begin with we were exceptionally lucky in our Chairman, Lord Strang, the former permanent head of the Foreign Office. I have never served under a better Chairman. He allowed full latitude to the Commission's members who were nearly all vocal and liked giving forcible expression to their often divergent opinions, but I cannot remember any occasion when Strang's patience failed to secure a unanimous decision, his own views being felt rather than heard. We were equally fortunate in our Deputy Chairman, Pauline Dower, and in our Secretary, Harold Abrahams. Pauline had been born a Trevelyan from Northumberland and had all the brains and energy of that remarkable family. Her knowledge of the English and Welsh countryside was as great as was her devotion to the Commission's cause of its preservation and enjoyment and her tact in dealing with local planning authorities. Harold Abrahams, the former Olympic gold-medal sprinter and the outstanding authority on athletics, was a most delightfully extrovert character who brought a refreshing non-bureaucratic independence of view to his job.

The Commission's Information work which was my particular charge presented a special difficulty. We had, of course, to try to make the general public aware of the existence of the Parks and of what they offered in the way of scenic beauty and open-air recreation, and also to create a public opinion so strongly in favour of the Parks as to make Parliament less indifferent to their welfare and to discourage official or private interests from satisfying their needs by robbing or despoiling the Parks. On the other hand, even if we had the money required, which we certainly did not have, to embark on national publicity or advertising aimed at inviting the public to visit the Parks *en masse* would be to risk destroying the very object of providing enjoyable recreation in unspoilt surroundings for which the Parks had been designated and which was already being threatened by more motor-cars and more people with leisure.

When I joined the Commission I found that little more had been done in the information field than to draw up and give some publicity to a Country Code of behaviour for the public to follow, dealing with such matters as litter, shutting gates, keeping dogs under control, avoiding the risk of starting fires and so forth.

After cogitating my problem in the light of the very limited funds available, I recommended to the Commission that the primary aim of our information work should be to try to ensure that all who visited a Park should have readily available all the information that would enable them to get the most enjoyment and interest out of what the Park had to offer in the way of scenery, fauna and flora, hiking, pony-trekking, climbing, camping and so on. For this purpose I proposed that each Park authority should be asked to appoint an Information Officer and establish Information Centres, both static and in mobile vans, the Commission aiding them with finance and with the supply of information material. I was especially pleased with one poster series which I devised for the Commission to produce. Thinking that some of our great British water-colour painters of the

late eighteenth and early nineteenth centuries must have
painted scenes in all of the Parks which would still appear
unchanged today, John Burbidge, the officer on the Commission's staff who had been selected for information work,
and I succeeded in finding in the Victoria and Albert and
other galleries a picture for each Park which fulfilled this
condition. We had the pictures really well reproduced in
small poster form under the common title of 'Our Heritage',
the letterpress below the picture saying that the scene
painted so long ago had remained unspoilt for our present
enjoyment and that it was our business to see that it stayed
so for the enjoyment of our descendants. The series attained
a great success not only in schools but also in display free of
charge by public authorities. Over the litter problem and
in many other aspects of the Parks' Information facilities
Park Wardens afforded great help. Low as the salaries were
that the Treasury allowed the Parks to offer with the aid of
a grant from the Commission, there was no difficulty in
finding enthusiastic and devoted men who besides acting as
friendly guides and guardians in the summer months would,
in winter, give talks and film shows on the Parks to schools
and other bodies.

Apart from my official duties on the Information side, I
represented the Commission at a number of Public Inquiries
in order to help oppose developments which we and the
local Park authority thought would be injurious to amenity
and the character of the Park. My most interesting experience was in support of the Oxfordshire County Council who
had rejected an application for developing ironstone working over a large area in the historic and lovely neighbourhood of Great Tew. The would-be developers, representing
powerful commercial interests, had then appealed to the
Minister who had ordered one of his Inspectors to hold a
Public Inquiry. A few weeks before its date, I visited the
area in the company of a local land-owner who had organized a strong resistance committee. There had been
ironstone workings some miles to the north and I was horrified to see the devastation wrought to the landscape by the

removal of the top twelve feet of soil, leaving roads and buildings perched precariously above the rest of a hedgeless and treeless wilderness. The evening before the Inquiry I went by rail to Banbury where it was to be held and was interested to hear my taxi driver from the station to the hotel express his strong views as to the necessity of forbidding the development. When I checked in at the hotel, the girl at the reception desk at once inquired if I had come to attend the Inquiry, and if so, which side was I on. On my telling her that I was supporting the County Council, 'Oh good,' she replied, 'I'll give you room Number Five.' I don't know to what attic she would have consigned me had I said I was on the other side, but the incident made it clear how strongly local opinion had been roused.

At the Inquiry next day the large hall was packed with County Council supporters, and every kind of local organization gave evidence against the development. I myself had an easy passage as a witness, the Q.C. employed by the developers refraining from trying to dispute my evidence. His appeal was based on the great importance to the national economy, especially in event of war, of his client being allowed to develop the workings in order to replace ore imports from abroad. But the very able Q.C. employed by the County Council was able by his cross-examinations completely to demolish the validity of the developer's case, much to the satisfaction of the local audience. As a result the Inspector advised the Minister to reject the appeal and the Minister followed his Inspector's advice, in spite of a strong parliamentary lobby having been busy on the developer's behalf.

There were, however, other cases with which I was concerned where the Minister rejected his Inspector's report so that the whole business seemed a great waste of time and money. I came away from Banbury convinced of the importance of really strong local opinion being mobilized over such issues, since it seemed that only the threat of losing votes would have any effect on Governmental indifference to landscape protection. Indeed, the derisory low priority given by Parliament to questions of amenity and non-material considerations was shown by our National Parks grant which, in its annual total, amounted to less than a penny per head of the population, even though it might have been thought that the preservation of the ever-more threatened natural beauties of our landscape was of considerable importance to the very valuable economic asset of our tourist industry.

The Commissioners were each appointed by the Minister for a renewable term of three years, and by 1966 I was in my fourth three-year term. Both being now well over 70, Lord Strang and I agreed that it was time for us to resign at the end of our current terms even if the Minister should offer to reappoint us. Harold Abrahams had already retired, and although I respected his successor as the Commission's Secretary, an able and conscientious permanent Civil Servant from the Ministry, I missed the personal relationship I had enjoyed with Harold. The Information side of the Commission's work was now functioning well and I had also been able to play a leading part in the designation of two Areas of Outstanding Natural Beauty in which I had a particular interest, Chichester Harbour, where my brother Michael had his home, and my own Cotswold area.

Early in 1965, in the course of many discussions, the Commission had come to the conclusion that with a million more motor-cars coming on the roads every year and with a rapidly rising population enjoying shorter hours of work, longer holidays and higher wages, it was time to make a fresh appraisal of the whole problem of leisure and countryside amenity in our overcrowded island. We considered that a negative policy of restrictive preservation of the Parks and Areas of Outstanding Natural Beauty through planning control would not much longer be sufficient to withstand the ever-mounting pressures, even if, as seemed likely, motorcar access to the remoter areas of the Parks had to be forbidden. We felt that a more positive solution had to be sought through the forward planning of open-air recreation as well as preservation on a nation-wide basis. In other words, if the weight of the numbers of people and cars crowding into the Parks was not to destroy the very object for which they had been designated, special recreation areas would have to be provided within easy reach of the big conurbations to attract those who just wanted somewhere to go in their cars for a day or weekend outing and to whom the company of crowds of their fellows and the noise of motor-boats and water-skiing and other such open-air pursuits would be a positive attraction rather than a drawback. All our evidence showed, indeed, that the majority of people were happiest in such surroundings and did not desire the solitude and quiet favoured by the minority. We therefore drew up a paper on these lines which we submitted to Mr. Willey, the Minister for Land and Natural Resources in the new Labour Government, impressing on him the urgency of the problem and the need for fresh legislation to give the Commission wider functions and more money to implement our recommendations.

All through 1965 I had been busy as a member of the study group on 'information' for the Duke of Edinburgh's Conference on 'The Countryside in 1970'. The Conference took place in November, the Duke presiding throughout in person with outstanding tact and ability. At it, Mr. Willey, following our recommendations, announced the Government's intention to set up a Countryside Commission and to establish 'Country Parks' as special recreational areas. He followed this up by issuing a White Paper, 'Leisure in the Countryside' at the beginning of 1966. We warmly welcomed the White Paper as going far to meet our wishes and promising early action, though we drew the Minister's attention to various important points which we hoped would be taken into account when the legislation was being drafted to give effect to the intentions expressed in the White Paper.

In May Mr. Willey announced his first steps towards the reconstitution of our Commission into the wider Countryside Commission envisaged in the White Paper. To our complete surprise and consternation they involved the appointment of Lady Wootton in replacement of Lord Strang and, with two exceptions, the resignation of all the other members of the Commission including Pauline Dower, the Vice-Chairman, all of us receiving out of the blue a curt letter asking for our resignations, accompanied by a brief and colourless expression of thanks for our past services. Since I had intended to resign in any case a year later I did not feel that I had any personal cause for grievance, and I think that Lord Strang felt the same, but we all considered that such abrupt dismissal of Pauline Dower was outrageous, apart from the folly of losing her great experience and knowledge at the same time as Strang was being replaced as Chairman by Baroness Wootton who seemed to have little qualifications for the post.

It also seemed stupid to change all the Commission's members on the eve of the implementation of the measures which they had put forward in the light of their experience and after so much thought. I remember Lord Bridges coming up to me at the Athenaeum to express his disgust at the whole proceeding and also his surprise that Strang had refrained from any public protest. As I knew, however, Strang had too strong a sense of public duty to risk damaging the influence of his successor on the new Commission. Now called the Countryside Commission it had only nine members, few of whom, apart from the two old members whose services had been retained, appeared to be qualified by experience or knowledge. My own belief was then and still is that our dismissal was due to Ministry officials who disliked the way in which the Commission was controlled by its experienced, independent-minded, outspoken and unpaid members instead of by paid fellow civil servants. So far, however, as I was personally concerned, I could look back without regret on nearly twelve years of thoroughly interesting, enjoyable and rewarding work in the company of highly congenial colleagues.

The harvest in the varied fields of the personal side of my life has been a rewarding one during the post-war years. First, there has been Elspeth's ever-growing reputation as a writer and as an authority on African affairs. Amongst her many books the *Flame Trees of Thika* and its sequel gave a picture of her girlhood in Kenya. Only Karen Blixem's *Out of Africa* has ever matched Elspeth's evocation of the early years of white settlement. Besides her books she contributed many articles to newspapers and magazines, was for some years a member of the B.B.C. 'Critics' team, and was the only woman member of the Monckton Commission to Central Africa. At home she became a Justice of the Peace and started and ran a small dairy farm.

Elspeth's very active life, involving as it did regular visits to Africa so as to keep abreast with African affairs and to amass material for her writing, as well as all her other activities, in no way affected the happiness of our marriage. On the contrary it enhanced it, since her work and travels made a great addition to our mutual interests. I had, too, all the enjoyment of discussing with her the proofs of her books and the excitement of reading in the newspapers with vicarious pride the almost invariably glowing reviews which they received. She was, too, a superb letter-writer and when apart we always kept in very close touch by correspondence.

Nevertheless what made it possible for Elspeth to lead such an active and varied life without any neglect of our son Charles' or my welfare was our good fortune in the recruitment of Miss Clague—or 'Cleggie' as we always called her —to our small household as Charles' nurse. She was excellent with Charles, kind but firm and standing no nonsense, and, when he started going to school, she stayed on with us, taking over the Woodfolds house-keeping and kitchen. Lacking any family ties, Woodfolds became her home as much as ours and she had no interests other than our affairs and those of our visiting relations and friends. This dependence made her, however, the more determined to assert her independence by making a virtue of brusqueness of speech and manners. But she was completely trustworthy and reliable and had other sterling qualities, notably great courage which made her bear pain and ill-health without self-pity or complaint and enabled her to get the better of a crippling attack of arthritis.

Her death was a very sad one. She had always said that she would go on working until she reached seventy and, to her great satisfaction, we then gave her the use of our furnished cottage just outside the gate leading to Woodfolds. It was the first home of her own that she had ever possessed and with her savings and pension she could afford to live there in comfort. But hardly had she moved in when headaches which she had stoically endured for some time became so bad that she was forced to consult our doctor. Suspecting a tumour on the brain, she was sent to hospital in Bristol, where after faulty diagnosis which caused her much unnecessary suffering, the tumour was found to be inoperable and ended her life.

Meantime, in 1954, when I was sixty, I had begun my own efforts as a writer. I had always derived satisfaction from putting words on paper in logical and orderly fashion, and in the course of my work I must have written the equivalent of several books in the shape of reports and memoranda. As a legacy of my tour with Amery, I had published two little descriptive articles in magazines, but I had been far too busy to attempt anything else. Apart from this, my knowledge of and admiration for Elspeth's sheer dedicated professionalism made me very conscious that I could never aspire to any writing that involved imagination, plot or dialogue and that I did not possess Elspeth's gifted use of words.

After 1952, however, having given up most executive work, I did have more leisure. For a good many years I had been indulging in the hobby of collecting eighteenth-century porcelain of the four great English factories of Bow, Chelsea, Derby and Worcester, and, for obvious reasons, had specialized in their tea wares. Many authoritative books had, of course, been written about the products of these factories, but none, I found, had brought out their special connection with tea-drinking. My analysis of contemporary sale catalogues showed that the manufacture of tea ware had been the factories' main line of business, so as to cater for the popularity of tea-drinking among the wealthy and fashionable. After some further social research into eighteenth-century tea-drinking habits, I wrote and arranged for the Tea Centre to publish an illustrated booklet, *Tea in Porcelain*, which dealt with this eighteenth-century tea and porcelain link, and listed the 'Tea Equipages' (as tea sets were then called) which the various factories offered. My little book brought in the added interest of an invitation to join the English Ceramic Circle.

A couple of years later I was approached by Thames and Hudson, the publishers, asking whether I would write for them a short popular book on the social and economic history of tea. I felt that this was entirely up my street. As with *Tea in Porcelain*, I found both the research and the writing of *Talking of Tea* a thoroughly agreeable pursuit and I was very pleased with the charmingly produced and illustrated little book that Thames and Hudson brought out in 1956.

Before *Talking of Tea* was published I had, however, begun on a very much more ambitious writing project. Elspeth had inherited a large portrait group painted by Van Dyck in 1632 depicting her ancestor, Endymion Porter, his wife and their three elder boys. I found that Anthony Wood, the seventeenth-century antiquarian, had described Endymion as 'tho' obscure, yet he was a great man and beloved of two kings, James I for his admirable wit and Charles I (to whom he was a servant) for his general learning, brave stile, sweet temper, great experience, travels and modern languages', but the only biography of him was a very feeble and sketchy one published some seventy years ago. Believing that biography might be within my grasp I decided to attempt to write Endymion Porter's definitive life.

It was a task that was to occupy my every spare moment for the next three years, but one that I much enjoyed. My research into original and unpublished documents proved to be as interesting as it was pleasant, often giving me all the excitement of a detective story as I followed up clues that might lead to the discovery of new useful material. What I found especially agreeable was the kindness of all those to whom I turned for help. Noel Blakiston and his staff at the Public Record Office gave me the greatest assistance and took a personal interest in my task of examining the mass of Endymion's private papers which furnished the basis for my book. Then Oliver Millar, the Deputy Keeper of the Queen's Pictures and the leading authority on the art of the period, placed all his knowledge unreservedly at my disposal, this being of special value since Endymion's chief role at Court had been to act for King Charles in forming the superb royal collection of pictures. Veronica Wedgwood, too, best of all seventeenth-century historians, as well as other historians, gave me much excellent advice and suggestions for sources and seemed in no way to resent the intrusion of an amateur into their professional sphere.

Endymion Porter, the Life of a Courtier was published by Chatto's in May 1959 and was a Book Society recommendation for that month. My apprehensions that my book might be ignored or castigated by the critics had already been allayed by the very kind comments that Veronica Wedgwood had made to me after reading it in proof, but I was not prepared for the amount of space and praise that *Endymion* was accorded; *The Times* on the day of publication; next day two columns by Veronica Wedgwood in the *Telegraph* and a positively 'rave' signed review in the *Yorkshire Post*; on Sunday three columns by Raymond Mortimer in *The Sunday Times*, followed during the week by splendid notices in all the leading provincial papers; then the weeklies with notable reviews by Sir Charles Petrie in *Time and Tide*, by Howard Spring in *Country Life*, and by Dr. Christopher Hill in the *Spectator*, with even the anonymous *Times Literary Supplement* being most kindly. No wonder I went about in a haze of smug vanity.

Meantime I was already engaged on another book. Lady

Denman had died in 1954, and her daughter Judy (Lady Burrell), believing that a biography would form her mother's best memorial was employing a most competent woman to assemble material for it from documents and interviews. Judy felt, however, that the book should be written by someone with close personal knowledge of her mother and asked me to undertake it. Lady Denman's main fields of public work in the founding and development of the Women's Institutes, the Family Planning Association and, in the Second World War, the Women's Land Army, all provided interesting material as did her highly individual and remarkable personality.

Lady Denman, G.B.E. was published by Chatto's in 1961. It was widely and very favourably reviewed, but I derived most satisfaction from the appreciative letters sent me by Lady Denman's relations and friends, and most of all from the inscription which Judy wrote in the specially bound copy she gave me, reading 'with gratitude for exceeding my highest hopes'.

Biography now seemed to me well within my limited range as an author and I was lucky enough shortly to find the opportunity for embarking on another book. Elspeth's mother was a member of the Grosvenor family, her father having been Lord Richard Grosvenor, a younger son of the 2nd Marquess of Westminster and younger brother of the 1st Duke. He had been created Baron Stalbridge in 1886 for his political services as Gladstone's Chief Whip, and he had inherited one of his father's Dorset estates, Motcombe near Shaftesbury, rebuilding the house which was now a school.

One day when my mother-in-law was visiting us from Kenya we drove over to Motcombe and in the churchyard saw the grave of Elspeth's great-grandmother who had died in 1891 at the age of 94. After the death of her husband the 2nd Marquess, she had lived at Motcombe and at near-by Inwood with her youngest daughter Theodora to whom she had left all her large personal fortune and her possessions. Theodora and her husband, Merthyr Guest, had had one child, a daughter, who, on her death, had left Inwood and its contents to Count Guy de Pelet. None of us had met him, but when we went on from Motcombe to Inwood he gave us a most hospitable reception. In showing us over the house Count Guy told us that among the Grosvenor possessions which he had inherited were the 2nd Marchioness' diaries and a large number of letters mostly to and from her mother, the famous Duchess—Countess of Sutherland. Would I, he asked, be interested to read them? Returning home with a suitcase packed full of letters and diaries, I thought that they might form the basis for a book about the 2nd Marchioness (known in her early married life as Lady Elizabeth Grosvenor) and her times as a member of the wealthy Whig aristocracy.

Fortunately Lady Elizabeth turned out to have been a most entertaining and outspoken correspondent and diarist, and I got to work to try to recreate her background, dividing the book into subjects such as country and London life, travel at home and abroad, politics, shooting and hunting, instead of treating the book as a chronological biography. In the course of seeking more material for my book I got in touch with Lady Elizabeth's great-grandson, the 4th Duke of Westminster, and went to stay with him and his wife in Cheshire. Thus began a most happy personal friendship, apart from my being given complete access to all the Grosvenor archives, none of which had been published.

Both Gerald, the Duke, and Sally his wife, took great interest in my researches and presently Gerald asked me if I would go on to write the life of his grandfather, the first Duke who had died in 1899. Although *The Times* in its obituary notice had described his name as being 'a household word throughout the land', his very varied and hardworking career as politician, philanthropist, supporter of forward-looking causes and sportsman—he had been probably the most successful race-horse owner and breeder in the history of the Turf—seemed to have been almost wholly forgotten and his biography had never been written.

Both my *Lady Elizabeth and the Grosvenors* and *Victorian*

Duke were published by the Oxford University Press in 1965 and 1967 respectively. Their writing had agreeably occupied my leisure for five years and both were very well reviewed and achieved a modest success in sales. My one great regret was that Gerald, the 4th Duke, did not live to see my life of his grandfather published. In the few years I had known him I had come to feel great affection and admiration for the sheer goodness of his character, his integrity, generosity, fair-mindedness and utter lack of pretentiousness and for the courage with which he overcame the handicap of the severe wounds he had received in Normandy in 1944, and which were the cause of his early death.

All in all, my career as a part-time author, only embarked on when I had reached my sixties, had afforded me the greatest interest and satisfaction. The money my books earned would have left me starving had I been dependent on it, but I had found it highly flattering to my ego to be published and well reviewed. I never had the slightest belief, however, that I had missed my vocation or that I could ever have rivalled Elspeth's professionalism which my own amateur efforts only made me respect the more.

The purchase of Woodfolds in 1938 was the best investment I have ever made, not just financially—though it has appreciated fantastically in value—but much more because of the happiness it has given us. While working in London after the war I usually slept at the Oriental Club but almost always managed to get home for a long weekend which became longer after I had given up executive for advisory work, and the peace and quiet of the country was always a wonderful restorative to mind and body.

Woodfolds farm, when I bought it, had no garden other than a small vegetable patch and a few old apple trees. On the east side of the house, which was the obvious area for a garden, there were pig-styes and the remains of decayed sheds. I had therefore the rewarding task of designing my garden free from the shackles of any legacy from the past. The land, unfortunately, only consisted of a flat field with a slight upward slope to the south. Its one feature was its background of the grey stone walls and roof of the house itself to which the whole garden had to be related. The soil, however, was a good heavy loam with a clay subsoil, but acid-soil loving plants such as azaleas and hybrid rhododendrons had to be ruled out. When the builders were at work on the alterations to the house, I got them to terrace the slight slopes so as to give some variety, and to build a wall on the west side for protection against the prevailing wind. Otherwise I contented myself with a very modest plan of lawns, beds, shrubs, yew and box hedges and fruit trees which could later be enlarged and new features introduced.

During the war I had the very active help of Harold Raymond, the head of Chatto and Windus, who frequently came down with me from London for weekends and who was only really happy when toiling the whole day long at ambitious garden construction work using the wealth of grey Cotswold stone which was to hand. As a result the garden is now too big for the present-day availability of labour, but for nearly thirty years I was lucky in having the whole-time services of Sid Cook who lived in the village. He had never been a gardener but had the countryman's knowledge of vegetables and flowers. He was—and still is—a great raconteur, and while working with him I was entertained by long stories of earlier times at Oaksey and of Sid's own career in World War I from enlistment to the day his battalion reached the front line in Flanders when his pal, declaring that 'this was no place for an honest Englishman', had promptly rubbed some dirt into a cut he made in his leg and had got himself evacuated sick to return much later and much to Sid's disgust as quartermaster-sergeant in charge of the rum ration.

In making the garden I committed many mistakes, so that Elspeth was later often complaining that no sooner had a tree or shrub become established than Gervas had it dug up. On Boars Hill I had made roses my speciality. Here at Woodfolds the soil was ideal for them so that they became the garden's principal feature and I now have over 500 planted of all kinds : hybrid teas, floribundas, climbers and old-fashioned specie varieties. My belief that Miss Jekyll had done a disservice to English gardeners when she started the fashion for herbaceous borders was confirmed at Wood-folds, when I initially made a long one. It used to be tidy enough in May but by mid-July it had always become an overgrown jungle impossible to weed or control. In the end I abolished it, making in its place a square cutting garden intersected by stone paths centring on a sundial, where I grew all my herbaceous plants but which I could easily keep tidy and free from weeds. It was a step I have never re-gretted.

After more than thirty years at Woodfolds I am convinced that gardening is the most rewarding of all hobbies as well as being one of the least expensive. Elspeth, whose interest in the garden is mainly the utilitarian one of providing fresh vegetables and fruit for current eating and for her deep freeze, was recently asking me why I so fully shared the love of non-utilitarian gardening, of flowers and shrubs, which has become so widespread among all classes in Eng-land and which has caused such an expansion of the seeds-men's and nurserymen's businesses, although the days of great gardens have almost vanished and paid garden help is virtually impossible to obtain. My answer was that the first reason lay in the English climate. However much we all abused the weather, it was one of the kindliest climates for gardens in the world with its absence of extremes of heat and cold and with its ample rainfall. Thanks to our climate, the love of growing flowers had always been, I believed, a particularly English trait, though the industrial revolution had for a long period debarred masses of our population from giving it expression. Now the opportunity had returned with the affluent society and its increased leisure, while the cheapness and easy preparation of frozen vegetables, now everywhere obtainable, were causing even the villager to give up his allotment and think of his garden in terms of flowers and not mainly as a source of food. Because, too, of the length of our grey and dreary winter, the English, like myself, found relief in looking forward to the glories of

240

spring flowers, daffodils, hyacinths and tulips, in the smallest patch of garden or even in window boxes, and in planning ahead for the summer flower succession in however small a space. Both prospectively and retrospectively his flowers helped the gardener to live by the comforting motto on my sundial, 'Horas non numero nisi sirenas'.

In 1952 I followed Elspeth's example in taking up farming, buying a 120-acre dairy farm in the next parish some three miles away from Woodfolds and installing a working manager. We established a herd of high-yielding Friesians and I gained first-hand experience of the problem of trying to make an economic unit, using paid labour, out of one of the small farms that account for 85% of all our dairy holdings. In spite of all the hard work and skill of my working manager, my farm proved a far from profitable venture, but thanks to the increase in the price of farm land I was able to get back my original investment and subsequent losses when I sold the farm some ten years later.

Woodfolds provided the happiest and healthiest of backgrounds for the early years of our son Charles, well looked after by Miss Clague, but spending much of his time with Sid Cook the gardener and with the young son of our neighbouring large farmer. Sending Charles away to a preparatory boarding school at the age of 8½ seemed, when it came to the point, a singularly cruel practice only indulged in by the British upper and middle classes. But he had reached a stage when, having no brothers or sisters, he needed more competition, wider companionship of his own age and more discipline than was afforded either by his home or by the little day school he attended in Cirencester. I did, however, take great pains to try to find a school where small boys would be better treated than Aldous and I were in our first years at Hillside. Eventually we chose Westbourne House, a school of some sixty boys near Chichester. Charles was never the type to whom school appealed, but he was, I think, as happy there as he could have been anywhere else, doing well at all games and leaving with a Rugby scholarship. Fifty years earlier I had found Rugby a highly civilized and comfortable place after the Borstalian atmosphere of my prep school, but, after Westbourne House, Charles must have thought it distinctly tough. However, he did well there, ending in the VIth form and playing cricket for the school at Lords, when I had the thrill of seeing him clean bowl the number one Marlborough batsman with his first ball. From Rugby, too, he succeeded in getting a place at Oriel. But Oxford's atmosphere was, I thought, very different from the one I had found so pleasant in 1913. Industry, headed by Morris motors, had taken Oxford over. So far as college life was concerned the mere increase in numbers in each college seemed to have put an end to the intimate relationship of dons and undergraduates that had been such a feature of my year at Balliol. Charles read P.P.E. without any great interest except for political history and achieved an honours degree.

Recalling the stimulus that America had always given me, I then thought that the atmosphere and tempo of the United States, so different from that of Oxford, would prove helpful to him. Charles agreeing, I wrote to Earl Newsom and Elmer Roper, and was delighted to get an immediate reply from Earl saying that he had been lunching with that very remarkable Englishman, David Ogilvy, who had invaded Madison Avenue and by sheer advertising flair had created his highly successful advertising agency, and that Ogilvy had offered to take Charles on as an 'advanced trainee' at a salary which would meet all his needs. It was, however, clearly to be understood that Ogilvy was taking on no passengers and that if Charles failed to make good he would promptly be sent back to England.

From the moment he got to America Charles found the way of life and work very much to his liking and stayed in New York for eighteen months, after which he had to return to England to avoid being liable for the American armed forces. He had, however, found advertising to be congenial and on his return to London was taken on by the large English agency which had just joined forces with David Ogilvy in New York. Nor was his job the only fruit of

Charles' American stay. In New York he met and later in England married Frederica, a daughter of my first cousin David Huxley, Julian's and Aldous' half-brother, who had married an American wife and was working in New York. It seems to be a most successful marriage and Elspeth and I are delighted with our daughter-in-law.

A new element came into Elspeth's and my life with her purchase of a very derelict cottage and the eighteen acres of land that went with it in the Brecon Beacon National Park on the Brecon–Monmouthshire border and less than two hours by car from Woodfolds.

Middle Gaer is 1,100 feet up on the steep slope of the 1,400-foot Gaer mountain and its site is a superb one. Facing due south the land falls steeply down through woods to the River Honddu in the lovely Vale of Ewyas which leads from Crucorney to Llanthony and beyond to Capel-y-Fyn. To the south-west across the valley rises the 2,000-foot Sugar Loaf, its upper slopes dark with heather ; in front, due south, 1,300-foot Brynawr bounds our view, its gentle bracken-covered slopes dotted with may-trees, and behind Brynawr to the south-east stands the long ridge of the 1,600-foot Skirrid mountain falling away to the east to the rolling Herefordshire plain with its mile after mile of chequerboard fields, stretching to the distant line of the escarpment of the Forest of Dean. Behind the cottage to the north the Gaer rises steeply with an ancient British fort on its summit and from it one looks west over the wooded Patrishow and Hermitage valleys to the unbroken wildness of the Black Mountains with sheep the only inhabitants and with peaks rising to 2,600 feet.

Staggered as I was by the magnificence of the view when Elspeth first took me to see it after she had bought the place, I wondered how on earth she was going to make the cottage habitable. It was falling to pieces, the only amenity being that it had main electricity, while its only approach was up half a mile of overgrown stony lane, so narrow as to be impassable to any builder's lorry. Several builders refused to attempt the very considerable work of reconstruction, but

Elspeth was eventually fortunate to find the two Jones brothers of Llanbedr who, bringing up all the material in a small van, made a really splendid job of carrying out Elspeth's ideas for one combined sitting-room and kitchen, two small bedrooms, bathroom, larder and cloakroom, with night-storage central heating and soft mountain water by gravity along a polythene pipe from a spring in the mountain behind. Bulldozing away the earth at the back of the cottage and facing the banks with local stone both made the cottage dry and created a sheltered sun trap of a patio.

Accompanied by our dachshund who much enjoys the walks, we try to go to Middle Gaer for a week every month from April to October. Though so near in distance it offers the most complete change from Woodfolds, in its remoteness, its mountain air, its glorious views, its walks on short springy turf and in the character of the people with their pleasant friendly charm and lilting accents. It is a place in which to relax, with Elspeth's household chores cut to the minimum, with no telephone to answer and no garden for me to feel compelled to tender.

In bad weather, rain and clouds completely blot out the view, but I am writing this on a sunny evening in mid-June and from the big south window I see the cloud shadows chasing each other across the green slopes of Brynawr, while the whole wide distant landscape is shining bright in the evening light and the air is filled with the scent of the white may-trees in full flower.

EPILOGUE

Pleasant as Middle Gaer is as a change, it is Woodfolds that forms the core of our lives. With oil central heating and wood fires from one of the old ash trees on our land, the winters pass snugly enough, and though the garden is dead except for winter-flowering shrubs, the house is full of plants grown in my small greenhouse where I can spend many a happy hour even in the coldest weather.

Our long living-room is lined with books and I now often find that re-reading the works of favourite authors is as rewarding as was their first reading, while the Wiltshire County Library van, which visits Oaksey every fortnight, brings a supply of new books. Several of our shelves are devoted to poetry and when we are alone on winter evenings I read aloud to Elspeth from the poets, a performance which she professes to enjoy. Wisely, I feel, the television set has been installed in Charles' old nursery, now an extra sitting-room, so that to view television requires a conscious effort of will.

During these post-war years death has made gaps in my family. First my elder sister Marjorie, followed a few years later by her husband Edward Harding. Then the sudden death of my youngest brother Kit, with whom my ties were always of the very closest, and who with his wide interests and tremendous sense of fun was the most entertaining of companions. Leaving the army after the war with the rank of Brigadier he had been employed by the Nuffield Foundation and was doing work exactly suited to his outgoing nature and love of his fellow men.

There was, too, sudden tragedy when my niece Henrietta, my younger sister's daughter, was killed in an accident just six months after her happy marriage.

In 1963 Aldous died. I had managed to see him on most of the few occasions on which he had come to London from California and he had once stayed at Woodfolds. As always our old intimacy would be renewed; as always, the essential goodness and sweetness of his character would shine out; and, as always, I would be fascinated by the wit and range of his talk covering so many subjects that his amazingly many-sided genius had explored. The memorial gathering for him at the Friends' House in London at the end of 1963 was a very moving affair, with tributes by David Cecil, Kenneth Clark, Stephen Spender and Julian and with a memorable rendering of Bach's chaconne by Yehudi Menuhin.

Friends have also died in these years. 'Friendship' is, however, a loose word. If it embraces men and women whom I am always glad to meet again and who seem to have an equal pleasure in meeting me, I have a host of 'friends' in many parts of the world, even if a Christmas card is our only regular annual contact. If, however, the word means the kind of relationship of whose interruption or cessation I would constantly be reminded, I have few 'friends' outside my family circle, and the people with whom I am now in frequent touch. The old adage 'out of sight, out of mind' is only too true in my case, and so my 'friends' have throughout my life changed with change of scene and circumstance. But if the result has been few enduring friendships, it has also spared me from enmities. I hope, indeed, that I shall be remembered—albeit very temporarily —with affection by the very many people whom my life has touched.

My lack of ambition has given no one cause for jealousy and I have always had a hatred of quarrelling. This might be because I am far too much of a 'yes-man', always seeking agreement, always inclined to see the other point of view and always reluctant to stand firm in opposition, especially over matters of principle. But this is not wholly due to weakness, since I have long been convinced that the pragmatic is the sensible approach to affairs, whether in my work or in general, and that conduct should be governed not by some principle for which a line of action is taken but by the practical consequence of taking that line. I do not have the qualities that make for greatness, but my modest ambitions have never extended to anything of the kind, and such as they are they have been well satisfied. What I should most like to be remembered for would be kindness, tolerance, generosity and trying to fulfil what R. L. Stevenson called his 'great task of happiness'.

Conscious that, at 75, the time for my own departure as well as that of my contemporaries should be approaching, I have now formed the habit of looking through the death notices in *The Times* before settling down to the crossword puzzle on the same back page, and am surprised at finding so many men and women who have lived on into their nineties. For myself, I believe in my Grandfather T. H. Huxley's words, that 'the great thing one has to wish for as time goes on is vigour as long as one lives and death as soon as vigour flags'. Although my mental powers seem to show little decline I am already constantly irked at my physical inability to walk at anything but a very slow pace or to do a day's work in the garden. I have no special fear of death itself; it is only the thought of a painful or lingering end and becoming a burden on those I love that disturbs me. I have always believed in and tried to live up to the Christian Ethos, though I have never felt able to subscribe to the dogmas of any Christian Church.

Brought up in T. H. Huxley's great tradition, I call myself an agnostic, the word that, as he wrote, he coined 'not as a creed but as a method, the essence of which lies in the single principle which positively may be expressed, in matters of intellect follow your reason as far as it will take you without regard for any other consideration; and, negatively, do not pretend that conclusions are certain which are not demonstrated or demonstrable'. As my grandfather also wrote, 'I neither deny nor affirm the immortality of man. I see no reason for believing it, but on the other hand, I have no means of disproving it.' Like my grandfather, however, just because the majority of mankind has always had such a strong desire for life after death, I suspect evidence put forward on its behalf and find the balance of credibility much against it. This does not in the least enhance any fear of death, and the last lines of a poem that my grandmother wrote in 1889 often come into my head and express my own feelings.

> 'And if there be no meeting past the grave,
> If all is darkness, silence, yet tis rest.
> Be not afraid ye waiting hearts that weep,
> For God still giveth his beloved sleep
> And if an endless sleep he wills—so best.'

It was the last three of these lines that her husband, T. H. Huxley, desired should be inscribed on his gravestone.

INDEX

INDEX

INDEX

Great Enton, 104, 111, 115, 117, 122

Grierson, John, 148–9, 170

Gurdon, Gladys, 103, 117

Haldane, J. B. S., 69, 71

Haldane, Mrs., 71–2

Haldane, Naomi (later Lady Mitchison), 71–2

Harding, Sir Edward, G.C.M.G., 153, 157, 190, 209, 245

Harlow, Professor Vincent, 207

Henderson, Keith, 134

Hillside Preparatory School, 31–42

Huxley, Aldous, 18, 32, 34–8, 40–2; character as a boy, 34–5, 53–4; loss of eyesight, 67; at Balliol, 68–72, 79–80, 121, 159, 212–13; death, 246

Huxley, Anne (later Mrs. Geoffrey Cooke), 14, 115; marriage, 184; 209, 210, 245

Huxley, Charles Grant, 208–9, 232, 241–3

Huxley, Christopher, 14, 26, 115, 209 245

Huxley, Elspeth, 149, 154–5; marriage to Gervas Huxley, 156, 157; starts career as author, 157; 159–60, 166, 170; makes name as author, 173; 175, 177, 181–4, 186, 199, 208; birth of son, 208–9; 212, 220; books and post-war activities, 232; 234, 236, 238–41, 243–5

Huxley, Frederica, 243

Huxley, Gervas, birth and lineage, 11–14; childhood, 14–30; at preparatory school, 31–42; at Rugby 42–54; schoolboy holidays, 54–61; in Leipzig, 63–6; at Balliol, 68–72; in World War I, 73–115; commissioned in East Yorkshire Regiment, 78; in the trenches,

80–100; in Humber Garrison, 101–4; with 38th Division in Flanders, 104–9; with 30th Division, 111–15; with Alfred Booth & Co., 116–23; marries Lindsey Foot, 117–18; Secretary Publicity Committee Empire Marketing Board, 126–60; tours Dominions with Amery, 137–48; visits West Indies 149–50; break up of first marriage and divorce, 153–6; marriage to Elspeth Grant, 156; starts career in Tea marketing and visits Ceylon, 158–64; travels in India, Africa, Canada and U.S.A., 165–72; forms International Tea Market Expansion Board, 172–3; further travels, 173–6; Tea market promotion in U.S.A., 174–183; with Ministry of Information, 195–6, 202–8; originates Y.M.C.A. Tea Cars, 196–8; originates service of tea in factories, 199–201; adviser to Ministry on relations with American Forces in U.K., 202–7; head of Empire Division, 207–8; creates Tea Centres, 211–12; adviser on public relations to Colonial Office, 216–18; member of Drogheda Committee, 218–19; chairman of committee of enquiry into Uganda's information services, 220–1; on British Council's Executive Committee, 222–3; on National Parks Commission, 224–31; as author, 233–8; as gardener, 238–41

Huxley, Dr. Henry, lineage, 11; professional gifts and work, 11–15; marriage, 14; 57, 60, 66, 76–7, 104, 122; retires from practice and moves to Boar's Hill, 122; 184, 186, 209–10; death, 210

INDEX